SUPER POP!

POP CULTURE TOP TEN LISTS
TO HELP YOU WIN AT TRIVIA,
SURVIVE IN THE WILD,
AND MAKE IT THROUGH
THE HOLIDAYS

DANIEL HARMON

ZEST BOOKS

35 Stillman Street, Suite 35
San Francisco, CA 94107
www.zestbooks.net

Young Adult Nonfiction / Humor / General
Library of Congress control number: 2012943318
ISBN: 978-1-936976-36-2

Cover and interior design: Marissa Feind

Manufactured in the U.S.A.
DOC 10 9 8 7 6 5 4 3 2 1
4500407168

Connect with Zest!

zestbooks.net/blog
zestbooks.net/contests
twitter.com/ZestBooks
facebook.com/ZestBook
facebook.com/BookswithaTwist
pinterest.com/ZestBooks

ACKNOWLEDGMENTS

Here is a partial list of people, places, and things (aka "nouns") without which this book would never have happened: Dave Letterman's list of the "Top Ten Numbers from One to Ten," the new canon being established at Criterion Collection, the continual surprises at NYRB Classics line, and the life-saving "Saturday Night Movies" series on New York public television (which in the year 2005 aired such new classics as *I'm Not Afraid* and *Eat Drink Man Woman*). Also, libraries like the SFPL's Taraval branch, the St. John's College library in Annapolis, the Westport library in Connecticut, and the Mechanics' Institute Library in downtown San Francisco. Also (more recently), email, panic, coffee, jokes about the necessity of coffee, the necessity of coffee itself, more coffee, and podcasts (especially the "endorsements" and "what's making us happy" segments from the *Slate Culture Gabfest* and the *Pop Culture Happy Hour*, respectively).

On a more personal note, I owe a special debt (payable in special dollars) to the vicious dog that hounded me throughout the writing process (Beatrice), the real laughter and equally real skepticism of one Caroline Caviness, and all of my collaborators, including, in particular, Ann Edwards, Eddie Lee, Nikki Roddy, Michael Caviness, Pam McElroy, Nick Harmon, Wyatt Harmon, Dilip Aidasani, Ethan Alter, the Zest teen advisory board, and the irrepressible Dr. Internet.

There's no way I would have ever been so devoted to this task (or so excitable when discussing the 400th item) without the example set by Greg Harmon, and there's no way I would have tried to make an argument about "why *Armageddon* matters" without the dubiousness of Anita Harmon (who also stocked our home with an endless supply of truly great romantic comedies throughout the 1990s). Also, thanks to everyone at Zest Books and at Houghton Mifflin Harcourt for sticking with this book even after I revealed I was thinking of writing it myself.

TABLE OF CONTENTS

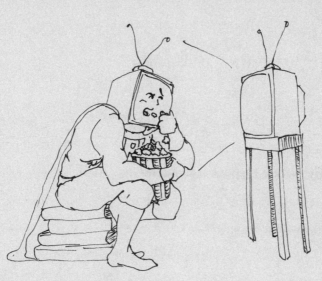

>> PART II: GET SMART(ER)

>> PART III: STOP DOING IT WRONG

>> PART IV: FIND HAPPINESS

>> PART V: SURVIVE THE HOLIDAYS

INTRODUCTION

There are a lot of things going on in this book. There are words, there are numbers, there are lists, there are illustrations, and there are probabably some typoos, too, but there is also, beneath and above all that, a genuine desire to turn readers on (. . . keep reading) to exciting new things and underappreciated old things and to make entertainment edifying. But before beginning, I wanted to take a moment to explain where this book came from, what it's meant for, and where it falls on the Arbitrary Spectrum. Why? Because a book without an introduction is like a movie without an overture—and I miss overtures in movies. So without further ado or explanation, I give you the first of many top ten lists . . .

THE TOP TEN THINGS TO BEAR IN MIND WHEN READING THIS BOOK

10 HOW THIS BOOK IS ORGANIZED

Things are a lot less fun when you feel terrible after they are over (cf. Mardi Gras, warfare, New Year's Eve, and celebratory cigars on all occasions). That's the problem with a lot of pop culture: It goes down way too easy, and four seasons of Real Housewives later, you wonder where your humanity ran off to and why it has your credit cards. The lists in this book are organized into five different self-improvement categories—"Be More Interesting," "Get Smart(er)," "Stop Doing It Wrong," "Find Happiness," and "Survive the Holidays." Not every item in every list is equally instructive, but there really is a lot of value in the things that entertain us, and sometimes, by just paying attention to that fact, we can remove a lot of the guilt from our "guilty pleasures." Not always, *Top Gun*, but sometimes.

9 TO WHAT EXTENT I THINK POP CULTURE CAN ACTUALLY BE USED FOR SELF-IMPROVEMENT

I'm serious! This is the way I, for one, actually relate to pop culture. I have a very hard time enjoying a book or a movie unless I feel it's in the service of some greater good—sounding informed, for example, or feeling better about myself, or actually learning something new. And with a little planning and ambition, I am convinced that pop culture can lead to a more fulfilling existence. But even if this were not my real belief—even if this were a giddy contrivance—it would still have some value here; because if you can find a way to connect ten different pop-cultural phenomena under a single coherent category—no matter what that category may be—then even the most debased of those ten items will gain something by its connection to everything else. That's the theory, anyway. (This theory brought to you by *The Weakest Link*.)

8 HOW ARBITRARY THE NUMBER "TEN" IS

Very arbitrary! This is a book of "top ten" lists in the most literal sense only. Each of the 40+ lists included here begins with the number ten and ends at the number one, but the order of the entries is 96 percent arbitrary at least 50 percent of the time. The point here isn't to dictate what the best revenge movie is or what the most magical fantasy landscape may be, but rather to consolidate and organize the best, most popular, and most exciting stuff from pop culture.

Ten is a totally arbitrary number that's nicely round. It's big enough to let some fun outliers in, and yet not so big that the lists lose their coherence. Ten is a starting point and nothing more. (Ten is also net spelled backwards. For what it's worth.)

7 HOW ARBITRARY THE RULES FOR INCLUSION ARE

The rules aren't arbitrary at all, because there are no rules. If something is good and it's relevant to a list that I thought had some merit, then I tried to include it. If that something was first a book but was then turned into a movie that was then further adapted into a video game (like, say, *The Great Gatsby*), then I tried to either pick the best of all these versions or, short of that, pick the shortest and most consumable iteration. If you feel like there are things that should be in these lists but aren't, perhaps you are a gumshoe. Or some other more modern form of detective. I don't know, but whatever the case, you definitely have a nose for the truth, and I could not agree with you more. A surprising amount of material was left on the cutting room floor. But everything that *is* in here is intended as a sincere recommendation (with the single exception of item #4 in the "Sleep with the Fishes" list).

6 WHY I WANTED TO WRITE THIS BOOK

The answer to almost every question is, of course, "the internet." I am aware of this, but the fact remains that, with a very few exceptions (A.V. Club's "Inventory" series, for instance, or the Criterion Collection's "Top 10s"), most lists and recommendations on the internet are pretty unsurprising. In December you get the Christmas movie lists, on Valentine's Day you get the romantic movies lists, and on every other day of the year you see the same basic set of books, movies, games, and songs, no matter where you read your news. Some of the titles may change, but it's hard to find anything that's really going to open your eyes.

For me, this phenomenon became most frustrating when I was looking for a few new movies to add to my annual Christmas movie marathon party (a twelve-hour "party" which, according to tradition, only I am able to enjoy). It was almost impossible to find any list that went much further than all the old standards and a few new staples. The fact that it was so hard to search for Christmas movies that went beyond the classics was, on the one hand, frustrating, but on the other hand, kind of exciting. Because there are a lot of great movies about snow and dysfunctional families—so where was that list!? That is Christmas! And what's true for Christmas is doubly or triply true for Mother's Day, for instance.

I wanted to write a book of lists that took recognizable occasions (like holidays) and genres (like historical fiction, say, or survival books) and offered some new ideas. I relied heavily on said internet in order to populate these lists with relevant entertainment options, but my goal was always to create lists that would resonate with people, but which the internet would not be able to populate on demand.

5 WHO "I" IS

"I" am a guy who grew up craving pop culture but consuming very little of it. I read a lot as a young person, but most of what I read was written by the white and the dead—and not in a fun, zombie way. Luckily, I was also sick a lot, and in the course of my sick days, I got sick unto death of entertainment that was not actually entertaining. At the time (pre-Google), I was at a loss. But then I realized that someone at my local library cared enough to get old movies that were actually good, and I was officially back in business. From curated library collections I moved on to curated internet recommendations and podcast endorsements, and although I don't have any shortage of recommendations these days, I still feel like the more lists there are, the better. Especially if they're even just a little bit different. (I use the word "different" here in both the complimentary and the insulting sense.)

"I" has a tendency to be kind of intrusive in nonfiction books, so I tried to keep me out of it for the most part. I pop up when occasion demands, but the recommendations included here are not just things that I like. In fact, very few of the books on my shelves or the movies in my Netflix history even appear in this book. I have consumed at least some significant part of every item included in this book, and I heartily recommend them all, but I also made sure that I was not the only one who was a fan. I used online review forums, the advice of friends, and, of course, any number of canonical lists—from IMDB's Top 250 to *Rolling Stone*'s Top 500 to the Modern Library's top 100 novels list—to ensure that this wasn't simply a listing of things that I had once crushed on in the privacy of my own home. Because that list would be embarrassing in the extreme.

4 WHAT "I" MEAN BY "POPULAR CULTURE"

By "pop culture," I mean whatever is convenient for me at any given time. We know it when we see it, so I don't see much benefit in worrying about it. There's some very high culture in here and some very low culture, too, but basically what I'm going for, with every item in every list, is something that people can reasonably expect to consume for fun.

3 HOW VIDEO STORES INFLUENCED THIS BOOK

Once upon a time, before discs began popping out to us from mailboxes and before videos came streaming into our homes through internet tubes, we had to rely on actual, physical stores. And since these stores had limited space—and since Blockbuster had all the new releases on lockdown—the mom and pops of the world had two ways of keeping their customers interested: They could either carefully curate their collections and rotate their titles into and out of different categories ("Flemish Neo-Noirs," "Musical Westerns," and "ALF-inspired Space Comedies," for instance), or they could just say to hell with it and let the movies fall into a general state of chaos.

Curation is great, but there's still an order to it; only in the chaos shops did you feel that anything was possible. It wasn't like the good movies were over here and the bad movies were over there and the rated x movies were behind that curtain; instead, everything was everywhere, so you really had to look. Nothing could be dismissed out of hand. Hopefully this book can be read in the same way that those old video stores were browsed. Hopefully you can open up to any page and find something of interest. (Or, short of that, at least something to laugh at.)

2 WHERE AND WHEN THIS BOOK MIGHT COME IN HANDY

Where? Oh, just all manner of places. Just all manner. If there is a bookshelf or a computer or a television or even a smartphone available, then this book should come in very handy indeed. So I guess the real question is, where does it not come in handy? Aha! That list is much shorter: in space (especially when plummeting through it), under water (unless in a submarine vehicle of some kind), in any kind of vehicle, whether sub- or super-marine (because focus on the road!), and in the future when the machines turn against us.

When? Well, my hope is that this book will have something to offer whether you're looking for a new recommendation or just hoping for a new take on an old favorite. My hope is that if you haven't heard of the given thing before, that you'll want to check it out, and that if you have, then you'll want to check it out again.

1 HOW MANY OF THESE ITEMS YOU ACTUALLY NEED TO BEAR IN MIND WHILE READING THIS BOOK

Approximately zero. But now that it's over, I hope you enjoy the book! (Also, "bear in mind" is a terrifying phrase.)

PART I

BE MORE INTERESTING

LIVE LIKE AN ARISTOCRAT
THE BEST PLACES TO MINGLE WITH THE ELITE

— ROYAL FLUSH.

As James Bond has demonstrated time and time again, you don't have to be a baron to live like an aristocrat. Instead, you just need a superior demeanor, a stiff upper lip, and a distinctive slogan to go along with your favorite drink order. ("Make mine a milk. Boiled, salted, and in a pan," to give one example. Or: "Tequila. Now. And a bacon straw for sipping.") But if you're not yet adept at tying a bow tie or landing a line, don't lose hope. Even failure can work in your favor (since past inbreeding did, after all, set a fine precedent for eccentric mannerisms). So settle in, keep an open mind, and select the aristocratic tic that works for you!

10 THE LEOPARD
DIRECTED BY LUCHINO VISCONTI (1963)

It's hard to talk about this movie without talking about its director: Luchino Visconti was born into a noble Italian family, but he made his first big international splash with *La Terra Trema*, a chronicle of life in a Sicilian fishing village that was so authentically rendered that subtitles had to be added so that Italian audiences could understand what the amateur actors were saying. At the time, that naturalistic style was all the rage, but Visconti's own personal style was always something a bit more . . . elegant. *The Leopard*, a historical epic chronicling the political turmoil of nineteenth-century Sicily, is saturated with color and moves fluidly from opulent scene to opulent scene—until the walls come crumbling down and a new, more democratic country is born. Through it all, the Prince of Salina, Don Fabrizio (played by Burt Lancaster) strides over this chaos with Bendicò (his loyal Great Dane) behind him. He is the perfect gentleman, and he is going down with the ship.

9 RIGHT HO, JEEVES
WRITTEN BY P.G. WODEHOUSE (1934)

Jeeves is a man whose mother named him Jeeves; and, therefore, Jeeves is also, necessarily, a butler. Bertram "Bertie" Wooster, on the other hand, is not much of anything at all. He "is not" almost by profession. He is not employed. He is not unhappy. He is not especially intelligent. And he is not overly bothered by much of anything—except his overbearing aunts. But without Jeeves, Wooster would not be Wooster; and without Wooster, Jeeves would not be Jeeves. They are a master and servant, yes, but they are also a perfect pair. Bertie has the problems and Jeeves has the answers, over and over and over again. But the familiar setup operates in the same way that "the apartment" or "the coffee shop" operates in so many classic sitcoms: It simply allows us to settle in and pay attention to what really matters—namely, the interactions among the characters (and the inspired ways they denigrate each other).

8 BRIDESHEAD REVISITED
WRITTEN BY EVELYN WAUGH (1945)

It's too bad that Evelyn Waugh was named Evelyn, because if he had simply been named "George" then "George Waugh" would be famous for having written one of the funniest and most truly enjoyable books in the English language, instead of being mocked for having a name that appears to have been stolen from an elderly English lady. But that's just the way things go sometimes.

"Brideshead" is the estate of Lord Marchmain and his family—including, most notably, the young Sebastian Flyte and his teddy bear, Aloysius. (Note to Sebastian: If you are old enough to drink and troubled enough to brood over all of your many drinks, you are also probably too old to have a teddy bear, just as a general rule.) Sebastian's difficulty in coping with his privileged existence is telling, however. This is one of the funniest books ever written, but it's also deeply somber. The drunk scion's teddy bear is a good indication of that tension. The family is old and rich and powerful, but they are also at the end of their rope. Luckily, ropes are much more interesting toward their ends, and the book's narrator, Charles Ryder, is on hand to account for Flyte's dissolution (via grain alcohol and whimsicality) and to give a full accounting of both what the family stood for and what they really were.

7 CASINO ROYALE
WRITTEN BY IAN FLEMING (1953)

James Bond is not a member of the aristocracy in anything but the most metaphorical sense—but if anyone has ever had a stiffer upper lip than 007, I would like to meet this person, shake his hand, and offer to break the spell that has turned him into a statue. Ian Fleming didn't waste any time in establishing the key elements in his first Bond novel. *Casino Royale* has it all: sangfroid, Russians, shaken martinis, expensive accoutrements, alluring strangers, dangerous new friends, sadistic villains, confusing plots, and torture. And on that note, if anyone ever invites you to strip down and make yourself comfortable on a chair that has no seat, DO NOT DO IT; but if you do sit down, and if someone does then cane you from below, take it like a spy. If you can get through that with style, then you truly have arrived.

6 THE AGE OF INNOCENCE
DIRECTED BY MARTIN SCORSESE (1993)

It's hard to imagine how Daniel Day-Lewis (the hyper-intense method actor), Martin Scorsese (the artiste behind America's best gangster films), and Edith Wharton (the turn-of-the-century American author who obsessed over questions of decorum and social class) could ever find a common ground. Day-Lewis and Scorsese? That one's easy: *Gangs of New York*. Wharton and Day-Lewis? Sure: They both share a genius for saying a lot with a little. Wharton and Scorsese, however . . . that's where things begin to fall apart. But in an interview with Roger Ebert in 2005, Scorsese revealed the tie that binds them all together: "What has always stuck in my head is the brutality under the manners." Sticks and stones may break my bones, in other words, but words may do the same. (And looks may do even worse.) If you want to learn how to stab someone to death with a pen (verbally, I mean) this is where you need to go to school.

5 THE TALENTED MR. RIPLEY
WRITTEN BY PATRICIA HIGHSMITH (1955)

Mr. Ripley is very talented at knowing what he wants and then pursuing it. According to many self-help books, this should make Mr. Ripley a very healthy, very wealthy, and very wise man, indeed. And by the end of the book, Mr. Ripley has in fact made himself far better off and far better situated than he was at the outset, but his greatest attribute is luck. His compulsion to take what he wants and be what he desires (and to do so without delay) makes him very prone to errors, but time and again a little stroke of luck stands between him and his always imminent (but never actual) punishment. The devil is in the details, however, and there are a lot of details in Mr. Ripley's story. (Principle among them is the fact that he is not afraid to indulge in an occasional bout of murder.) From the selfishness to the cynicism to the strange blending of love and homicide, this is the story of a budding aristocrat, if ever there was one . . .

4 DAMAGES
CREATED BY DANIEL ZELMAN AND BROTHERS GLENN AND TODD A. KESSLER (2007-)

Russia has its counts and countesses, England has its dukes and duchesses, and we in America, what do we have? Well, high-powered trial attorneys for one, corporate kingpins for two, and media celebrities for three (and the win). *Damages* gives us all of the above. If you're wondering what the American struggle for power looks like when it's dressed up and ready for dinner, this is it. And if you want to know what the American struggle for power would look like after it has been shoved into an alley, handed a broom, and told to get ready for a knife fight, keep your eyes fixed on Rose Byrne in every single season premiere. Each new season plunks her down in a rat-infested bag of trouble, and the plot twists don't let up until the finale, the cliffhanger upon which a new season will begin. Because this is America, where winning matters more than blood (and where blood only matters if it kills you). This is the rebirth of the aristocracy, all dressed up in red, white, and blue.

3 KEEPING UP WITH THE KARDASHIANS
STARRING THE KARDASHIAN FAMILY (2007-)

Once upon a time there was a thing called the aristocracy. It was a loose affiliation of nervous people who did what they could to "keep it in the family" so as to maintain their wealth and prestige. The aristocracy was not always loved, and people called it names, but it was feared and admired for a while (due to its success), before it was violently overthrown. Once upon a time there was also a television show called *The Brady Brunch*, which chronicled the conflicts and resolutions that occur when two distinct families (a father with three sons and a mother with three daughters) try to combine their respective parts in the California suburbs. This show was not always loved, and people called it names, but it was feared and admired for a while (due to its success), before it was violently overthrown. Then it was put into syndication and turned into a movie franchise, because duh.

Keeping Up with the Kardashians is the sum of these two ideas. The show is a fairly bald means of increasing the Kardashian family's fame and prestige, but it's also a sitcom, a reality show, and a place where reality seems to play no significant role. Most but not all of the children born to Kris Jenner (the matriarch) have names that begin with the letter K. Kourtney is the oldest, Kim is the famousest, Khloe is the most accented, and Rob is the K-lessest; but there's also Brandon, Brody, Kendall, Kylie, and a rotating cast of American celebrities and superstars, from Reggie Bush to Kanye West to Lamar Odom. Some people love this family, other people hate it; but all in all, it has to be said that they are a pretty big deal. They are rich, attractive, famous, self-involved, and crass. They are who America wants to be. (But imitate them at your own peril.)

2 DOWNTON ABBEY
CREATED BY JULIAN FELLOWES (2010-)

Season 1 of *Downton Abbey* was phenomenal because it was like being allowed to spend even more time on the grounds of Gosford Park (the setting of the film of the same name where Julian Fellowes first made his reputation). It was a place where rich people made decisions slowly, judged people rapidly, and fought against any and every possible change to the status quo—no matter how big or small. It was the entertainment equivalent of a rearguard action. But if Lady Grantham (played by Dame Maggie Smith) is playing defense for you, then hope is far from lost. For proof of this fact, see Season 2, in which Europe is ravaged by the First World War, influenza, and a variety of upstarts, but in which Downton also remains a stoical, implacable host to all. (And if you're looking for proof of how sadistic an entertainer Fellowes really is, see Season 3.)

1 GAME OF THRONES
CREATED BY DAVID BENIOFF AND D.B. WEISS (2011-)
BASED ON THE NOVELS BY GEORGE R.R. MARTIN (1996-)

EXTENDED LOOK!

So with the possible exceptions of *Keeping Up with the Kardashians* and *Casino Royale*, all of the works mentioned above are really more about the death of the ruling class than they are about the existence of the same. They are all looking back at aristocracy. Thus, in order to find something that engages with the nobles on more or less equal terms, we have to move to a parallel universe: We have to move to the Seven Kingdoms, and play the *Game of Thrones* . . .

And in order to avoid losing ourselves in the murky political waters of this impressively epic TV series, let us just say that here, in this universe, might is almost always right. The only problem is that it's often very hard to tell who is mighty and what exactly makes them so. The family that seems to have the firmest grasp on what it takes to achieve real dominance is the Lannisters. They are unquenchable in their thirst for power and merciless in their execution of it (no pun intended). There are many families who possess some share of political significance, or money, or dragons, but the Lannisters are the only real aristocrats in the show. (And how do we know this? Just listen to their accents!)

Like any number of great fables, *Game of Thrones* never strays very far from its central idea, but it is never held in thrall to that idea either. So to put it another way, *Game of Thrones* is about power in the same way that Peter Pan is about boyhood—that is to say, entirely and not at all. And although GOT is ostentatious where Peter Pan is wry, they both use the leash of their central theme as a means of keeping nearly everything relevant.

Game of Thrones takes place in a world where, like ours, anything is possible because everything is up for grabs—with sufficient means, that is. And thus, in a family that contains an uncompromising father, a charismatic son, a domineering daughter, a Joffre, and a dwarf, the Lannisters contain something for us all. Like the aristocracy, the only thing the Lannisters don't contain within their ranks is the populace they trample underfoot. Oh, and dragons. (Which could be a problem . . .)

DIVE INTO THE UNDERWORLD
ESSENTIAL TOURS OF GANG WARS, THE DRUG TRADE, AND OTHERWISE FELONIOUS LIVING

ALRIGHT, ALRIGHT. I'LL GIVE YOU A TOUR.

If you're at a party and you can tell a story about how your old friend Jack "Rumballs" McMannard once accidentally stole his favorite sister's favorite car (on her birthday, no less!) you're going to go home a winner. Street cred is the best cred, and it's not just the rat-racers who invest in their criminal affiliations. After all, where would the merry men be without Robin Hood? (Answer: Stuck at Euro Disney.) Who would count all 40 thieves, if it weren't for Ali Baba? (Answer: Count von Count . . . he alone.) Everyone wants to know the right kind of wrong people, and everyone wants to know the secret password. But there are a lot of ways to say "Open Sesame." It's time to start getting fluent in the streets . . .

10 BREAKING BAD
CREATED BY VINCE GILLIGAN (2008-)

The most exciting—and most terrifying—thing about the criminal element in *Breaking Bad* is that it is everywhere. Walter White gets his initial "baking" supplies from the high school where he teaches; he gets his motivation from the American health care system (which essentially abandons him after his cancer diagnosis); he finds his customers everywhere; and he hides his captive-taking, drug-dealing, murderous second life in plain sight. This is the state of the American underbelly, the show seems to say. It's everywhere. *Weeds* put it in the suburbs, but *Breaking Bad* goes one step further and puts it in the desert—the place where pretty much nothing lives (a suitably ominous setting for the increasingly morbid, increasingly pessimistic, and increasingly brilliant show).

9 GRAND THEFT AUTO IV
DEVELOPED BY ROCKSTAR NORTH (2008)

The underworld, wherever it's found and by whatever name it's known, is always reliant on a secret code—because the walls have ears. In *Grand Theft Auto IV*, the necessity for a secret code is reflected not only in the game's dialogue (which one *New York Times* reviewer said possessed a "mastery of street patois to rival Elmore Leonard's") but is also evident in its icons and landmarks. "Swingers" (aka the New York Yankees) and the "Algonquin" (aka Manhattan), for example, help to reproduce New York in satirical miniature as "Liberty City," a place where prostitutes, smugglers, drug dealers, pimps, murderers, robbers, carjackers, racists, stereotypes, con-men, and thieves all come together to pay homage to the American dream—sometimes by another name, and sometimes not. It's the place where, in one scene, you've made it, and in the next scene, they've made you. It's rough, it's tumble, it's America—virtually.

8 CITY OF GOD
DIRECTED BY FERNANDO MEIRELLES (2002)

Brazil is big. Rio is big. But Rio's slums are enormous. Almost a quarter of the city's six million residents reside in the favelas, which are not, by all accounts, a very safe place to be. Drugs are big business, guns are everywhere, and the police have little control. For Rocket, the main character in *City of God*, this is his world. We follow him as he grows up here, and what we wind up with is a picture of a completely believable adolescence in a completely unbelievable place. When the violence or the threat of violence gets too intense, Rocket manages to find little moments of escape by going to the beach, smoking pot with his friends, and taking pictures of the world as he sees it. But as the drug wars intensify, escape gets harder and harder to come by, and at one crucial moment, escape and captivity combine: He's stuck taking pictures of a live gunfight. And one way or another, you know that this is going to be his way out.

7 TOKYO VICE: AN AMERICAN REPORTER ON THE POLICE BEAT IN JAPAN
WRITTEN BY JAKE ADELSTEIN (2009)

It seems improper to write anything at all about "the underworld" without mentioning the Yakuza—Japan's very organized collection of organized criminals. You know, the guys with the tattoos, the rigorous code of behavior, the pervasive cultural influence, and, of course, the finger-shortening. But at the same time, because the culture is so entrenched in Japan, it's hard to make it accessible to American audiences. Gangster films are for America, and Yakuza comics (and TV shows, and movies, and exposés) are for Japan. But then Jake Adelstein happened.

Adelstein was the recent college graduate who ate ramen for a year, studied religiously, and eventually passed the standardized test for Japan's biggest daily newspaper, the *Yomiuri Shinbun*. After that, the strange American talked his way through several interviews and actually got himself hired. Then he made friends with the police who covered the Yakuza. Then he made friends with some actual Yakuza members. Then he uncovered a huge human trafficking story. And then things got dangerous. Jake Adelstein is crazy—crazy like a psycho fox on crack cocaine after three hours spent jumping on a trampoline. And his education (in how to be a Japanese journalist, how to find sources, how to win a drunken fight, how to impersonate an Iranian, and how to survive among the Yakuza) is comprehensive, vicious, and edifying in the extreme.

6 SIN CITY
WRITTEN BY FRANK MILLER (2005)

Now, of course, everyone knows that comic book characters aren't real. But if they were real, and if they were all really seedy, I think we can all agree that they would look, act, and talk like the characters in Frank Miller's *Sin City*. This is a complete world; and the movie adaptation takes everything that's great about the comic but then ups the ante by adding Elijah Wood as a cannibalistic murderer. (Gack!) Middle Earth was one thing, and there were real dangers there, sure, okay; but when the actor who played Frodo Baggins starts swiping at people with homicidal fingernails, then you know it's about to get real. (Real murderish.)

5 GOODFELLAS
DIRECTED BY MARTIN SCORSESE (1990)

Gangster movies are often about style as much as they're about crime. *The Godfather* had style, certainly, but a conservative kind of style. It looked classic, whereas *Goodfellas*, from the very first, looked and sounded fresh (in the early '90s sense). In fact, it's telling that when Henry Hill first starts getting involved in mob activities, his mother identifies his nefarious ways by looking at his suit. The point of Martin Scorsese's iconic gangster movie isn't moral or practical. He doesn't care what Hank Hill could have done differently or better. Instead, his movie is about lines like "I always wanted to be a gangster." It's about "Layla" and bodies in dumpsters; it's about making a grand entrance to the Copacabana and eating a good dinner in prison. It's about looking good, no matter what the cost. This is the movie that brought sexy back to American gangster films.

4 THE SOPRANOS
CREATED BY DAVID CHASE (1999-2007)

For almost every one of the entries on this list you can make a pretty reasonable claim that it represented "the mob for its time." In a way, though, that doesn't hold true for *The Sopranos*. It's great not because of its relevance—not because it features a psychologist or a homosexual, or because it takes place in the ruins of industrial America—but because it's a really great, really expansive mob show. It's got everything you want: double dealing, paranoia, power struggles, strip clubs, machismo, changing times, drugs, politicians, and great female characters—but it's also got the one thing you absolutely have to have: iconic individual scenes. Because after all, when we're talking gangster, if the whole thing is perfect but there's no shot of Al Pacino screaming into outer space (as there was in Michael Mann's *Heat*), or of Robert De Niro standing, triumphant, beneath a swinging light bulb (as he did in *The Godfather, Part II*), then you've come up short.

For it to be a gangster film—which *The Sopranos* certainly is (despite the fact that it aired as a series on HBO)—you need to see the bottle of orange juice exploding and Tony just barely escaping in Season 2; and you need to see the lights go out in the finale. Then you know it's really gangster.

3 THE FRIENDS OF EDDIE COYLE
WRITTEN BY GEORGE V. HIGGINS (1970)

The Friends of Eddie Coyle is the fly on the wall for every conversation you ever wanted to hear. That's the essential difference between it and the other books of "realistic" crime dialogue: It's usually hard to tell if what you're listening to is from the streets or from a writer's workshop. With George V. Higgins (an assistant US attorney for many years), however, there's never any question. Eddie Coyle is the Boston Irish gangster friend you never had. Robert Mitchum played the role in the excellent film adaptation, and if he did any research for the role it was a waste of time, because Eddie Coyle is what Eddie Coyle says. (Even when he's lying.) And his story is unnerving because, for once, the life of crime—the life of lies, betrayal, and murder—seems really mundane. It's as normal as a bag full of groceries . . . and as abnormal as a grocery bag filled with guns. (Both are relevant here.)

2 THE WIRE
CREATED BY DAVID SIMON (2002-2008)

It's the show that needs no introduction. "The best TV show of all time." It's *The Wire*, and the only reason why it's not number one on this list is because there's always a chance that this minor slight will lead to a confrontation with the show's creator, David Simon—and that is very much to be wished for. But moving on: It's often noted that although the show takes place almost entirely in Baltimore, each season of *The Wire* takes place in a different kind of eco-system, moving from the streets, to the docks, to City Hall, to the schools, and finally to the newsroom. The show is so complex and so nuanced that no summary will ever be complete, but a pessimist could reasonably say that the show demonstrates the thoroughgoing corrup-tion of American city life. A pessimist might also note that, when it comes to the characters on *The Wire*, whether you fight crime or engage in it, teach school or cut it, you are guilty. An optimist, on the other hand, could say it's about how we're all connected. Either way, if you want to be up on the state of the art of the American drug trade, this is the place to go.

1 THE GODFATHER: PART II
DIRECTED BY FRANCIS FORD COPPOLA (1974)

EXTENDED LOOK!

Common sense tells us that it's always best to begin at the beginning—but sometimes that's not the way time works. *The Godfather: Part II* makes a case for the end being the beginning, and the beginning being the end. *The Godfather* is usually the first movie most people think of when they think "mob movie," but of course, the real story of *The Godfather* doesn't really begin until its sequel. That's where Don Vito, the Godfather himself, does his growing up, and—thinking in genre terms—it may also be the first instance of the origin story in American blockbusters. (This was before *The Dark Knight* and *Watchmen* and *The Incredibles* had really hit it big, after all.) Old Marshmallow Mouf (aka Marlon Brando) had turned Don Vito into an icon in the original Godfather, and by returning to Don Vito's formative years, Coppola was able to both indulge his newfound die-hard fans and also add a new layer of depth to Michael Corleone's story. (Savvy move, winey man.)

And although it seems kind of petty to argue over which of two masterpieces is the better masterpiece, suffice it to say that *The Godfather: Part II* is flawless entertainment. It provides a brief education in how to write dialogue, manage parallel plots, and light a murder scene; not to mention how to start and manage a mob family, how to uncover a mole, and how to get away with murder (tip: live beside a lake).

Because it works so well at the most superficial levels—as an amazing mob movie, mystery film, and melodrama—it also seems possessed of endless depth. Its profundities are smuggled in while your eyes are focused somewhere else. And so it turns out that, while you're watching a movie about the American mob, you wind up hobnobbing with American politicians and financiers, Jewish gangsters, the Italian mafia, and even Diane Keaton. If it's in America, it's in *The Godfather: Part II*.

DRINK THE KOOL-AID
TOUCHSTONES FOR QUIRKY, LIKE-MINDED PEOPLE

The wrong kind of cult is a scary thing, but that is not the kind of cult we are talking about here. We're talking about the right kind of cult, where people get to maintain their status as thinking individuals but also have the opportunity to spend a few days every year dressing like aliens, drinking scotchka, or screaming at movie screens. "What's the deal with that guy," people will wonder. And let them wonder, because that's the moment when we don our Spock ears, deliver a rousing speech on the topic of intergalactic farming subsidies and their relationship to American economic policy, and stun everyone around us with our broad set of interests, passionate public speaking style, and ears. Live long and prosper, y'all. We're out. Critical thinking and debate are all well and good for the most part, but sometimes we also just need to demonstrate our capacity to sob over the fate of an alien planet.

10 THE ROCKY HORROR PICTURE SHOW
WRITTEN BY RICHARD O'BRIEN AND JIM SHARMAN (1975)

The Rocky Horror Picture Show is the movie that set the standard for cult classics. Not only does it have aliens, transvestites, and poor production values, but it also helped to usher in the era of the midnight movie (a time slot and a genre that has since blossomed into a small cottage industry). It's easy to look back now and think, "Sure, a campy movie musical with a naive young couple and lascivious aliens was always destined for cult status," but that kind of fatalistic thinking removes everything that's magical about this movie. Tim Curry was cast in the lead role because he bumped into Richard O'Brien on the way to the gym; the movie had a $400 promotional budget for its opening run at New York's Waverley Theatre. And now nearly everyone who attends a screening dresses as their favorite character (and also throws food willy-nilly and screams expletives at the screen). If that's not a miracle, then I don't know what is.

9 STAR TREK
DIRECTED BY J.J. ABRAMS (2009)

Not to put too fine a point on it, but *Star Trek* is home base for nerds, dorks, dweebs, and whatever the word for "space-jerks" is in Vulcan. I am confident that if Spock were available for comment, he would say the same. *Star Trek* has always had a devoted following (its first fanzine appeared in print in 1967), but after it went into syndication things changed materially. In addition to its core audience (again, of "the nerds"), it gained "the kids." The kids, that is, who were watching TV episodes about outer space at home, while everyone else was watching the news about Watergate, Vietnam, the Iran-Contra affair, the fall of the Berlin Wall, White-water, Monica Lewinski, O.J., and something about internets and blogospheres . . .

Personally, I remember being confused by the very concept of *Star Trek*—because who would want to watch stars walk around pointedly, if instead you could see stars war? J.J. Abrams found a way to satisfy both the space jerks and the space idiots in his 2009 reboot. His movie accommodates the old guard by integrating old cast members via time travel and (in traditional sci-fi style) a parallel universe; and it accommodates newbies with a more or less linear plot, strong characters, sexy alien on human action, and a lot of compelling battle scenes. So if you've ever wondered why tens of thousands of people attended the last Trekkie convention, this is probably the best place to start.

8 "ONCE MORE, WITH FEELING"
FROM BUFFY THE VAMPIRE SLAYER,
WRITTEN AND DIRECTED BY JOSS WHEDON (2001) ♫ 🖥

Joss Whedon writes comics, directs winking mini-musicals, and, of course, is legendary as the man behind *Buffy the Vampire Slayer, Firefly, Angel,* and *Dollhouse.* He is a one-man generator of cult phenomena. But he also recently directed *The Avengers* (currently the third-highest grossing feature film of all time) along with an episode of *Glee,* and has thus solidified his standing as a maker of serious Hollywood bucks. The cultish fervor of Joss Whedon's fan-base is never likely to completely abandon him (just as he's not likely to ever abandon his sense of the absurd), but the more success he achieves, the harder it will be to remember that once upon a time he really did, in true cult style, lack a budget.

"Once More with Feeling" leaves a lot to be desired in terms of production values, but it more than makes up for it with the sheer amount of "things that are happening." After all, this was just another episode in a long-running, much-loved, well-reviewed, and poorly rated television program, but in this one episode you will find: original music, real actors really singing, real actors really dancing, a bright blue suit on a bright red demon, snappy dialogue, countless double entendres, an impressive amount of character development, and a coherent rationale for having the characters of this fantasy show suddenly break into song spontaneously. That is a lot for one episode. That is the stuff that cults are made of. And although it's currently tough to attend a public screening (due to a dispute with the studio), hopefully we can all look forward to a future with a hefty dose of *Buffy* sing-alongs.

7 THE SOUND OF MUSIC
DIRECTED BY ROBERT WISE (1965) 🎞

The Sound of Music has beautiful songs (by the legendary duo of Rodgers and Hammerstein), charming lyrics (by the same), a thrilling plot (involving Nazis), an incredible backdrop (the Alps), and incredible performances from a top-shelf cast (including Julie Andrews and Christopher Plummer). But all of these ingredients do not traditionally add up to cult status. Where's the freakishness? (It has none.) Where's the struggle for acceptance? (It won a basketful of Oscars.) What's the deal!?

The deal is that it's a genetically engineered freak. It's a great WWII escape movie with insane cinematography and pretty much perfect songs. Speaking of the songs, not only do they sound good, they also advance the plot, take us inside the minds of the characters, and they're lighthearted when they need to be and elegiac when they don't. And when people hear these songs they want to sing along. (Key phrase: sing along.) If you could sing along to a fire alarm, a fire alarm would be a hit, and there would be a cult around it. *The Sound of Music* is a fire alarm sent down to Earth from Heaven.

6 TWIN PEAKS
CREATED BY DAVID LYNCH AND MARK FROST (1990-1991) 🖥️

"Interesting" is a funny word, because it can be used as both a compliment and as an insult without having to really change its meaning at all. For example, if someone says, "That hat sure is interesting" to someone who is wearing a tie-dyed rodent on his head, then "interesting" is clearly intended as an insult. Whereas if someone says, "That hat sure is interesting" because someone else is wearing a perfectly normal top hat which happens to be speaking grammatically correct Middle English and saying quite compelling things about haberdasher culture in twelfth-century London, then it is clearly meant as a compliment. But in both cases the word means the same thing: Both hats are interesting! And David Lynch is like both of these hats, in both of these ways. He is interesting, brilliant, bizarre, and true without being sensible. Oh and PS: You know what else is interesting (in that same good-hat/bad-hat sense)? The suburbs. And that's what *Twin Peaks* is: a suburb of the mind. See you on the other side of the white picket fence.

5 THE EVIL DEAD
DIRECTED BY SAM RAIMI (1981) 🎞️

The Evil Dead has a classic cult pedigree: It was shot at a remote location, on an extremely limited budget, with two budding cult icons (Bruce Campbell and Sam Raimi), and on two different types of film stock. And, lastly but far from leastly, it has since morphed into an extremely lucrative film franchise. *The Evil Dead*, for its part, was your basic country cabin horror movie (but more so, and more better, and more edited by a Coen brother); it was followed up by *Evil Dead II* (1987), which was essentially a polished-up version of the original, and *Army of Darkness* (1992), a time-traveling, gussied-up remake of both of the earlier movies. Each of the three movies has laughs, terrors, and, of course, Bruce Campbell (as Ash Williams), and like a great pop album, even though you can't really tell the difference between the songs, you'll love them all the same.

4 TROLL 2
DIRECTED BY CLAUDIO FRAGASSO (1990) 🎞️

Troll 2 is often listed among the worst films ever made—it's even won the honor of starring in the documentary *Best Worst Movie*—but it contains one moment of real, indisputable horror.

This moment occurs when you, the viewer, realize that *Troll 2* not only has nothing to do with the classic 1986 movie *Troll* (and therefore fails completely as a sequel), but it also lied to you. There are no trolls here! You've been swindled out of your due portion of trolls! And instead, *Troll 2* only gives you goblins. This would be enough for a lawsuit, if the movie weren't so entertainingly bad. It takes place in a town called "Nilbog" ("goblin" spelled backwards); a suspicious police officer's name is "Sheriff Gene Freak" (because understatement is under-appreciated); and some common modes of death in the film include "death by popcorn," "death by Nilbog milk," and death by stilted dialogue (just kidding—but also not really). So perhaps someday, if the word "bad" ever makes a sequel ("Nu-Emosewa 2"?), maybe then we will finally be able to better understand what has happened to us in the course of this greatest, most awe-inspiring failure.

3 FREAKS AND GEEKS
EXECUTIVE PRODUCED BY JUDD APATOW (1999-2000) 🖥

Before he was declared King of Hollywood, Emperor of Pop Culture, and Lord of the Actor's Stable in the year 2007 (not really, but almost), Judd Apatow had already contributed to a string of cult hits, from *The Ben Stiller Show* to *The Cable Guy* to *The Larry Sanders Show*. But *Freaks and Geeks* is where the "Apatowian" world began to really take form. In addition to launching the careers (both big and small) for a huge number of actors—including Seth Rogen, Jason Segel, James Franco, Linda Cardellini, and Martin Starr—the series put real-seeming teenagers in a recognizable high school setting, and then began churning out laughs, drama . . . and very poor ratings. And thus a cult is born.

When the show died after shooting only 18 episodes (and airing even less), fans clamored for more, but no more episodes were ever filmed. Apatow then appeared to take it upon himself to advance the careers of everyone who had anything to do with the show by casting and utilizing all these people in *The 40-Year-Old Virgin*, *Knocked Up*, *Superbad*, *Forgetting Sarah Marshall*, and a string of other hits. So now, here we are: It's Judd Apatow's universe, and we are all freaks and geeks (and if we're not, we're probably not very interesting characters, either).

2 DOCTOR WHO
CURRENTLY PRODUCED BY STEVEN MOFFAT AND
CAROLINE SKINNER (2005-) 🖥

Mr. Rogers once told his viewers that "you can grow anything in the garden of your mind." It's a nice idea, but it doesn't go far enough for the Doctor, who will see Mr. Rogers his "garden of the mind" and raise him a "garden of the space-time continuum." Because when you leave this garden untended, anything is liable to happen. At the beginning of each new episode, you can see the weeds that have already sprouted up, threatening life, love, the universe, and emotional closure at every turn; luckily, just when things start to look dicey, the Doctor is on hand to prune, sow, and harvest as needed—so that, in the end, lovers will always find each other, families will always reunite, and time will be healed.

Before the show was rebooted in 2005 (its original 25+ year run on BBC television ended in 1989), it would have been difficult to imagine how the show would manage to stay current while remaining faithful to its geeky spirit, but it has more than done that. The changing times as well as the changing doctors (the Doctor has the power to regenerate and take on, essentially, a new persona and identity) are written into the fabric of the show, so that, in a way, the more things change, the more things stay the same. (Another instance in which the Doctor's reality bears an uncanny resemblance to our own.) If you haven't watched *Doctor Who* before, come for the guest stars, but stay for the TARDIS, the Daleks, the Master, the music, and everything else.

1 THE ROOM
DIRECTED BY TOMMY WISEAU (2003)

There are two basic ways to become a cult phenomenon: You can either be so deeply appreciated by so few people that they have no choice but to rally together and fight against the sands of time in order to ensure that someone else, someday, will also appreciate you ("you" in this case being *Twin Peaks*, *Star Trek*, Morrisey, etc.), OR you can be so uncannily, immaculately bad that your badness will exceed human understanding, and you will therefore only touch those jaded, ironic souls who seek profundity not only in what is ambitious and ineffable, but also in that which is profoundly awful.

The Room is in that second group. It will never be mistaken for a masterpiece, because it is awful. But its awfulness has a kind of internal logic that is hard to resist; it draws you in. Audiences now have a litany of chores to perform when they attend a screening. They chant "Go! Go! Go!" as the camera tracks across the Golden Gate Bridge (because it rarely makes it all the way across, but it never serves a purpose). They throw footballs around, because that is what Tommy Wiseau (the writer, producer, and star) tends to do when left alone with other men. And when the audience sees spoons on the screen, they have to yell "Spoons!"—but not for any reason, really. They yell "Spoons!" because there is no reason for framed pictures of spoons to keep appearing. But time and again, there those pictures are. And therefore, the people yell "Spoons!" And therefore, they throw spoons. And in that moment, they also find each other. Life is absurd, and so is *The Room*.

Welcome to the cult of Tommy Wiseau. PS: Spoons!!!!

DISCOVER NEW WORLDS
EXPLORERS WHO CAN TAKE YOU INTO THE UNKNOWN

Have you heard about this thing, exploring? It is an activity that humans sometimes engage in, wherein they leave behind what they already know and attempt to advance into what lies . . . beyond. But here's the thing: When you don't know what's around the corner, anything can happen next! And although it's always possible that you'll run into a delightful and charming new species of sea-rabbit (good news for sea-Easter!) when you're 20,000 leagues under the sea, it's also possible that you'll be consumed by a prehistoric squid—one that has suction cups of death! No one knows! But as in all things, there are pluses and minuses to this state of affairs. On the negative side, sometimes explorers suffer serious injuries (or worse); but on the positive side, when explorers do suffer serious injuries, man, do they wind up with some great stories. And as nonexplorers, we, the sane, will always be around to pick up the pieces (the story-pieces, I mean).

10 MARCO POLO IN *THE TRAVELS OF MARCO POLO*
WRITTEN BY MARCO POLO (THIRTEENTH CENTURY) 📖

It's kind of funny that we still use the phrase "the known world"—as though there were a portion of the earth that was still unknown. Spoiler alert: There is not. If you wanted to, you could open up Google Earth right now and plot a route from the Arctic North to South Africa using nothing but public transportation. But of course, it wasn't always that way. Once upon a time, all you could be sure about, as a tourist, was that sooner or later you were going to enter the land of sea-monsters, upside-down humans, and mutant beasts. They were on the maps of the time not as decorations, but as real warnings. They were out there, somewhere. Also out there somewhere, circa AD 1271: Kublai Khan, the Mongol Empire, and very well-established boundaries between Europe and Asia.

These truly were the dark ages in Europe, but Marco Polo braved all of these dangers (real, imagined, and imagined but real) to try and find some light. He survived shipwrecks, thirst, hunger, and barbarous borderlands, and made his way into the court of Kublai Khan, where he thrived, personally and professionally, for over 15 years. He encountered much that was unusual there (including the use of sand as money and poison as remedy), and much that was familiar (including political ambition and courtly intrigue), but by putting his experiences into words, he managed to not just expand the known world, but also enliven and augment it. Before Marco Polo there was Europe on the one hand and Asia on the other; after Marco Polo, there was the wider world.

9 CARL FREDRICKSEN IN *UP*
DIRECTED BY PETE DOCTER AND BOB PETERSON (2009) 🎞️

Back in the old days—back in 10,000 BC, for instance—you didn't need to have money to be an explorer. So long as you were a strong swimmer and brave enough to set out on the water before anyone else did, you could very well find yourself on an island that no other human had ever seen before. (And then, once the island was discovered, you could plant your land stick in the earth and declare yourself President and Sole Resident of Mud Rock Sea Place.) But after we figured out how to construct a boat and calculate longitude, exploration became a rich-person's game. Nowadays, whether you want to plumb the depths of the ocean or rocket into space, you need to have capital first. Luckily, Pixar has that. And even more luckily (luckily-ier?), they know what to do with it, once they have it. They know how to spend it, and where to go.

In *Up*, Pixar goes to the undiscovered country of the mind. Ed Asner plays Carl Frederickson, aka Ed Asner (the archetypal grumpy old man). And after a heaving sob-inducing opener, in which we see Carl go from wide-eyed kid to starry-eyed lover to married gent to bereaved widower in the blink of an eye, it seems as though the dreams of Carl's youth are dead and gone forever. His wife is dead. They never traveled. He is about to get assistance with his living. But then he sets his house afloat (via balloons) and dares to see the world. Metaphor alert: The dreams of our youth and the uncharted territories of the map occupy the same territory. They are both the lands of unfulfilled potential.

8 JACQUES COUSTEAU IN *THE UNDERSEA WORLD OF JACQUES COUSTEAU* STARRING JACQUES COUSTEAU (1966–1976)

If you're an explorer and you're not able to tell a good story, then you're really not much of an explorer. "Oh, yeah, I borrowed a few boats and we headed west, and then we wound up in a stormy set of islands." NO. "My name is Cristobal Colon. I fought desperately against the King and Queen of Spain in order to secure the ships I needed to challenge the very limits of the globe and discover what I now call 'The New World.'" YES. That's the ticket. Facts + flair = a future in exploration. And in that respect, Jacques Cousteau was the man with the golden ticket. A born entertainer and a lifelong wonderer, he wasn't the most brilliant scientist ever, but he certainly made a real contribution to his field (by inventing SCUBA gear, among other things), and he never, ever, stopped selling his brand. When we watch nature programs today and marvel at the shots they get and the straightforward manner of explaining technical concepts, we are watching the legacy of Jacques Cousteau: the most French of all possible underwater explorers.

7 THE AMERICAN ASTRONAUTS IN *FOR ALL MANKIND* DIRECTED BY AL REINERT (1989)

So yeah, TV's pretty weird. It used to be the case that if humanity couldn't see something with its own eyes, it pretty much didn't exist. Then, around the nineteenth century, humanity started taking pictures and stopping time in its tracks. And then, in the twentieth century, the pictures started moving and talking, and Lucy loved Ricky, and Ricky loved Lucy, and you could watch sports at home, and then man was on the moon, and then we were there with him, and then . . . WHAT?! That is where we went too far. The war was cold, the medium was hot, and everyone was confused.

But no, it's true: When Neil Armstrong, Buzz Aldrin, and the Apollo 11 crew landed on the moon, we were there with them. We were on the moon. We also, of course, remained on Planet Earth. That is a strange thing. *For All Mankind* tries to make a kind of sense of that strange thing, showing how these people got there, what they thought there, and what we saw when they stepped off a spaceship (a ship that flies through space!) there. On the moon. Where that weird man lives. (PS: How did he feel when humans stepped on his moon-face? Will we ever know?)

6 ERNEST SHACKLETON IN *SOUTH*
WRITTEN BY ERNEST SHACKLETON (1919)

It's hard to top the mysterious aura of outer space. Or at least it would be, were it not for Antarctica—a place where frozen ants reign over us all! No, just kidding, but it's still pretty bizarre. Ice is everywhere; cold is everywhere; murderous, camouflaged predators are everywhere; and oh yeah, no, seriously, the cold will literally murder you all on its own. Nevertheless, Captain Ernest Shackleton thought it would be cool to hang out down there, and in August 1914, he set sail for the great white South aboard his soon-to-be infamous ship, *The Endurance*. But before he and his crew reached the Antarctic mainland, they were trapped in pack ice. Then the ship was crushed by the surrounding ice, and sunk. Then they had to figure out a way to get home before everyone froze to death, or starved to death, or was bored to death, or all of the above. Then Shackleton got everyone back home alive, where he realized he was broke. Then he decided he had to write a book, and *South* is what we wound up with. Fair trade? Who knows. Exploration, huzzah!

5 DIAN FOSSEY IN *GORILLAS IN THE MIST*
WRITTEN BY DIAN FOSSEY (1983)

It's no coincidence that so many classics from children's literature and film take place in the animal kingdom. Animals are not human, so it's magical when they act human; but it's also deeply uncanny. And the closer we get to Homo sapiens on the evolutionary spectrum—and you can't get much closer than the mountain gorillas that Dian Fossey studied—the more uncanny things become. (How uncanny, you ask? Answer: More uncanny than Fido's guilty demeanor after his latest gas-blast.) Over her 13 years in the African jungle, Fossey was able to explore the prehuman world. She was able to see what friendship, love, fatherhood, motherhood, dinnertime, and war look like before a species has achieved a spoken language. And the answer is, it looks the same but very different. This is not a children's book. Fossey navigated the worlds of two very different species simultaneously, and in the end, the world that she shows us is a new one: It's not entirely human, and it's not entirely animal, but it is entirely our own. (And she leaves it to us to decide who "we" are in this context.)

4 RED ORM IN *THE LONG SHIPS*
WRITTEN BY FRANS G. BENGTSSON (1941-1945) 📖

When it's good, historical fiction is capable of two major benefits: It can either take a famous moment and offer an alternative or expanded account (as in *Wolf Hall*, for instance), or it can take an unexamined or obscure moment and attempt to shine a new light on it. Both options can yield thrilling results, and in *The Long Ships*, both options do. Swedish author Frans G. Bengtsson provides, on the one hand, an immersion into Viking life and culture (a topic of perennial interest and curiosity), and on the other, an illumination of the way European and Arabic cultures combined during the tenth century. Red Orm, the character at the center of this saga, is brave, hilarious, lucky, and, above all, Viking. But as you'll discover, Red Orm has a very open (one could almost say "global") notion of what it is to be a Viking, and what it means to be Red Orm . . .

3 LINK IN *THE LEGEND OF ZELDA: OCARINA OF TIME*
DEVELOPED BY NINTENDO AND GREZZO (1998) 🎮

From the very beginning, video games have always had an exploratory bent to them. Even when the screen rolled unrelentingly forward—in *Super Mario Bros.* for instance—there was always the chance that you could squat down on a pipe and pop into a netherworld (as one is wont to do when one is a Mario). But until video game technology really began to blow up in the late 1990s, you could only "explore" a video game in the way that you were able to "explore" a painting. In both cases, you were limited by what the artist wanted to show you. But then *Ocarina of Time* happened, and all of a sudden gamers all over the world were moseying along rolling hills, probing into dark corners, and moving on to the business of slaying enemies and saving the world when they well and truly felt like it. And as it turned out, the bumper stickers were right: a lot of people really would "rather be fishing." Even virtually.

2 CABEZA DE VACA IN *CHRONICLE OF THE NARVAEZ EXPEDITION*
BY ÁLVAR NÚÑEZ CABEZA DE VACA (1542) 📖

In 1527, any trip to the New World was a pretty intrepid act of exploration. The country was less than 50 years old to Europeans, and each trip required passing over what had previously seemed an infinite ocean, docking in a tumultuous harbor (usually in the storm-tossed Caribbean), and then trekking over strange new lands, peopled with strange new people. And that was what was on the menu if your trip went as expected. In Cabeza de Vaca's case, the trip did not go as expected. First comes shipwreck; then comes hunger; then comes battle, slavery, escape, and a nearly unending trek across what we would now recognize as the southern United States. On every step of this incredible journey, from Cuba to Florida, Texas, Guadalajara, and Mexico City, de Vaca encounters an America that is pre-Spanish, pre-English, and pre-American. If ever there was a time-travel novel, this is it. It's nonfiction as science-fiction, and it's the craziest vacation ever.

1 SCROOGE MCDUCK IN *DUCKTALES*
CHARACTERS CREATED BY CARL BARKS (1987-1990)

It's all well and good to fly to the moon, or dive to the bottom of the sea, or discover America, or be "first" to some place else, but let's give credit where credit is due: namely, to the ducks of *DuckTales*—and, of course, to that king among ducks, Uncle Scrooge McDuck. These brave ducks do it all. In addition to traveling all over the animated world, they also pop into other centuries and other cultures at the drop of a hat. And in addition to fending off real-world dangers (like crooks, robbers, and thieves), they also readily confront imaginary perils from the world of pop culture (like harpies and the malevolent forces in Homer's *Odyssey* . . . and the Beatles). It's easy to get lost in such a post-modern landscape, but these ducks don't care. To put it another way: They don't give a flying duck. To rephrase: They don't give a Launchpad McQuack. For all these reasons and more, they are the greatest explorers that the world (whether real and imagined) has ever known. *DuckTales*. Woo-ooh.

FIND YOUR CALLING
ALL-CONSUMING HOBBIES FOR YOUR CONSIDERATION

*L*ook, there's no denying that it's cool to do big, bold things. You're definitely going to land a few dates if you can reflect on that time when you negotiated a peace treaty, or invented the iPhone, or wrote and performed (in public) "Your Body Is a Wonderland." Those things all take vision, courage, and a sense of purpose in this life. But if you really want to be admired, you have to also show a quirkier side. Because it's one thing to be a Supreme Court justice, but it's something else entirely to be a Supreme Court justice who performs as a clown at birthday parties for celebrity pets. The former is impressive, the latter is the stuff of legends. The latter is also the stuff of this list. Heed these suggestions, and prepare yourself for legendary status.

10 KES
DIRECTED BY KEN LOACH (1969)

Featured hobby: Falconry.

In medieval Europe, falconry was a status symbol. If you could hunt with a raptor, you were probably a noble. In 1970s Britain, this was no longer the case, at all. Billy is fifteen years old and the son of miner. He does not have much to look forward to, but he does at least appear to have a special bond with a wild bird. The education that he and the kestrel provide to one another is expansive and profound. The movie has been named one of the top ten British films of the twentieth century by the British Film Institute, and the acclaim is deserved. Like *Brief Encounter* (number two on that same list), it takes a small character in a small situation and shows us the world. (Bird's-eye view.)

9 THE MOST DANGEROUS GAME
WRITTEN BY RICHARD CONNELL (1924)

Featured hobby: Big-game hunting.

The Most Dangerous Game is a modest, genteel title for an elegant little novella. The villain of this book—an aristocratic landowner—is so extremely cultured. He is Eastern European. Very. So we settle right in, hoping that "maybe this book won't be about a literal manhunt, after all!" As a result, when the main character (aka "the hunted") does start hurtling himself through a terrifying island landscape (filled with natural hazards and man-made knife pits), everything becomes that much more upsetting. Since its publication in 1924, the story has become hugely influential (I'm looking at you, *Hunger Games*), but even so, it's worth learning how to construct a Burmese tiger pit now, before the Europeans and their hats get any more eccentric.

8 TINY FURNITURE
WRITTEN AND DIRECTED BY LENA DUNHAM (2010)

Featured hobby: Photographing tiny, useless furniture.

If your parents are successful and you're a young adult, there are two basic paths you can take in order to maintain your self-respect: You can either strive ambitiously for success through traditional routes (making money as a lawyer, saving lives as a doctor) or you can deny the very idea of success, and insist on something smaller (as an artist, most commonly). Or you can do both. You can be Lena Dunham and achieve success and celebrity by making small artworks like tiny furniture (or making the tiny furniture in *Tiny Furniture*, as Aura does). And then you can make *Girls*.

7 AMÉLIE
DIRECTED BY JEAN-PIERRE JEUNET (2001)

Featured hobby: Lies, theft, and home invasion for the greater good.

High production values, a beautiful leading lady, poignant voice-overs, profound emotional impact, and Paris, France. These elements, combined, are enough to make any pessimist scoff heartily (should said pessimist be possessed of a heart). But *Amélie* is more than just a pretty face. It also takes the time to figure out how the staples of romantic comedy (cute people, meet-cutes, delayed gratification, and whimsy) can be converted into real poignancy. The answer, in a sense, is lies. Amélie is a shy, sheltered being who markets herself as a Paris phenomenon. She sends a garden gnome on a global tour in an effort to get her dad out of the house again. She constructs a false narrative about her neighbor in order to demonstrate, to said neighbor, that love still matters. And she, for her part, finds her beloved by first thinking about who he could be, and then tracking him down via Polaroids. Amélie, in sum, is a great lover because she's a great liar—and God bless her for that.

6 PRIMER
WRITTEN AND DIRECTED BY SHANE CARRUTH (2004)

Featured hobby: Time travel.

Primer is a fun little time travel movie in the same way that time travel is a fun little hobby. The film (which won the Sundance Film Festival's Grand Jury Prize) was shot, in the director's words, for "the price of a used car," or roughly $7,000. But it's smart, it's tense, it looks great (even though, due to budgetary constraints, many of the scenes could only be shot in one take), and it centers around a concept so mind-blowing that you'll probably need to consult a diagram in order to talk about the movie afterwards. A plot that's hard to comprehend normally isn't a point of pride, but in this case it is, and it ought to be. *Primer* deals with time travel as it deals with science and life more generally—as things that, for at least the duration of this miraculous film, have an equal share in reality.

5 FOLLOWING
DIRECTED BY CHRISTOPHER NOLAN (1998)

Featured hobby: Following humans. Because. (PS: Look behind you.)

Before *Batman Begins*, before *Inception*, before even *Memento*, Christopher Nolan made *Following*—a film that was shot on an even smaller budget than *Primer*. As with *Primer*, almost every take had to be used, but Nolan relied on intense rehearsals to ensure that, despite the budgetary constraints, the film still maintained a certain polish and style. *Following* follows a follower (obviously) named Bill, whose strange hobby eventually sets him up for a very serious fall. It already looks and feels like a Chris Nolan film; from the chopped and mixed chronology to the pessimistic outlook to the white-knuckle intensity, it's pretty much all there . . . and it's pretty much all great, already.

4 VERONICA MARS
CREATED BY ROB THOMAS (2004–2007)

veronica MARS

Featured hobby: Amateur sleuthing.

Veronica Mars sounds like the kind of great idea—a high school student in "Neptune," California, begins sleuthing around after her best friend is murdered—that's great in theory and abysmal in practice. It's just hard to imagine a network television show being sufficiently well acted, written, and managing to balance all of the priorities of plot and pathos. But not only does *Veronica Mars* succeed as a mystery show, it also works as a compelling high school drama, a postmodern comedy, and as a classic prime-time soap opera. And it's a great place to go for celebrity sightings: There's Kristen Bell in the title role, Amanda Seyfried (as the dead girl), and a litany of other future stars (and *Party Down* cast members).

3 MY MAN GODFREY
STARRING WILLIAM POWELL AND CAROLE LOMBARD (1936)

Featured hobbies: Scavenger hunting; buttling.

William Powell isn't that well known today, but he remains one of the most charming actors ever to don a moustache. In *My Man Godfrey,* he plays Godfrey, a strangely refined hobo on the fringes of Depression-era New York. Godfrey becomes an item of value (as a "forgotten man") when two sisters (played by Carole Lombard and Gail Patrick) need him to finish first in a perverse game of scavenger hunt. Godfrey sides with Carole Lombard, who, in her gratefulness, enlists his services thereafter as a butler. And then falls in love with him. From that description alone, you can probably figure out how the movie ends, but the process of getting to that foregone romantic conclusion has hardly ever been more enjoyable.

2 THE LEAGUE
STARRING MARK DUPLASS, NICK KROLL, JONATHAN LAJOIE, PAUL SCHEER, KATIE ASELTON, ET AL. (2009-) 🖥

Featured hobbies: Fantasy football; adopting scary telephone voices (although "Bobbum Man"—he who threatens your "equipmunk"—is already taken).

It's hard to think of a more offensive show than *The League*. It's also hard to think of a funnier one. That's because the cast of Duplass, Kroll, Lajoie, Scheer, and Aselton, are given free rein to say what they will after the scenes are set up—and because they all have horrible, filthy, ridiculous minds. The show is ostensibly about fantasy football, but it's really about the stupid obsessions that control our lives, and no matter how old we get, keep us all behaving like children. Children with no manners, no decency, and very few limits—especially when it comes to the Shiva.

1 VERTIGO
DIRECTED BY ALFRED HITCHCOCK (1958) 🎞

Featured hobby: Turning people into ghosts, and vice versa.

Vertigo was recently voted the best film of all time by the *Sight and Sound* poll (which is conducted once every ten years). It is, in a lot of ways, a perfect movie. But that makes it sound stuffy. It's also a perfect entertainment. To say the same thing a different way: From up close, it's a deeply suspenseful, deeply mysterious thriller; and from far away, it is a profound reflection on life, guilt, time, and desire. All of the film's metaphors and themes have a way of echoing one another, and Hitchcock also manages to express these ideas and their relationships in profoundly visual terms. To give one example: At the film's midpoint, Kim Novak looks up at a church tower and runs toward the steps. James Stewart looks up at the same tower and begins to run after her. That single tower has two separate meanings, simultaneously, and when Kim Novak runs up the steps, she is both an accomplice to a murder and a citizen just looking to help. These dual realities, of course, will eventually come home to roost, in the single person of Kim Novak. Every scene in the movie is a little miracle, and the movie as a whole is a big one.

It also looks incredible (thanks to Hitchcock), sounds incredible (thanks to Bernard Herrmann), and has an iconic title sequence (thanks to Saul Bass). It's good. You should watch it, if you haven't seen it. And if you have, you should watch it again.

OUTWIT DEATH
ESSENTIAL LESSONS IN SURVIVAL

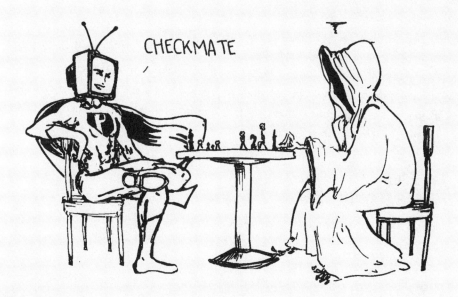

CHECKMATE

Do you know what's dangerous? Human existence, that's what! Every day we get out of bed (already dangerous), commute somewhere via trains (which derail) and cars (which crash), do some work (which leads to stress, which causes heart disease), and then socialize over drinks (a kind of poison) with other people (our natural enemies) before going to sleep (. . . aka "a pleasant death!"). And that's without even accounting for rabid possums, poisoned pens, or electrified manhole covers. Still, it's worth remembering that, although Death's been gunning for us since Eden, we've been plotting our escape for just as long. Let us count the ways . . .

10 ROBINSON CRUSOE
WRITTEN BY DANIEL DEFOE (1719)

Parents wisely tell their children never to turn their backs on the sea (because it's clearly out to murder us); but when our fronts are to the sea, our backs are to something else. After being shipwrecked, Robinson Crusoe doesn't turn his back on anything. Instead he identifies his resources, turns everything to account, and never stops planning. The tension in the book is endless because nothing is ever guaranteed. Today's solution is tomorrow's problem, and that's as true in America today as it was in England in 1719, when Defoe's book (which many claim is the first novel written in English) was published. The only book that Crusoe had on his island was a copy of the Bible, but whether you're looking for spiritual or physical sustenance, it's hard to do better than Defoe's masterpiece. It's a thousand books in one, and every time you read it, you learn something new.

9 THE EDGE
WRITTEN BY DAVID MAMET (1997)

Elle Macpherson, David Mamet, Alec Baldwin, Sir Anthony Hopkins, and a bear. I mean, stop it. It's too much. David Mamet's trademark brand of obscenity-laced machismo gets its perfect outlet here, as Anthony Hopkins has to somehow (1) survive a crash landing, (2) stave off bear attacks, (3) eat maggots, (4) tease out the difference between bosom companion (Alec Baldwin) and cuckolding murderer (Alec Baldwin), and (5) rediscover civilization. Fortunately, Hopkins's character is a great reader and knows how to make a compass from scratch. Unfortunately, he doesn't realize that when you're stuck in the wild with Alec Baldwin, the only direction worth going is: away from Alec Baldwin.

8 INTO THE WILD
WRITTEN BY JON KRAKAUER (1996)

Most behavior guidelines consist almost entirely of No's: Don't hit your classmates. Don't pee in the pool. Don't eat poisonous snacks. And so on. These are good rules, but every once in a while even the best rules need to be tested. Christopher Johnson McCandless was a very brave, very smart guy who said no to all the No's, headed into nature, and sought to live a wilder, more natural life. Four months later, he was dead. This wasn't a necessary outcome to his life philosophy by any means, but it does show just how critical every decision becomes when you leave civilization's safety nets behind.

7 LORD OF THE FLIES
DIRECTED BY PETER BROOK (1963)

Childhood is a brutal business: Adults give you food (aka "lunch"), but the bullies take it from you. Parents give you a name, but the wiseacres give you a new one. And then gym class comes along, and your "teachers" stand idly by while other kids fire bouncy red missiles at you. The torture never ends, and then you're expected to somehow grow up. *Lord of the Flies* is about that strange blend of brutality and civility that we call "childhood," but it's also about the primal forces that lie beneath all of civilization, no matter how old you may be. The novel of the same name (written by William Golding) offered an alarmingly convincing portrayal of what children would be like when stranded on a desert island and stripped of all oversight; but the film went one step further: Peter Brook took a fairly random sampling of aspiring child actors, put them on an island, removed almost any sense of supervision, and started filming. In his words: "the only falsification in Golding's fable is the length of time the descent to savagery takes. His action takes about three months. I believe that . . . complete catastrophe could occur within one long weekend." (Note to self: Everyone on earth is or has been a child, therefore, RUN.)

6 127 HOURS
DIRECTED BY DANNY BOYLE (2010)

So yeah, it's one thing to make it through childhood or lunch at Chevy's, but it's something else entirely to survive in the wild when the biggest threat to your survival is the fact that your arm is still attached to your body. This movie—which, again, is about a man sawing through his own arm—was commercially and financially successful. That is a miracle. Or, as we will probably say in the future: That is a James Franco. So, the next time you go hiking, please heed this film's warnings and remember to bring along a cell phone, a cell phone tower, morphine, grenades, a doctor, your mom, a car, food, water, extra batteries, and a light saber (in case you do actually need to amputate something). Or stay home, watch this movie, and never trust nature again.

5 UNBROKEN: A WORLD WAR II STORY OF SURVIVAL, RESILIENCE, AND REDEMPTION
BY LAURA HILLENBRAND (2010)

In chapter 1 of *Unbroken*, Louis Zamperini—a former track star and an Army Air Forces bombardier—survives a crash landing, gets on a small raft, and travels hundreds of ocean miles with little more than wits and oars at his disposal. The shark attacks are relentless. The sun is relentless. And at the end of the journey, only two of the original four men in his party are still alive. Again, that is just the first chapter of a much, much longer survival tale. In the course of Laura Hillenbrand's thrilling account, you learn how to survive at sea for 43 days and how to kill a shark with pliers (when oars aren't available). You learn how survival is possible when death seems inevitable, and you also learn that if something is possible, Louis Zamperini will do it. He is now 95 years old.

4 DELIVERANCE
WRITTEN BY JAMES DICKEY (1970)

Deliverance is a sinkhole of terror, but it's written like a potboiler, where every new solution leads to a whole new set of problems. As a result, the book veers wildly from bizarro travelogue to horror story to adventure tale to crime novel, and yet somehow it all hangs together. The movie version has the "Squeal!" line and "Dueling Banjos" (one of the weirdest songs to ever win a Grammy), but the book lasts about six hours longer—so if you savor suspense (and tips on how to kill with a crossbow) you've got to go back to the original.

3 THE WALKING DEAD
WRITTEN BY ROBERT KIRKMAN (2003-)

Which of the following do you think is more of a threat to your survival: a global pandemic, terrorism, heart disease, or a zombie apocalypse? I would definitely say zombie apocalypse, even though I know in my brain-parts that zombies is "profoundly incorrect." But so be it. Zombie-apocalypse prep is still a worthwhile hobby, because even at the end of days people still need to eat food, drink water, and find a place to sleep. Also, though a zombie apocalypse might sound outlandish at the moment, the fact that so many different books and movies have prescribed the same remedy for the undead (braining 'em) is more than a little disturbing. If zombies aren't real, then why do we know so much about them!? Why are we so good at killing them!?

2 THE ROAD
WRITTEN BY CORMAC MCCARTHY (2006)

In Cormac McCarthy's version of the future, it is very cold. There are no resources. Looting is life. Most of the survivors in this world are on a barbaric and never-ending hunt for other human beings, because when it really comes down to it, people are edible. McCarthy's novel follows a father and his son in this hellscape, and [spoiler alert] the two do not share many laffs together. (Where did all the laffs go! And how do you survive in a post-laffs world?) It's not easy, but it seems like morals might be the answer. You need morals on the road. Oh, and it also helps to start out with a bathtub full of clean drinking water. Everything in the book is described in stark, stripped-down language, and it's all very vivid, and very believable. This book will haunt your dreams.

1 THE SHAWSHANK REDEMPTION
DIRECTED BY FRANK DARABONT (1994)

We've reviewed survival tactics in the face of zombies, cannibals, hillbillies, childhood, rocks, the sea, bears, and Alec Baldwin. But there is one arena that still needs to be discussed: jail. The movies teach us that jail is the scariest thing ever. It is even scarier than the previous terror champion: landsharks on motorcycles, wearing fur hats—no, those aren't hats! My god! They're swarms of furious killer bees! So let us thank Stephen King (who first wrote the novella "Rita Hayworth and the Shawshank Redemption") for the existence of this now classic prison film, in which we learn how to deter rapists, find a cushy job, embezzle funds from a warden, find an understated narrator, and escape a high security facility. Also, if you're ever in a bind outside of jail, just start talking about how much you love *The Shawshank Redemption*. It will turn your enemies into your friends, and turn everyone—friends and enemies, robbers and robbees, wardens and inmates alike—into Morgan Freeman–quoting machines. Seriously. It works every time.

PUT ON A POETIC AIR
SOURCES OF WEIRD AND WONDERFUL WORD COMBINATIONS

The Moon, July 21, 1969: Neil Armstrong leans over his space-desk, takes a bite of astronaut's ice cream, and plans his first words: "I take small footsteps, yet look how far I go, Earth friends!" [Mutters to himself, crosses it out.] "Baby steps, you say? No! These are moon-bounds!" [Shakes his head. Throws paper away.] And then he has it: "That's one small step for a man; one giant leap for mankind." And even though he flubbed his lines when he finally exited Apollo 11, that little bit of poetry went a long way. (Another victory for the Astro-Poet Guild.) So whether you're planning your own moonwalk or just planning a weekend, it's time you learned how to smash your words together, better! Poetry!

10 THE ROYAL TENENBAUMS
DIRECTED BY WES ANDERSON (2001)

Whether you hate Wes Anderson, love Wes Anderson, or don't know who Wes Anderson is, this is the Wes Anderson movie for you. This is the film that you'll actually be able to relate to. Here it doesn't matter how font-savvy you are or whether or not you get the French film references or appreciate the soundtrack; here, you just need to have a family. Because once you have that, we can more or less take it on faith that you also have a family member that you love, hate, and find embarrassing.

Gene Hackman as Royal Tenenbaum is the epitome of the much-beloved, much-despised, much-mocked father type. But despite his pretensions to grandeur, it's worth noting that he is nothing without his words. His personalized brand of whimsical, aggressive, defensive jargon makes him the kind of person—the kind of individual—that we all want to know. His failure as a parent is perfect and complete, because he fails so completely in his own way. Without his jive-talking, ass-shagging, brick-throwing style of address, he is just another stereotype; just another distant, entitled, egocentric patriarch. But with his true-blue-isms, he's become an icon.

The best line: "I'm not talking about dance lessons. I'm talking about putting a brick through the other guy's windshield. I'm talking about taking it out and chopping it up."

—ROYAL TENENBAUM

9 BRICK
DIRECTED BY RIAN JOHNSON (2005)

The first rule of *Brick* is: Brick is not a brick. Just like in the golden days of film noir, almost everything here is a double entendre, and just like in the golden days of noir, there is no black and white. In high school, as in life, you need to know the right people, ask the right questions, and ask those questions in just the right way. The only major difference between high school and the real world is that, before you graduate, the alert level is higher, and the stakes are lower. Not at this Southern California high school, however. Here, high school tactics (code words and cliques) meld with gangland politics (eat or be eaten) to create the perfect environment for surprisingly authentic, high-octane wordplay. Brendan's (Joseph Gordon-Levitt) ex-girlfriend has been murdered, and if he wants to stay safe and find some answers, he'll first need to find a way to start blending in. When in Rome, speak Latin. When in high school, find something more exclusive.

The best line: "When the 'Upper-Crust' does shady deeds, they do them all over town, and the pitch is, they got these little symbols so they can tell each other without word getting around."

—THE BRAIN

8 DEADWOOD
CREATED BY DAVID MILCH (2004-2006) 🖵

Shakespeare is often referenced in praise of *Deadwood* because the language is so very highfalutin'. On the other hand, *Deadwood* has a character named Al Sweringen (played by Ian McShane), and he does exactly as his name would have him do: He swears like an engine. "Cocksucker" is the fuel that Al runs on (because, as I'm sure he's noted, he eats cocksuckers for breakfast), but it is not his only weapon.

Al swears when he shits, and his shit swears when it lands. When Al swears, a devil gets its horns; and when Al swears, he does it like an angel. He is the Walt Whitman of ball-busting, shit-pounding, all-out Wild Westernry. End of fucking sentence. His obscenities are inspired and inspirational. They sound amazing, and they get things done. And although the American West in *Deadwood* isn't realistic by any means, Al's f-bombs still have the kind of inner life that we should all aspire to. They are open-ended, poetic, natural, and true.

The best line: "Here's my counteroffer to your counteroffer: Go fuck yourself."

—AL SWERINGEN

7 JUNO
WRITTEN BY DIABLO CODY (2007) 🎞️

Diablo Cody (nee Brook Busey) is the screenwriting talent behind *Juno, Jennifer's Body*, and *Young Adult*. So on the one hand, yes, Diablo Cody is a human being on Planet Earth (honest to blog she is!); but Diablo Cody is also a dialect: a distinctly bloggy network of internet jokes, pop culture references, and puns. In an early scene of Cody's debut feature, Juno (Ellen Page) offers her parents what may be the movie's one straight line: "I'm pregnant." After that, the quips come out in force—and it actually makes a lot of sense, in context. Her characters are vulnerable, and jokes act as their most reliable form of self-defense. And luckily, when the jokes fall flat, then Juno's dad is always available to "punch Paulie Bleeker in the wiener," because whether you're dealing with pregnancies, comedies, or bank robberies, you always have to have a backup plan.

The best line: "That ain't no Etch A Sketch. This is one doodle that can't be undid, Homeskillet."

—ROLLO

6 "C·R·E·A·M· (CASH RULES EVERYTHING AROUND ME)" BY THE WU-TANG CLAN (1993) 🎵

There's no way to quantify the value of our poetry and poets, but still, if someone put a gun to your head and said "quantify our poetry and poets or I'll blow you away!" then word creation would not be a bad standard to go by. Shakespeare, for instance, is notable for the sheer number of words and phrases that he created (or popularized) and which we still use. And by a similar accounting, American culture as a whole owes a special debt to hip-hop—and to groups like Wu-Tang Clan in particular. They have popularized and expanded upon existing slang in such a way as to literally augment the English language.

Wu-Tang consists of a variable crew of rappers (often superstars in their own rights) based in and around Staten Island (aka Shaolin), New York. Their lexicon is so extensive that they've created their very own dictionary. And although "C.R.E.A.M." is just one song, it puts many of the group's best traits on full display. RZA's sample evokes the mood of a dark, empty barroom; the lyrics fall into one another easily and casually, like drunken patrons; and the words, even when they're foreign, are always clear. It's a beautiful, harsh, desolate song. And for the record, the world would be a better place if everyone referred to everyone else as "God."

The best line: "We got stickup kids, corrupt cops, and crack rocks . . . / and stray shots, all on the block that stays hot."
   —Inspectah Deck

5 "JABBERWOCKY" WRITTEN BY LEWIS CARROLL, PUBLISHED IN THROUGH THE LOOKING-GLASS, AND WHAT ALICE FOUND THERE (1871) 📖

Why struggle to find an existing expression when you can just make up a new one? Why are we always fraboodling with all these old words? That was Lewis Carroll's opinion, anyway, when he penned his iconic seven-stanza poem about the Jubjub bird, the Bandersnatch, the Jabberwock, and the beamish boy who dared to face them. Carroll's so-called nonsense poem vibrates with life; his meaning is palpable. And even though it harkens back to an older form of English, it still remains a step ahead of the language today. After all, who among us can find suitable terms to describe the Tumtum tree! No one! And why bother? We can simply feel it in our bones.

The best line: "O frabjous day! Callooh! Callay!'/He chortled in his joy."
   —Lewis Carroll

4 THE MIGHTY BOOSH
STARRING JULIAN BARRATT AND NOEL FIELDING (2004-2007) 🖥

The Mighty Boosh often has the feeling of being an inside joke. Vince Noir (played by Noel Fielding) and Howard Moon (played by Julian Barratt) don't seem overly perturbed by the possibility that their audience may not "get it." Oh, you don't really get my meaning yet? Well, just hold your horses, tiny eyes! Season 1 is loosely oriented around a zoo. Season 2 is loosely oriented around a curiosity shoppe. Lots of comedy shows rely on a consistent sense of place (the coffee shop in *Friends*; the bar in *How I Met Your Mother*), but in *The Mighty Boosh*, these settings act more like launching pads, as a point of origin from which the show can blast off to outer space or another alternate universe. So why go back to these places? Who knows? Why does Old Gregg like Bailey's so much? What is a crack fox, and why is it so emotionally volatile? What is "crimping"? And why are Vince and Howard so susceptible to spontaneous, coordinated lyricism? It's all nonsense, I suppose (quite literally so, in the case of crimping), but it's a beautiful nonsense.

The best line: When the zoo owner Dixon Bainbridge refers to the zoo's python as "the windy-man! The long mover!" Or, any crimp, ever.

3 A CLOCKWORK ORANGE
WRITTEN BY ANTHONY BURGESS (1962) 📖

Children love things that rhyme. The rhymes are ridiculous, the children repeat them seriously, we all laugh and they cry and we all fall down. Everybody wins. But then Anthony Burgess came along and built the "goo-goos" and "ga-gas" of baby talk into an entire adult language called "Nadsat" (which is often derived from existing Russian words, but also benefitted from extreme permutations of existing English slang as well), and, what's worse, he gave that language to a terrifying gang of youths with a penchant for a bit of the old ultraviolence. *A Clockwork Orange* is profoundly uncanny. In its pages even milk ("moloko") has an air of menace, and "Home" becomes a house of horrors. If nightmares could talk, they would speak Nadsat. (Which makes it even more upsetting when you realize that, the more you read, the more fluent you become.)

The best line: "And then there was more smekking and another malenky tolchock, O my brothers, on my poor smarting rot . . . I knew I was going to get nothing like fair play from them stinking grahzny bratchnies, Bog blast them."
    —ALEX

2 FLIGHT OF THE CONCHORDS
CREATED BY JAMES BOBIN, BRET MCKENZIE, AND JERMAINE CLEMENT (2007-2009)

Bret and Jermaine are New Zealanders with big American dreams, and even bigger (and even more funky) Kiwi imaginations. Several times each episode their dreams and imaginations combine in the form of spontaneous, whimsical songs. Sometimes, as in the episode "Friends," these songs are apt, poignant, and take place in bowling alleys; other times, as in "Foux du fafa," they are apt and poignant, but take place in the linguistic gutter between French and English. The show feels in some ways like "the future of musical comedy!" (scare quotes used because I am literally terrified by the idea that musical comedy has a future), because the songs work so well as both melodies and as jokes (and as commentaries on genre, but space is limited here). In the end they give eloquent testimony to the fact that, in music as in politics: If it sounds good, then it makes sense . . .

The best line: "Foux du fafa, foux du fafa, fafa / Foux du fafa, ah ee ah."

1 EUROVISION SONG CONTEST
CREATED BY MARCEL BEZENCON ON (1956-)

Sometimes you have to just go back to the source. And whether you're talking about gibberish, American pop, *Star Search*, the Super Bowl halftime show, or reality television, the European song contest generally known as "Eurovision" (even though the program name varies from country to country) is the source. Since the 1950s, this contest has served as a proving ground for the likes of ABBA, Celine Dion, and France Gall. But what makes this contest so interesting—and so relevant here—is the fact that, since Europe has no unifying language, the less meaningful the words, the better. Who cares about the diction in a song about a dying breed of Estonian carpet-fitters if no one can understand the language or the cultural reference points? So as a result, what a lot of the songs wind up utilizing is a sort of Esperanto scat. A universal gibberish.

The best line: "Zaleilah-leila-lei, everyday, everybody!"

ADOPT A MORE OUTLANDISH CHILDHOOD
BECAUSE SOME KIDS HAVE ALL THE (BAD) LUCK

I hate to be the one to break it to you, but our grandparents got the jump on us. They realized long ago that there's no reason to get a ride to school if you can walk five miles instead. ("In the snow!" they insist.) And then they realized that it was one thing to have to walk five miles, but it was something else entirely to have to run because wild wolverines were chasing you and because you had to get to class in time to eat your boiled egg, scrub the floors, and glue your textbook back together before Teacher got to class and penalized you for "laziness and incipient rebellion." If grandparents know anything, then they know this: A childhood filled with danger, hardship, and something gross for dinner is a sure-fire route to respect; but we can't all be born at the bottom of the well. The rest of us have to look to fiction for a suitable past . . .

10 HARRY POTTER AND THE GOBLET OF FIRE
DIRECTED BY MIKE NEWELL (2005)

Hogwarts is a place where kids are taught spells and potions by a stunning cast of British character actors; it's a place where the bathrooms are filled with kooky, sexually adventurous ghosts, and where the annual commute to school is filled with beans of every flavor and chocolate frogs. It's a place where magic happens! But it's also a place where puberty happens, and thus, by the time the fourth film (fourth in sequence, first in entertainment) in the series rolled around, Hogwarts had become a very dark place indeed. For confirmation of this profound darkness you need look no further than the setting for the final event in the Tri-Wizard's Cup: a hedge maze. You know another movie that concludes in and around a hedge maze? *The Shining*.

9 EMPIRE OF THE SUN
DIRECTED BY STEVEN SPIELBERG (1987)

Steven Spielberg has a long history working in the "outlandish childhood" genre. He directed *E.T., Hook,* and *Jurassic Park,* and produced *The Goonies* and *Super 8*—and most of his other films (*Jaws* and *Close Encounters of the Third Kind,* for instance) still rely on children to emphasize the impact, and often the emotional ambiguity, of pivotal moments. But *Empire of the Sun* still stands out. It's the first film that Spielberg directed where the child in question was based on a real person: the author J.G. Ballard (aka Jim Graham). Ballard and his family were placed in a Japanese internment camp after the Japanese overran Shanghai in World War II, and 20 years after the fact he wrote a novel based on those experiences. "Those experiences" are rough.

The Lunghua camp, where Jim is captive, it's a dog-eat-dog world—and that makes it pretty tough for all the humans to survive. (Good material for a story though.)

8 THE WITCHES
WRITTEN BY ROALD DAHL (1983)

Like Maurice Sendak (the author and illustrator of *Where the Wild things Are,* among other things), Roald Dahl wrote children's books that were not very child-friendly. But whereas Sendak's stories and illustrations seemed lit up by a warm light, which, on reflection, seemed deeply weird and threatening, Roald Dahl wrote stories that took place in dangerous environments but infused those stories with a pervasive spirit of magic, warmth, and even love. Matilda, in the book by the same title, grows up in a family of rotten, selfish con-artists, but is herself a little miracle; James, in *James and the Giant Peach,* is attacked by anything and everything in the course of his travels, but he never loses his spirit; and in *The Witches*, not only is the main character orphaned and stalked by witches from morning to night, but the book also ends with the boy transformed into a mouse. Unfortunately, that drastically reduces his life expectancy; fortunately, it makes him a little less likely to outlive his beloved grandmother. That is a serious dose of melancholy for a "happy ending" in a children's book, but it's hard to deny the charm of that last scene.

7 CALVIN AND HOBBES
WRITTEN AND ILLUSTRATED BY BILL WATTERSON
(IN SYNDICATION FROM 1985-1995)

Calvin is exceptional to this list in that his daily life is fairly mundane. Getting to school is not a problem; dinner is on the table every night; and Calvin has no real enemies to speak of. But what he does have is truly dangerous imagination. He has Hobbes: a stuffed tiger who spends nearly every school day lying in wait for Calvin to return home (at which point Hobbes can launch himself from his hiding place and send Calvin sprawling back into the street). And again, that's Calvin's favorite toy. When it comes to his teacher, the food on his plate, the noises in the dark, and cardboard boxes . . . that's where things get out of control. That's where Spaceman Spiff pops up and where the leafy greens start talking back. In the end, nothing is safe from Calvin's imagination (least of all Calvin), which is one of the things that makes the comics so consistently recognizable and beautiful. *Calvin and Hobbes* is the place where nothing is static, and where your snowman is, in a very real sense, a commentary on conceptual art.

6 A HIGH WIND IN JAMAICA
WRITTEN BY RICHARD HUGHES (1929)

"So yeah, this one time my siblings and I were kidnapped by pirates (via a botched monkey operation—more on that later), and my brother died (via coconuts, I think?), and then we were all, like, pirates together, but then my favorite sister, the weird one, murdered this one dude, kind of by accident but also not, because she stabbed him a bunch, but yeah, it was still cool for a while. We all hung out for a few months, and shared stuff, and tried to find a way to live together, but then things started to get weird, and eventually the pirates got arrested, and we went back to England. And then my brothers and sisters and me all became adults one day. The end!"

That's basically it: That's what happens in *A High Wind in Jamaica*—except of course that summary lacks the book's poetry and ambiguity and the overwhelming weirdness of being born into a world that makes no sense at all. Summary: This book is everyone's childhood, plus real, live, PIRATES.

5 ADVENTURES OF HUCKLEBERRY FINN
WRITTEN BY MARK TWAIN (1884)

Huckleberry Finn is a normal American boy in the same way that the Mississippi River is a normal American river. They are archetypal; they are huge, eternal, effortless, natural metaphors. So, to put it another way, the Mississippi is made of water in the same way that Huck is made of humanity. That's a lot of responsibility to put upon a kid, but luckily Huck (as he is, and will forever be, affectionately known) is also able to set some time aside for himself. And luckily for himself, Huck has an eye for entertainment. He is thus able to fake his own death, escape his abusive father, borrow (and pilot) a raft, navigate a blood feud, and help to free his friend and helpmate Jim, a slave. The trouble doesn't end when the book does, but *Huckleberry Finn* was then and remains now a touchstone for the ongoing conversation about race, about freedom, and about American identity.

4 BRAVE
STORY BY BRENDA CHAPMAN (2012)

Pixar has made great movies about childhood, adulthood, toys, fish, robots, rats, bugs, and even cars. If they had to, I do believe they could turn the story of the Microsoft Paper Clip into an Oscar-worthy tale of insecurity and tragic isolation (tear); but they have not been so great about girls. *Brave* sought to remedy that fact. They started well, with an independent, red-haired free-thinker named Merida (Princess Merida, to give her full title), but then Merida turned her mother into a bear, and from that point on, the smart money was always going to be on a bear movie. But with that being said, *Brave* is also a movie about the power of nature, about the overwhelming power of who we want to be and who we really are. It's also a movie in which the main character has to deal with, quite literally, an angry mama bear. And that is a childhood that is going to come heavily laden with some very intriguing stories.

3 THE LION, THE WITCH AND THE WARDROBE
WRITTEN BY C.S. LEWIS (1950) 📖

The first book of *The Chronicles of Narnia* began when the Pevensie children (Peter, Susan, Edmund, and Lucy, by name) "were sent away from London during the war because of the air-raids." The Nazi blitz, to reiterate, is what happens before things start to go off the rails. That's what happens before a mythical lion goes "on the move again"; before freaky fauns called Tumnus start referring to themselves as "Mister"; and before everyone starts getting petrified by certain witches possessing certain devilish candies. (If it is not, in fact, delightful, why then is it called a "Turkish Delight"? Why is no one suing these people!?) *The Lion, the Witch and the Wardrobe* includes humans, lions, witches, wardrobes, and World War II. All between two book covers, and all in a way that makes some sense. If only every childhood could be so coherent.

2 SOUTH PARK
CREATED BY TREY PARKER AND MATT STONE (1997-) 🖥

No offense to Kenny (who experienced death on a disturbingly regular basis through *South Park's* first five seasons), but Eric Cartman is the kid whose licking-taking, keeping-on tick-ing tendencies are really the most impressive. And so if you want to establish your school of hard-knocks credentials, Cartman is the boy to see. (Cartman is also the boy to see if you suspect someone of having incited a national controversy, or an international incident.) Cartman's nose for conflict has regularly put *South Park* in face-to-face confrontations with Saddam Hussein, the devil, and almost every major pop-cultural flashpoint since the show first aired in 1997. The commentary is astute, the songs are memorable, the situations are absurd, and the comedy is, for lack of a better word, genius. Cartman is at the center of it all, and in the end he still winds up being a pretty recognizable kid. He's really not that far away from the insecure bully down the street—the one who dances to "Pokerface" while wearing an oversized NFL jersey. Because he loves Lady Gaga as much as he hates the Steelers. Yeah, that kid.

1 THE ADVENTURES OF TINTIN
WRITTEN AND ILLUSTRATED BY HERGÉ (FIRST PUBLISHED IN 1929)

EXTENDED LOOK!

Tintin is responsible, sober, well groomed, well dressed, intellectually curious, emotionally mature, and politically astute. Tintin also lives alone in a handsomely furnished apartment and is a dog-owner. He is thus an adult in every possible sense—except the most critical one, because he is also a boy reporter.

Now when it comes to boy reporters, Tintin has three major advantages over his peers: (1) as a comic book character, he never has to age; (2) as Tintin, he never has to deal with the stresses of high school (for reasons that are unknown) or sexual relationships (for reasons that are more ambiguous); and (3) as a character in Hergé's world, there is never any shortage of news stories for him to cover or villains for him to foil. When it comes to boy reporters, therefore, he is aces, the very tops.

But before probing more deeply into Tintin's accomplishments, let's take a minute to acknowledge some of his peculiarities. Like Kafka's Josef K., he is a man (or in this case a manboy) without context; like Peter Pan, he never grows old; like Ernie on *Sesame Street*, he is yellow and has crazy hair; and like Mickey Mouse, he is of indeterminate age and has almost universal appeal. He is, above all else, Tintin. (Rhymes with: Rin-Tin-Tin [but pronounced according to the French or English style, as you will.])

Over the course of dozens of books, Hergé's Tintin uncovered conspiracies, saved others, saved himself, flew to the moon, foiled murder plots, solved crimes, withstood the arias of Bianca Castafiore, and resolved political crises all over the globe. But no matter where he was or what he was up to, he was always surrounded by a living, breathing, and dynamic world—a world informed by real politics as well as living color. Tintin is a cartoon character, but his world is our world. And as a result, whatever past you would have liked yourself to have, the chances are you'll find it in the course of Tintin's never-ending boyhood. (Things you'll also find: one alliterative alcoholic, two bumbling detectives, several articulate animals, a thousand genres, a million plot points, and a million billion stereotypes . . . oh, and infinite joy. The end.)

TEN ESSENTIAL CATCHPHRASES FOR USE AT DINNER PARTIES

10.
"Did I do that?"
(Steve Urkel, *Family Matters*)

When to employ:
This is just something to keep in your pocket for any awkward moments. Or to use by way of an apology if you show up without wine, flowers, or the usual social graces.

9.
"What's up, Doc?"
(Bugs Bunny, *Looney Tunes*)

When to employ:
Whenever you see a doctor. Every time. (If Bugs Bunny has taught us anything, it's that jokes like this get funnier with repetition.)

8.
"Survey says . . ."
(The host, *Family Feud*)

When to employ:
Right before you lift the cover off of the green beans and bellow, "Green beans!!"

7.
"Get. Out!"
(Elaine Benes, *Seinfeld*)

When to employ:
If you're ever forced to wait outside the bathroom.

6.

"Hasta la vista, baby."
(The Terminator, *Terminator 2*)

When to employ:
Whenever children are put to bed. (But be sure to look baby dead in the eyes when speaking these words.)

5.

"Ain't I a stinker."
(Bugs Bunny, Looney Tunes)

When to employ:
Not when you think. No, that's inappropriate. So some other time, probably.

4.

"Sonic Boom!"
(Ken, *Street Fighter 2*)

When to employ:
If you feel you aren't getting enough attention but don't really know what to say. (Volume is key here.)

3.

"That's all, folks!"
(Porky Pig, *Looney Tunes*)

When to employ:
As soon as you finish your meal. To let people know.

2.

"D'oh!"
(Homer Simpson, *The Simpsons*)

When to employ:
As a pun, if the hosts happen to serve bread pudding for dessert. See who is smart enough to catch this one.

1.

"May the Force be with you."
(The good guys, *Star Wars*)

When to employ:
As an exotic way of saying, "Thank you for all the leftovers." Then leave with as many leftovers as you can carry. After all, it takes a lot of calories to sustain this level of charm.

GET UP TO SPEED
ESSENTIAL PODCASTS FOR ASPIRING KNOW-IT-ALLS

The word "podcast" connotes many things—a sport where contestants use fishing poles to heave alien sacs into outer space (where they belong!), or maybe a reality television series where strangers are forced to coexist for months in a single cubicle, to give just a couple of examples—but the word "podcast" doesn't help anyone understand what podcasts actually are. So for those who don't know: Podcasts are just radio programs, but with way fewer commercials, DJs, and dead air; and way more talking, swearing, and listener edification. If you have a commute in the morning or a mindless chore to do at night, that is prime podcast time. So line up the subscriptions, start downloading, and prepare to be a cooler, smarter version of yourself . . .

10 PLANET MONEY
PRODUCED BY NPR AND CHICAGO PUBLIC MEDIA 🔊

Podcasts are not, by and large, especially profitable enterprises. This means that a lot of the really great podcast content out there comes from either public radio stations (NPR, the BBC, etc) or from news outlets, like *Slate*, that offer podcasts simply as a supplement to the more traditional content they produce. But it also means that even when these shows do fit into a larger company mission, they tend to fight for as large an audience as they can possibly get. This is good news for people who want to know what's happening in areas like politics, science, technology, and (most pertinently here) finance, where the issues under discussion can often be quite complex.

Planet Money never shies away from complexity (in fact, it grew out of an hour-long *This American Life* episode that explained how the American housing bust went down), but it also manages to find entertaining ways of accessing complicated topics, from dark money to currency exchange rates to the perils and profits of free goods. They also manage to do proactive stories on larger financial questions like "What could a bipartisan panel of economists actually agree on in terms of tax reform?" that other mainstream news outlets would never consider. So in under 30 minutes, you'll get great stories, some surprising facts, and a new way of looking at the world around you. Not bad!

Essential for: Budding economists.

9 HANG UP AND LISTEN
PRODUCED BY SLATE, FEATURING JOSH LEVIN, STEFAN FATSIS, AND MIKE PESCA 🔊

Sports radio is famous for being brash, bullying, and for lack of a better phrase, dumb as a pigeon on stilts. You've got the one guy who thinks all goalies should be sumo wrestlers, the other guy who swears statistics killed JFK, and more first-time callers/long-time listeners than you can shake a stick at. But *Hang Up and Listen* says good-bye to all that. This crew of thoughtful, articulate, and very funny reporters goes deep inside the sporting week's three most interesting events, and when they do have a special guest on the program, it is usually not because that person has won a major trophy; instead, it's more likely that he has a realistic outlook on the meaning of a missed field goal or because she's written a book of haiku about curling. Each episode also concludes with the utterly unique (and often revelatory) "Afterballs" segment, where . . . well, just listen. If you love sports, you'll love *Hang Up and*

Listen. If you hate sports, same. And if you want to just sound superior when other people talk in sports-radio jargon, this is the place to find the sweet poison you need to shut those first-time callers up.

Essential for: Anyone who doesn't feel entirely at peace with the amount of tears America sheds during the televised Olympics coverage.

8 START THE WEEK
PRODUCED BY BBC RADIO 4, HOSTED BY ANDREW MARR 🔊

Aside from the high-profile guests it manages to snag for its roundtable discussions, there's nothing flashy about *Start the Week*. The themes are serious (they've recently tackled such topics as religious extremism, the relationship between science and politics, and nuclear weapons in the modern world), host Andrew Marr's questions are always in earnest, the bluster quotient is low, and at the end of most episodes, you get the sense that everyone involved in the discussion learned something new and taught something new to someone else. So it offers, in sum, a pretty beautiful picture of human conversation and cultural dialogue. The show has been running on BBC Radio since 1970, so a number of different people have served as host, but rest assured that Andrew Marr—the current host—will keep the guests on topic and devoted to a common goal: an interesting discussion of human culture in all its many forms.

Essential for: Serious cocktail party enthusiasts.

7 SLATE'S CULTURE GABFEST
PRODUCED BY SLATE, FEATURING STEPHEN METCALF, JULIA TURNER, AND DANA STEVENS 🔊

Podcasts are really all about personality. Whether you're one person jabbering into a solitary microphone in a suburban basement or part of a team collaborating on a weekly show in midtown Manhattan, you won't have much success if you can't get your listeners to like you. It doesn't matter how incisive your analysis is if your audience thinks you murder doves and smash old ladies' mailboxes on your nights off. And although I do think it's possible that host Stephen Metcalf may be up to no good right now (with a roguish band of baby-booming street poets), in sum, the gabfesters combine to form a kind of podcasting dream team.

Stephen frequently draws groans from Julia and Dana when he insists that the latest summer blockbuster is an offense to humankind, but when he backs up that same bit of hyperbole with a surprisingly poignant theory of American disintegration—which forces Julia and Dana to really make an argument for why *Iron Man 2* can't reasonably be considered a sin—then all is forgiven. And because each of the show's three personalities have such divergent interests, the endorsements at the end of the show really do wind up offering something for everyone.

Essential for: People looking for the next great show or for something new to say about an old, mediocre one.

6 WTF WITH MARC MARON
PRODUCED BY BRENDAN MCDONALD, HOSTED BY MARC MARON

If anyone has ever recommended the *WTF* podcast to you before, they've probably also told you to skip the opening ten to fifteen minutes (where host Marc Maron delivers a monologue filled with emotion, F-bombs, and enough honesty to make you question the virtue of honesty as a trait). But it's funny, because that same style is also what drives his interviews, which are just about the greatest thing ever. His interviews happen to be with comics and other "performers" (including not only Louis C.K. [famously] and Dane Cook [infamously], but also people like Dan Harmon, Ira Glass, and Judd Apatow), and although he goes very in-depth on questions of comic inspiration and how people managed to pay their industry dues, the podcast really does wind up being hugely expansive. (Probably because each new interview really is about what comedy is and means to each new interview subject, rather than a formulaic discussion of why someone or something is funny.) This is, in sum, Marc Maron's podcast, and he's a guy worth listening to (even when he's an asshole).

Essential for: Future comedians, failed comedians, comedic geniuses, and Friday night hacks. Also for anyone who wants a sense of what it takes to succeed in the entertainment industry and what it costs.

5 LEXICON VALLEY
PRODUCED BY SLATE, HOSTED BY BOB GARFIELD AND MIKE VUOLO

Lexicon Valley, a podcast that examines the whys and wherefores of language, is exceptional in this podcast list. Unlike the other programs—which tend to take complicated topics and explain them in an unusually direct and lucid manner—*Lexicon Valley* generally begins with a truly difficult question, and then makes it more difficult, and then adds a new wrinkle, and then gets one kind of an answer, but then reveals a problem, before finally solving the problem at hand . . . or not. But that's appropriate here! Language is a messy business, and *Slate's* new podcast lets language do its dirty thing on its own terms, without sacrificing any intellectual rigor or any entertainment value. You will be shocked at how much gendered nouns and historical tenses will turn out to have mattered to you.

Essential for: Anyone who uses words or has seen a word on TV.

4 ON THE MEDIA
PRODUCED BY WNYC, HOSTED BY BOB GARFIELD (AGAIN) AND BROOKE GLADSTONE

It sounds like a trade program (and it is a little odd that the title should be a problem for a program that's all about appearances and filters), but *On the Media* is much more than just a show about the media. And not because the show doesn't know where to stop, but rather because the media really is everywhere—and so is the media's influence. Teasing out the difference between facts, fiction, opinions, biases, trends, and "what the people want" is truly the devil's work—but Garfield and Gladstone go at it like saints. There are no easy answers here (at least not usually), but *On the Media* provides listeners with a real accounting of the stories that change the world, and the world that changes the stories. (And good luck figuring out which is which.)

Essential for: People who want more from their news.

3 IN OUR TIME
PRODUCED BY BBC RADIO 4, HOSTED BY MELVYN BRAGG

So here's the setup: Every week, Melvyn Bragg invites three experts onto his program to talk about a historical topic that is sometimes artistic, sometimes scientific, sometimes religious, and sometimes philosophical, but always of enduring interest and relevance. The experts are invited on the basis of their standing rather than their innate hostility levels (as is often the case on American roundtables), but because these people are passionate about what they do, you often get the sense that, in a way, you are listening to history in the process of being formed. Sometimes the areas of expertise will complement one another, so that an anthropologist and a linguist may shed light on different aspects of the same problem, but at other times, all three of the guests will view the same question through separate lenses—with combustible results. But no matter how definitive the conclusion may (or may not) be, the format allows listeners to ingest their history as real, vital material, rather than as dead weight. This show makes you excited to be a human being.

Essential for: Those who are skeptical of textbooks, but still believe in truth.

2 THIS AMERICAN LIFE
PRODUCED BY WBEZ, HOSTED BY IRA GLASS

Ira Glass believes in radio as a medium. That is, on the one hand, ridiculous, because look around; but it is also not so crazy after all, because even though *This American Life* doesn't have images (except when it's on television and it does), it works. It tells stories, and those stories are so well curated, produced, and told, that an hour later you're still sitting in your garage wondering why you are crying so hard about a man named Joe who lives in Illinois. But then, a week later, when the national media is covering a thousand guys just like Joe who just fought their way back to a living wage in the coal mines outside of Peoria, you're like, "Hey, yeah, I was right to call in sick that day. I was striking, and I did it for America!" But all exaggeration aside, *This American Life* has an uncanny knack for extracting human tears (and not just of sorrow, since a lot of comic writers and comedians are featured there as well), and a stellar reputation for beating the American media to the story that really matters. So if you need an excuse to sob, or just want to find your next small-talk go-to, Ira Glass has you covered.

Essential for: Americans.

1 RADIOLAB
PRODUCED BY WNYC, HOSTED BY JAD ABUMRAD AND ROBERT KRULWICH 📶

Pretty much everything that was said about *This American Life* can also be applied to *Radiolab*. Except instead of spending that lost hour in your garage crying your eyes out, if you're listening to *Radiolab*, the police will need to be called in: because your mind will have exploded 14 to 18 times. In most cases it would be a bridge too far to attempt to do a radio show on the topic of "mortality" or "time" or "memory," because WHERE ARE ALL THE PICTURES? But then a well-timed audio effect somehow actually helps you understand why the sky is blue, and then you are like, "Oh no, there go my brains all over the place again. Thanks a lot, *Radiolab*." But also, seriously: Thanks a lot, *Radiolab*.

Essential for: Things with ears, hearts. Also, aliens (as an instructive lesson in the fact that humans aren't so stupid after all).

THINK OUTSIDE THE BOX
PREPARATION FOR EVERY EVENTUALITY (AND SEVERAL ALTERNATE UNIVERSES)

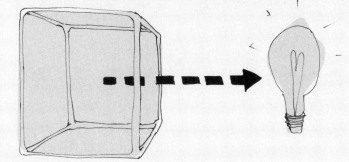

There are a lot of different kinds of intelligence: emotional intelligence, business savviness, common sense, street smarts, and book smarts, for starters—but there's also that little extra something that some people have, enabling them to solve the unexpected problem, unexpectedly. MacGyver style. Some people think that our dreams play a crucial role in honing that ability since they allow us to play out scenarios that are unlikely at the best of times and nonsensical at the worst; but we don't need to wait for night to fall before we start our homework. Instead, we can turn to science fiction and to Hollywood, where there's never any shortage of wildly outlandish situations for us to consider . . .

10 BLACK HOLE
BY CHARLES BURNS (1995-2005) 💬

Teenagers are known for their rebelliousness, but high school, for its part, just loves its rules. From what you can wear to how you can dance to whom you can eat with at lunch, you've got to know the boundaries. Together, these two contradictory impulses can be problematic, as students will always want to stand out and break the rules, but also fear compromising whatever status they may have already achieved. *Black Hole* takes that existing tension and ramps it up a billion by focusing its attention on the twin be-alls and end-alls of teenage life: sex and insecurities.

The setting is a small suburban town in the state of Washington, circa "the '70s." The situation here is normal (in the SNAFU sense), with one extra twist: There's an STD going around, called "the bug," which results in skin that sheds like a snake's hide, a little talking mouth that doesn't go where mouths belong, and a cute little tail, among other things. So basically a horror movie version of your worst dream, ever. All of which begs the question: What happens now? Yeah, that question, always. This incredible graphic novel earned Charles Burns a basketful of Harvey's and an Ignatz, and remains one of the all-time great comics. Check it out, and prepare for the coming of drug-resistant STDs from hell. (Seriously, do that.)

Lesson learned: Make fun-times with other humans at your own risk.

9 SPIRITED AWAY
WRITTEN AND DIRECTED BY HAYAO MIYAZAKI (2001) 🎬📽

"The witch Yubaba" is a phrase that, personally, makes me want to hide in a jar of succulent jelly beans for a thousand million years. (Jelly beans, because delicious and comfortable; succulent, because we need moisture to live and to consume more jelly beans.) This witch Yubaba is dangerous, and she lives in a truly dangerous world—a world in which not even universal blockbuster-hood can be counted on to keep the main character's parents from turning into pigs in the opening scene. But fear not: It all ends well. Everything returns to normal, more or less. So there's that. But once you've seen No-Face, you can't really ever go back. This is a movie that turns everyone into a Not-Child.

Lesson learned: Don't ever, EVER, take anyone you even sort of like to an abandoned amusement park. Also, if you do make that mistake, try and remember who you are. (Easier said than done.)

8 TUCK EVERLASTING
WRITTEN BY NATALIE BABBITT (1975)

Things that seem awesome to ten-year-olds on summer afternoons: unlimited Coca-Cola Classic; free movie passes; free pizza, forever; and immortality. But then, upon reflection, maybe not—because that fizzy, greasy, movie-laden summer already seems pretty boring by September 1, let alone 13 or 14 centuries from now.

I don't know if you've heard, but death is a pretty nasty customer. It kills us and frightens us and keeps us from being the gods that we feel we really kind of, sort of are. But not-death? That is not so cool either, when you really stop to think about it. That mind-blowing realization is at the center of *Tuck Everlasting*, where a normal American family happens upon a source of eternal life and then has to deal with the consequences. But this book is more than just a punch line; it's a chance to dwell in a world and with a family that are dealing with the repercussions of that dream, for better and for worse.

Lesson learned: Don't trust men in yellow suits, and don't make decisions you can't ever take back. From the playground to the Supreme Court, take-backs are essential.

7 CHILDREN OF MEN
DIRECTED BY ALFONSO CUARÓN, BASED ON THE BOOK BY P.D. JAMES (2006)

Most dystopian films and novels rely on simply upping the quantity of mean people and mean technologies in order to show how bad things can get, but *Children of Men* takes that same idea of a hostile future and puts the culprit inside our bodies as well. In this future, women can no longer have children. And in the film adaptation of P.D. James's incredible genre novel, Alfonso Cuarón manages to reflect the intimacy of this particular brand of pessimism by making the camera an almost living participant in the drama. Theo, the cynical main character played by Clive Owen, has been enlisted to help the earth's great hope—a miraculously pregnant young woman—make her way to science, safety, and protection. It's not an easy journey, but it's definitely a trip worth making. The dystopian future has never felt so real, nor so close.

Lesson learned: When times are dark, don't wait for help. (Also, keep your eye on the camera. Where'd that dude come from?)

6 ZONE ONE
WRITTEN BY COLSON WHITEHEAD (2011)

Zombies are metaphors, above all else. Whether that makes them more undead or less undead, you can be the judge; but it also, definitely, makes them ripe terrain for artists—for the people who trade in metaphors and meaning (and not always entertainment). Prior to *Zone One*, Colson Whitehead was an artist first and an entertainer second. With *Zone One* he sought to blend those two impulses, and what readers wound up with was a zombie-survivor novel that, for once, hadn't had its brain ripped out and eaten. Whitehead's essayistic style doesn't make it any easier for us to figure out what exactly is going on and what exactly it will take to stay alive, but at the same time, in the end, those aren't such easy questions anyway.

Lesson learned: Hope is for the hopeless.

5 A WRINKLE IN TIME
WRITTEN BY MADELEINE L'ENGLE (1962)

The main difference between our world and the world of Madeleine L'Engle's *A Wrinkle in Time* is the presence of what are called "tesseracts." I mean, there are also a number of oddly named old women, and "The Black Thing," and, of course, a Charles Wallace (Nota bene: There is nothing in this universe more charming or hilarious than a child who has the name of an accountant), but tesseracts are the real difference-maker. Once you go tesseract, you never go back. Or, well, you do, or you can, but it's not an easy journey. The space-time commute alone is pretty rough, but then there's the IT, the red-eyed man, and the space beasts to worry about as well. *A Wrinkle in Time* bears a lot of similarities to other books and movies nowadays, but that's because so many recent hits—from *The Golden Compass* to *The Never-Ending Story* to *Lost*—have borrowed from this iconic story. It's as old as time (it even begins with the words, "It was a dark and stormy night"), but as fresh as tomorrow's news.

Lesson learned: When confronting strange new enemies, remember what it is that makes you human.

4 THE HANDMAID'S TALE
WRITTEN BY MARGARET ATWOOD (1985)

There's no time-travel in *The Handmaid's Tale*, and no zombies, and no alterations to our fundamental biology. And as Margaret Atwood has herself pointed out, this fictional world differs in no essential ways from our own; but still, this is not our world . . . yet. The country of Gilead, where the narrator Offred serves as a handmaid (a woman who is responsible for bearing the children of the society's "Commanders"), has an extremely rigid caste system that prohibits her from reading, let alone making her own decisions and living her own life. But Offred is smart, resourceful, and curious. These are all dangerous qualities for a woman to have in Gilead, but there it is. The manner in which she manages to make a life for herself in such a circumscribed existence is both incredible and very believable. And that blend of traits is also, presumably, what enabled this novel to receive a nomination for the Booker Prize and win the Arthur C. Clarke Award.

Lesson learned: Don't let the bastards grind you down. (Not an easy task in a world where husbands and wives are prohibited from having their own children. Not an easy task where everyone is, speaking literally, a bastard.)

3 FLATLAND: A ROMANCE OF MANY DIMENSIONS
WRITTEN BY A SQUARE – A.K.A. EDWIN A. ABBOTT (1884)

There are two types of people in this world: people who separate things into two categories, and people who don't. (I am in the former group, as it happens. Which brings me to the point.) There are two types of things in this world: things that sound like what they are, and things that don't. *Flatland* falls firmly into the former group, taking its place there alongside words and phrases like "jumbotron," "salamander," and "Macho Man Randy Savage." *Flatland* is a book about a place (aka "a land") that is, by nature, flat. It exists in two dimensions. But the precision of the title belies all of the profound insights—insights into both society and dimensions—that Edwin Abbott provides in his novella. In *Flatland*, men are polygons, women are points, and the "square" who writes this story runs afoul of the authorities for insisting that there really is a place that contains another, third dimension. In the land of the blind, the one-eyed man is king. And in the land of two dimensions, it's pretty hard to understand what a "sphere" could possibly be. Geometry has never felt so alive.

Lesson learned: When a line is coming at you, it looks like a point. This is worth bearing in mind if you have infuriated any two-dimensional women recently. "Oh, what a cute little dot, and oh my God I'm being stabbed to dea—[is killed]."

2 MISFITS
CREATED BY HOWARD OVERMAN (2009-) 🖥

At first glance, *Misfits* sounds no different from any number of other recent sci-fi projects. A young group of ne'er-do-wells are struck by lightning and develop superpowers. ("Seen it!") And this familiar scenario is only made slightly more interesting by the fact that each of these super-powerful traits seems tied, in some way, to personality.

Then again, none of Jane Austen's books open with an especially original concept or offer an especially original plot; instead, Jane Austen is great because her characters are so compelling, her observations so acute, and her worlds so vivid. *Misfits* has a different set of attributes, but the show is equally reliant on quality. Each episode operates as a complete unit, with its own themes, rhythm, and plot—but each episode also sheds light on the larger questions of the series, such as: why these kids, why now, who's the masked man, and where are they going to hide all these dead bodies. It's dark, it's hilarious, it's imaginative, and it's on the BBC—so it's probably coming to America before too long.

Lesson learned: Don't ever sell your superpowers.

1 GROUNDHOG DAY
DIRECTED BY HAROLD RAMIS (1993) 🎞📼

For the most part, holidays get the movies they deserve. Christmas gets melodramas; Labor Day gets blockbusters; and Groundhog Day gets forgotten—because who cares about groundhogs! (No one. *Sky*hogs are where it's at.) But even though these animals are pathetic little dirt-scrabblers, and even though Mother Nature laughs at our attempts to figure out her plans, Harold Ramis still found a way to extract real meaning from this nonevent. How did he do this? Well, he modeled it after a Christmas movie, of course! After weatherman Phil (played by Bill Murray in much the same way that he had recently played Scrooge) realizes that he will be forced to repeat Groundhog Day endlessly, unless he can figure out some form of escape, he begins to try to live that day perfectly.

Lesson learned: This Bill Murray fellow has a future in comedy!

GET TO THE HEART OF THE MATTER
PITHY EXPLANATIONS OF REALLY COMPLEX THINGS

It's pretty annoying when humanity's fate is resting on your shoulders and all of a sudden you have to solve a complex physics problem, right? And as a result humanity is doomed?

No? That hasn't happened to you? Okay, then just forget it; but still, it's pretty annoying when people talk about super-complicated jargon-junk and you have no idea what a "categorical imperative" is or where a "Hadron collidor" would collide with things, right? Yeah, that is super annoying—for everyone. (Because those words are nonsense, I'm pretty sure.) So let's level the playing field a little bit. Let's fight fire with fire and pit genius against genius, using the wide world of books, documentaries, the internet, and dorks as our aides. Give us that sweet pith of genius, dorks! We're busy with other stuff! (Dorks oblige. [Nerds say thank you.])

10

"A HISTORY OF THE ENGLISH LANGUAGE IN TEN ANIMATED MINUTES"
DISTRIBUTED BY THE OPEN UNIVERSITY (2011)

English is the most convoluted, clanky, and complicated language since . . . Middle English, at least. It has some German in it, and some Latin, and some Greek, and some Twitter, and some hip-hop, and some slang, and some jargon, and et cetera and et cetera and et cetera. It is a frabjous, fabulous, fantabulous junkpile! And instead of an Académie Française to serve as guard dog, English just has a stack of dictionaries that are all too eager to expand and update. And so here we are, with hundreds of thousands of words, and no one to speak them sensibly.

So what does this mean, in sum? Culturally, we speak the language of a rudderless ship—but the Open University has volunteered to serve as Secretary as we wend our way to ship-wreck. To continue (fatally) with this long-winded metaphor, there are enough facts, and enough information, in this ten-minute, animated lecture, to sink a ship. And everyone who's anyone makes an appearance here—the Romans, the French, the Vikings, the Scots, and, of course, LOLcats. If you have ever wondered where our days of the week came from or why we use French-sounding words for the meats we eat but German-sounding words for the animals on the farm, you'll find your answers here. And before I forget, let me say again: This all happens in ten minutes. Less time than it takes to fold a fitted sheet! And it's animated! Plus William Shakespeare! #Winners! #Wieners! #Whiners! #Whoop!

9

PHILOSOPHY BITES
HOSTED BY DAVID EDMONDS AND NIGEL WARBURTON

The hard sciences are, as their name implies, hard to learn, hard to do, and hard to talk about. But once you know something, you actually know it! Two plus two is four, and force equals mass times acceleration, and next question, please! Philosophy, on the other hand, means literally "the love of wisdom"—but what is love, and what is wisdom, and can we use human language to approach a deeper truth? And so, what began as a thrilling concept about the hunt for truth and wisdom ends up, almost immediately, in a quagmire. Or, as Bertrand Russell put it once: "The point of philosophy is to start with something so simple as not to seem worth stating, and to end with something so paradoxical that no one will believe it." But that doesn't mean that it's not worth doing, or worth following.

Every generation has its own set of philosophical questions and answers and struggles, but whether you want to understand Plato's parable of the cave, gain some insight into the problem of evil, or investigate how philosophy can be practically applied, *Philosophy Bites* is the place to go. In this long-running podcast, hosts David Edmonds and Nigel Warburton conduct brief but incredibly compelling and provocative interviews with experts from a wide variety of fields on the Big Questions of human life and thought.

8 COSMOLOGY, CLARIFIED!
A BRIEF HISTORY OF TIME
WRITTEN BY STEPHEN HAWKING (1988)

Stephen Hawking is a smart person. (Very, very, very smart.) And since being diagnosed with a motor neuron disease in 1963 (when he was given two years to live), he has made a series of tremendous strides in helping scientists conceptualize the origin of the universe and the mechanics of such strange phenomena as black holes, light cones, and supergravity. With *A Brief History of Time* he also made his theories, proofs, and the basis for his thinking available to a popular audience as well.

This sounds impossible at first, because—well, here are a couple facts about black holes, just taken at random: They allow no light to escape, and so they're invisible; the "supermassive" black hole at the center of our solar system has a mass equal to four million suns. Its name is "Sagittarius A." (We named our black hole, I guess because otherwise we wouldn't be able to get its attention at a party.) This is crazier than the craziest Spock imitator at a *Star Trek* convention. And yet, when reading *A Brief History of Time,* you'll take all this in with a shrug, like, "Oh yeah, of course, that makes sense, because [some other crazily named phenomenon/fact you learned about earlier]." Stephen Hawking, creator of outlandish theories, prover of unbelievable facts, habitual blower of minds. And recurring character on *The Simpsons.*

7 THE MIRACLE OF CATS, SIMPLIFIED!
"CUTE CATS VS. PHYSICS"
FROM SMARTER EVERY DAY (2012)

Cats don't always land on their feet. But the myth of cats having nine lives isn't hurt much by the evidence that cats do in fact tend to survive falls from heights of more than seven stories, *after* achieving terminal velocity. "Terminal velocity" is a technical term, but it's also apt, because living beings that achieve terminal velocity are generally terminated. (*Operation Dumbo Drop* was a rare exception to this rule, but of course, that Dumbo was aided by a parachute and a Danny Glover.) So the question is, are cats actually little devils, capable of dark magic tricks at high speeds? How else could they manage this survival trick? The answer is found in the "conservation of angular momentum," but you'll have to watch the video to understand what that means. (And you'll have to grow a tail if you want to imitate their trick.)

6 THE HOUSING BUBBLE, TRANSLATED!
THE HISTORY OF CREDIT VISUALIZED
CREATED BY JONATHAN JARVIS (2009) [You Tube]

So remember a few years ago when all those banks went bankrupt and the housing market crashed and stock prices plummeted and suddenly all the new jobs dried up, too? It was, of course, no coincidence that all those things happened at once. Even if you were paying no attention to the news, the sense of a related series of unfortunate events was impossible to avoid. But at the same time, what's a CDO, how do credit default swaps work, and what do all the numbers really mean? There were a lot of explanations on offer at the time, and even though there was a consensus, more or less, even the briefest rundowns still left most people scratching their heads. That's where Jonathan Jarvis comes to the rescue. In a twelve-minute animated video, he supplements a nuts-and-bolts explanation with iconic characters and symbols, showing not only what all the concepts mean, but also how they relate to one another—both for better (at first) and (spoiler alert!) for worse.

5 THE MEDIA, DETAILED!
THE INFLUENCING MACHINE
WRITTEN BY BROOKE GLADSTONE, ILLUSTRATED BY JOSH NEUFELD (2011)

In comparison to modern economics, the physics of free-falling cats, or cosmology, the media isn't a very complicated concept. The media is, more or less, the way we communicate ideas, opinions, and art. But the way the media actually functions—the way bias works, the role of journalists, the manner in which information has to be balanced alongside profits—is very complicated indeed. Brooke Gladstone engages with these questions every week via *On the Media*, but in order to explain, in one sitting, how the media works, she had to take to a new medium: the graphic novel.

The Influencing Machine opens with a quick rundown on ancient media—showing how Mayan scribes operated as publicists and how Julius Caesar used an early version of the newspaper to rob the Roman senate of their mystique—and then moves on to show how American media managed to escape from the yoke of governmental oversight, and then, occasionally, fall back into that trap. But the real revelations arrive when she dives into concepts such as bias and objectivity and shows us how we can use these concepts to consume news media more intelligently and approach the media with a realistic rather than a cynical outlook. It's a worthwhile endeavor, for both her and for us, because, in her concluding words: "We get the media we deserve."

4 STATISTICAL ANALYSIS, STATISTICALLY ANALYZED!
"FIVETHIRTYEIGHT" (2008-)

Statistics are great because they are better at predicting the future than the previous technologies (crystal balls and faux-crystal balls), but they're also terrible because of all the numbers and math and enduring uncertainty. Nate Silver, however, is devoted to not just using statistics, but also explaining his process to the lay reader. It sounds a little boring—and when he was using statistical measurements to predict the win-loss records for Major League Baseball teams, he was certainly boring a lot of non-baseball fans. But when he took his zeal to the political arena and began working on a model to predict the 2008 and 2012 presidential elections, America at large began to take notice. Being "right" doesn't mean you had the right system in statistical terms, but being right also doesn't hurt. The "FiveThirtyEight" blog has been right a lot since 2008. The American political climate seems really volatile as a result of the normal media coverage, but Silver's blog uses math to get past a lot of the noise. Even when his predictions don't align with your political hopes, it's nice to just have a place where politics seems a little more like science and a little less like magic.

3 THE CITY, UNCOVERED!
THE WORKS: ANATOMY OF A CITY
WRITTEN BY KATE ASCHER (2005)

A city is like a Charlie Sheen: It's great until it breaks down, but then it's such a mess that you have to wonder how it ever managed to work in the first place. New York City is, above all else, a city, and whether it's functioning or malfunctioning, it does so on a grand scale. The subway system was the first in the world, and it's still running—on many of the same lines, over 100 years later. It was a marvel when it was first constructed and still remains an example for many other cities—and yet, if something happened to the water pumps (many of which are 100 years old as well), it would only take a few hours for the entire subway system to flood in serious rains . When Hurricane Sandy hit in 2012, all but one of the subway tunnels flooded, but almost the entire system was up and running within a week. *The Works* provides brief, heavily illustrated, and shockingly understandable explanations of New York City's infrastructure, allowing readers to see how things work, why things break down, and how they recover again. It's often disconcerting to learn how close we are to malfunction, but in sum, the book provides a remarkable portrait of an incredibly organic system.

2 THE ECONOMY, ILLUSTRATED (ECONOMICALLY)!
ECONOMIX: HOW AND WHY OUR ECONOMY WORKS (AND DOESN'T WORK) IN WORDS AND PICTURES
WRITTEN BY MICHAEL GOODWIN, ILLUSTRATED BY DAN E. BURR (2012)

Economix is the best crash course you could possibly imagine. It's got history (in pictures), theory (in pictures), definitions (in pictures), and straight-talk (in pictures), and if a picture is worth a thousand words, then this book is worth, like, 58 million words—plus however many actual words it has. With the aid of this book, business periodicals actually become interesting, and normal news coverage becomes engaging. Oh, so what's it about? Well, it is about economics, and in order to understand what I mean by that, please see the book. Agreed? Agreed. Next!

1 WORLD HISTORY, EXPLAINED!
A LITTLE HISTORY OF THE WORLD
WRITTEN BY E.H. GOMBRICH (1935)

When Ernst Gombrich was 26 years old (so after he'd received his doctorate in art history, but before he'd become a world-famous art historian), he became interested in writing a brief history of the world for young readers. A friend of his wanted to publish such a book, but in order to keep to the original schedule, they would need the entire manuscript within six weeks. Gombrich accepted the challenge. Less than six weeks later, he'd completed a masterpiece of both education and entertainment. *A Little History of the World* is an incredible story because human beings are pretty incredible creatures, with lots of bad habits, crazy ideas, horrible problems, and very creative solutions. This is our story. And in this version, it's unforgettable.

WATCH THE WORLD UNFOLD
HISTORY LESSONS THAT WILL KEEP YOU ON THE EDGE OF YOUR SEAT

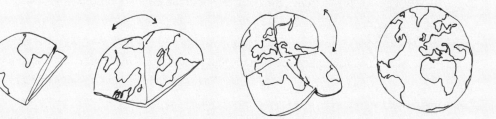

History, as a genre, has a sort of old-man smell attached to it—and that makes sense, because history is old, and it cares about old things. But history is also the source of almost all of our entertainment, from Shakespeare's medieval blockbuster *Richard III* to today's bestselling *Game of Thrones* series (both of which, incidentally, found inspiration in England's War of the Roses). History textbooks, for their part, are notorious for their sleep-inducing catalogs of dates and names, but when history is done well, it's much more than a lesson. It's a visceral reminder that the world that we live in now could very well have been very different.

It's thrilling to feel close to the people and events that helped form the world as we know it, but if we treat these phenomena as foregone conclusions, they lose all their vitality—they lose themselves. The items in this list remind us that the Middle Ages didn't think they were in the middle of anything at the time and that all history takes place in the present tense, not the past. This list is what happens when history stops being polite (and all old-mannish) and starts being . . . real.

10 ROME
CREATED BY BRUNO HELLER, WILLIAM J. MACDONALD, AND JOHN MILIUS (2005-2007) 🖥

Ancient Rome and HBO were kind of a match made in heaven. Rome was the site of orgies, drunkenness, violence, and general excesses of all kinds. Its biography is essentially the recipe for HBO's success. But *Rome*, the show, is more than just bare breasts and bloodied bodies (although both of those items play a significant role); it also takes you beyond the senate and the arena to the streets of a living, breathing city—with normal, everyday characters. And if those characters also happen to stumble into major historical events on an uncannily regular basis, well, sometimes that's the price you have to pay to keep things interesting. *Rome* only lasted two seasons (due to its running wildly over budget—something that certain failed empires can probably relate to!), but if you have to pick just one movie or miniseries to familiarize yourself with the ins and outs of Roman culture, problems, and influence, this is the one to choose.

9 THE NAME OF THE ROSE
WRITTEN BY UMBERTO ECO (1980) 📖

The Name of the Rose has to be one of the most unlikely bestsellers of all time. It takes place at a Benedictine monastery; it spends multiple chapters discussing the theological and political issues of the fourteenth century; it was the author's first novel; and it ends on a profound note of uncertainty and anticlimax. But in its favor, *The Name of the Rose* borrows from one of the all-time great genres (mysteries in enclosed spaces), features one of the all-time great detectives (the monk William of Baskerville), and most important, is just impossible to put down. Because when monks start popping up dead in unlikely places, people just want to know who did it, how, and why—and, if the answer happens to involve Aristotle, the Inquisition, literary puzzles, library chases, and debates over laughter and the value of learning, then so be it! Just give us the answers!

Who would have ever guessed that a week in a persecuted medieval monastery could be so interesting—or that so much would happen after dark!

8 THE DAUGHTER OF TIME
WRITTEN BY JOSEPHINE TEY (1951) 📖

There are mysteries and then there are *mysteries*—and *The Daughter of Time* is both. It investigates a murder, has a detective as its main character, and was written by a traditional mystery writer, so it's definitely a traditional mystery; but it also takes, as its subject, the personality of Richard III and, more deeply, the question of how much we can ever really know about our past. So to put this point another way: *The Daughter of Time* is a historical mystery in the profoundest sense. Alan Grant is a Scotland Yard detective of independent means who is, for the moment, bedridden at a London hospital. After considering a portrait of Richard III (the hunchback from Shakespeare's play, back again), he begins to wonder if this really is the face of a depraved homicidal maniac. With the aid of some friends he begins to investigate the historical record, and without giving too much away, it can at least be said that, if Shakespeare ever convicts you of a crime, it's going to take one hell of a detective to clear your name.

7 WOLF HALL
WRITTEN BY HILARY MANTEL (2009) 📖

Before 2009, Thomas Cromwell was a historical figure in need of a serious PR boost. As chief minister to Henry VIII, he was responsible for cutting England's ties to the Catholic Church, providing for the king's many marriage annulments (not an easy feat at the time), and persecuting the king's many enemies. Mantel doesn't dispute any of these points—as Josephine Tey denied the claim that Richard III was responsible for murder—but rather allows us to live with Thomas Cromwell and to see him as he may, potentially, have been: as an opportunistic and sometimes brutal man who was also intelligent, curious, and above all, pragmatic. Through his eyes, we get to see a world that is at once very different from our own, but at the same time quite recognizable. It was a very dangerous time to be alive and a very dangerous place to live—but it's not at all a bad place to visit. Both this book and its sequel, *Bring Out the Bodies*, won the Man Booker Prize.

6 I, TITUBA: BLACK WITCH OF SALEM
WRITTEN BY MARYSE CONDÉ (1986) 📖

There was in fact a real Tituba, who was tried and convicted of witchcraft in Salem, Massachusetts, in 1692. That much we do know. What we see in the course of Maryse Condé's incredible account of survival—and of life—under some of the most difficult circumstances imaginable is more than just an expansion of what we do know, however; it also offers the voice of a person who had been almost entirely erased by history. The odds are so thoroughly stacked against Tituba throughout her story that her presence on each successive page is a small miracle in its own right. She will not go away. And although it's often hard for us to put ourselves inside the heads of such a tragic figure, Tituba's vitality as a character makes the pain that we feel less a burden than a strange kind of reward. Sometimes pain like that is the cost of progress.

5 FAREWELL MY CONCUBINE
DIRECTED BY KAIGE CHEN (1993)

Farewell My Concubine has a great title—one that combines tenderness and coolness, possession and release, and love and resignation in just a few deeply evocative words. So kudos for that. But this poetic title also begs the question: How many movie titles have similarly gotten away with using a phrase that is unlikely to have ever been used in real life? Five? Fifty? Five hundred? Something not in a multiple of five? I don't know. The point is, if anyone has ever said "farewell, my concubine" to another actual human, then I will eat snakes on a plane. That's a promise.

But back to the movie. The film provides a beautiful, heartfelt, and heartbreaking portrait of China in the twentieth century via Xiaolou and Dieyi, two young orphan boys who, after a brutal training regimen, become the stars of the Peking Opera. Dieyi is raised to play the role of the beloved lady on stage, and his homosexuality does not make that performance any less confusing. Similarly, the commentary on the currents flowing through Chinese culture between the 1920s and the 1970s is never quite distinct from the identities and struggles of these two characters, which means that one is never quite sure about what is history and what is melodrama. Either way, it all works. Whether you know a lot about twentieth century or nothing at all, you'll learn a lot more here.

4 THE GHOST MAP: THE STORY OF LONDON'S MOST TERRIFYING EPIDEMIC - AND HOW IT CHANGED SCIENCE, CITIES, AND THE MODERN WORLD
WRITTEN BY STEVEN JOHNSON (2006)

London in the middle of the nineteenth century was a true marvel. After the Industrial Revolution, it was home to wealth, innovation, ambition, and some 2.4 million people. It was the biggest city in the world, but it was also (less marvelously) full of poverty and years away from having a proper sewage system. The removal of waste in all its many forms was thus the source of a bustling mini-economy (which is discussed in thrilling detail in the book's first chapter), but since there was no real direction to this effort, people's drinking water often suffered from contamination. That's a polite way of saying that the water was like unto a corrupt politician: entirely full of shit. The inefficient removal of waste also meant that the city, as a whole, smelled disgusting.

Consequently, cholera epidemics were not at all uncommon, but since scientists had yet to discover how bacteria could make people sick, many people—including most of the medical and scientific establishment—believed that it was the smell itself, the miasma, that was spreading this deadly plague. *The Ghost Map* is the story of how a physician named John Snow and a clergyman named Henry Whitehead managed to first identify the real source of the 1854 cholera outbreak and then track it down to a specific pump. As a result, the book is a logic puzzle, a treatise on urban planning, a social history, a medical mystery, and, as it turns out, a bestseller as well. Check it out, and then thank your lucky, flushy stars for proper plumbing and sewage.

3 BAND OF BROTHERS
EXECUTIVE PRODUCED BY TOM HANKS AND STEVEN SPIELBERG (2001)

World War II remains the centerpiece of twentieth-century historical discussion and debate. Hardly a year goes by where we don't have a bestselling book or blockbuster movie come out that's set in those pivotal years. *Band of Brothers* is noteworthy, however, because it manages to tell an important military story—the story of the 101st Airborne Division—through the lens of real people (or believable characters based on real people, anyway). The result is eleven hours of compelling, revealing, and memorable television entertainment.

2 MAUS: A SURVIVOR'S TALE
WRITTEN AND ILLUSTRATED BY ART SPIEGELMAN (COMPLETED IN 1991)

Maus is, in brief, Art Spiegelman's attempt to account for how his parents survived the Holocaust, in graphic novel form, using his father as the primary resource, and with animal species standing in for races—so Jews are mice, Germans are cats, Poles are pigs, etc. But there are times when these metaphors show their cracks or reveal their arbitrariness—as when Art visits his own psychiatrist wearing a mouse mask (just like his psychiatrist). *Maus* is not, in any sense, a straightforward history. The levels of guilt, blame, responsibility, and meaning weave in and out repeatedly, but in the end Spiegelman created something that was much more than just a great comic book. It was a great work of art. It won, among other things, both the Eisner Award and the Pulitzer Prize, and it remains one of the most popular (and saddest, and most thought-provoking, and controversial) graphic novels ever written.

1 THE BATTLE OF ALGIERS
DIRECTED BY GILLO PONTECORVO (1966)

Battle of Algiers was intended as a sort of corrective. It offered an account of the Algerian struggle for independence from the Algerian (rather than the French) point of view. And on that front it certainly succeeded, but as in *Lincoln* (to take an example from American politics) or the famous thriller *Z* (to take an example from Greek politics), the director was much more interested in making a movie than in offering a history lesson, and the result, in this case, is nearly two hours of beautiful, unbearable tension. Although it's shot in black and white and has a political agenda, this is not a dated art film. Instead, it does what only the greatest thrillers can do: It makes it impossible for you to turn it off if you have stumbled across it. And if any greater praise can be offered for a movie, then I don't know what it is.

CATCH A PREDATOR (AND MORE)
PROCEDURALS TO AID IN NEARLY EVERY ENDEAVOR

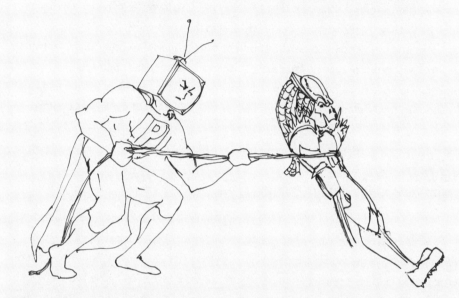

There's nothing better than a good routine. From lather/rinse/repeat to wax-on/wax-off, they keep us running smoothly. (Because seriously, sometimes good enough really *is* good enough.) But what is simply efficient in our daily lives also has a tendency to achieve a kind of genius in more ambitious settings. No one thinks about it much anymore, but police procedure and the scientific method and even an accountant's due diligence have come, over time, to achieve real wisdom. It's invisible for the most part, but when push comes to shove—or when someone makes a movie or writes a book—we have a chance to appreciate this ingrained aptitude. And it's at those times that procedure has a lot to teach us: not just about how government functions or how crimes are solved, but about how to get things done! So, without further ado, let's do it! Let's talk process and do how-to!

10 HOW TO WORK WITH WHAT YOU GOT
COLUMBO
STARRING PETER FALK (1971-2003)

There have been a lot of police procedurals over the years, but if you're a TV detective and you've got your own show, chances are that your success rate is right around 100 percent. So in that sense, it's hard to pick a standout. They all always win. So if you're going to leave aside the question of efficacy, then it comes down to style—and then you have to pick *Columbo*. He's polite, he's canny, he dresses comfortably, and he moves at his own speed. Each episode begins, as usual, with a murder; but in the case of *Columbo,* we actually get to see who the murderer is. It's a testament to the character's charm that, even though the audience knows who did it about an hour before anyone else, it always seems like Columbo is right on time.

9 HOW TO PUT ON A SHOW
THIS IS IT
DIRECTED BY KENNY ORTEGA (2009)

There's something kind of magical about a big event venue or arena when it's not in use. It's like seeing a whale's skeleton—even when you're staring right at it, it's unbelievable because it just never stops being huge. And like the whale's skeleton, it forces you to wonder how such an immense thing could ever have managed to work. *This Is It* takes you inside the Staples Center as Michael Jackson rehearses for an ongoing concert series in London. Jackson died before those shows ever happened, but the impact of his music and his moves are, of course, still very much alive. He spent almost his entire life in the public eye and was obviously a hard person to know, but this movie doesn't attempt to get inside his head. Instead, it offers a vision of the icon when he was at his most iconic (and maybe most himself) up on the stage. It gives you the chance to look inside the whale's skeleton while the body is still in motion.

8 HOW TO WATCH A MURDER TRIAL (ANSWER: SUSPICIOUSLY)
THE STAIRCASE
DIRECTED BY JEAN-XAVIER DE LESTRADE (2004)

In 2001, North Carolina novelist Michael Peterson found his wife at the bottom of a staircase and soon thereafter found himself embroiled in a murder trial. He was the one who found his wife. He had been cheating on his wife. And, as it turned out, he had discovered another woman that he knew dying at the bottom of another staircase many years before, in Germany. This is the setup for a sensational case, a truly unbelievable trial, and an equal parts illuminating and befuddling documentary about the things we know, the things we don't know, and Michael Peterson.

Director Jean-Xavier de Lestrade's previous documentary, *Murder on a Sunday Morning*, had earned him an Oscar and led to the release of another murder suspect in Florida, and as a result of these credentials (and his promise not to air any of the footage until after the trial), he was given special access to not only Peterson and his defense team, but also to the police and prosecution as well. Lestrade has said that he could never have made such a movie in France, because people there are "more suspicious" of movie cameras, but in an ironic twist, the more you learn in this case, the less you know. And the less certain you become, the closer you get to the end.

7 HOW TO ASSASSINATE A NATIONAL ENEMY
ZERO DARK THIRTY
DIRECTED BY KATHRYN BIGELOW (2012)

Kathryn Bigelow made her name with action-thriller films like *Near Dark, Point Break,* and *The Hurt Locker*, which are traditional in the sense that things explode and people bleed and stronger men succeed where weaker men fail. As a result of her choice of genres, she has earned a reputation as a director of "men's films," but *Zero Dark Thirty* shows that what Bigelow was really interested in wasn't so much masculinity or gender, but rather the question of what it takes to do "the dirty work." In *The Hurt Locker*, the work at hand is defusing live bombs in Iraq; in *Zero Dark Thirty*, it's finding and killing America's enemy #1: Osama Bin-Laden.

Jessica Chastain plays the CIA operative behind the mission, and she does an incredible job of becoming the character in the same way that her character (Maya) becomes her job. We sympathize with Maya because that kind of devotion seems necessary—it seems like the only way she can "do the job" at all. But devotion in itself doesn't justify decisions, and the pressure to do the right thing but also get the job done applies a tremendous kind of spiritual pressure to the movie; the movie's physical pressure, of course, doesn't need any help. Every second is nerve-racking. Not every decision is the right one, and not all decisions are justified (or justifiable), but every decision needs to be made, and Maya has to make them. And then live with them. This is a revenge story that seems, for the most part, actually moral.

6 HOW TO BUILD AN IGLOO
NANOOK OF THE NORTH
DIRECTED BY ROBERT J. FLAHERTY (1922)

In 1922, when *Nanook of the North* was made, there were no "documentaries" as we know them today, and in many ways it would be inaccurate to use that modern term to describe this movie. What Flaherty produced was, instead, simply a moving picture of life in the Arctic. Some elements of this moving picture were staged and some were (for lack of a better word) real—but every scene illustrates the challenges and solutions involved in surviving in the Arctic. When Flaherty arrived in the Arctic, the Inuit people had already begun adopting Western clothing and technologies, but when we see Nanook build an igloo, we are really watching how an actual igloo is made. And it would be one thing to describe this process, but if you watch one how-to video in your life, make it this one. It may not come in handy where you're living, but it offers an incredible testimony about humanity's ability to make something from nothing.

5 HOW TO BUILD A TELEVISION EMPIRE
LAW & ORDER
CREATED BY (DUN DUN!) DICK WOLF (1990-2010)

Okay, so the show itself isn't about the process of building a television empire, but the history of the show remains an object lesson in that process. Of character development, there is little or none; of ripped-from-the-headlines-ness, there is much; and of entertainment, episode after episode, year after year, there is a seemingly endless quantity. *Law & Order*—in its original and purest incarnation—is a miracle of plotting, efficiency, and entertainment: In the first thirty minutes, Someone does a crime-murder, and although Someone is hard to find, eventually the cops find Someone, and Someone is arrested; then, in the second half of the show, Someone is prosecuted, and just when it looks like they're about to get away, the screw is turned, and the show is like, DUN DUN! And you are like, "WHA!?" Someone got served!!! And then it happens again but differently in the next episode, but you are always, always like "WHA!?" PS: It's great.

4 HOW TO RUN A POLICE DEPARTMENT
PRIME SUSPECT, SEASON 1
STARRING HELEN MIRREN (1991) 🖥

Before *The Wire* and before *NYPD: Blue*, there was *Prime Suspect* and its lead character, Jane Tennison, played by Helen Mirren. Incidentally, these three shows are also more than just gritty crime dramas; they are also all on a continuum of shows that used the police force to examine larger cultural issues as well. Each season of *Prime Suspect* (save Season 4) takes up a new case and, in most cases, a new cultural flashpoint, but Season 1, of course, is where it all started, and it still stands up. In addition to having an incredible script and cast (including Tom Wilkinson and even Ralph Fiennes, briefly), it also manages to blend the issue of sexual politics at the police department with the facts of the case under investigation. The investigation is the star of the show, but Helen Mirren also managed to turn Jane Tennison into something more than just an ambitious and determined detective—she turned her into an icon.

3 HOW TO FREE AN INNOCENT MAN
THE THIN BLUE LINE
DIRECTED BY ERROL MORRIS (1988) 🎞

When it comes to documentarians, Ken Burns generally falls into the camp of directors who make movies about things that have passed. The Civil War is over, and Burns provides a compelling portrait about what happened, when, and why. Michael Moore, on the other hand, makes documentaries about things that are happening now—about issues like gun control, the health care debate, and the war on terror. And then there's Errol Morris. His documentaries seem to deny the existence of that split. He makes movies about the present doubts that our past has given to us because, in his words, "Nothing is so obvious that it's obvious." *The Thin Blue Line* opened a case that was closed—the conviction of a man named Randall Adams on murder charges—and showed not only how dubious the conviction was, but also how likely it was that his younger companion had, in fact, committed the crime. It offers viewers a journey into a past that seemed definitive, and then shows how that past can, through careful consideration, be resuscitated and offer us the possibility of a new, more truthful future. It's a kind of miracle.

2 HOW TO SELL THE BESTSELLING BOOK OF ALL TIME
SALESMAN
DIRECTED BY ALBERT MAYSLES, DAVID MAYSLES, AND CHARLOTTE ZWERIN (1968)

For as long as there's been an America to dream about, people have talked about the American dream—and about its imminent demise. In fact, because the American dream is all about individual initiative and accomplishment, you could argue that our national mission thrives on the suffering of people like Willy Loman in *Death of a Saleman* or Jay Gatsby in *The Great Gatsby*. The threat of failure, both small and large, is what gives the dream its power, and although we look up to the people who do make it, the poignancy is all with the losers. The Maysles' brothers' documentary *Salesman* is full of small (you could even say petty) victories and minor humiliations. These men are trying to sell the Bible, the bestselling book of all time, to normal people in normal homes who are also trying to make ends meet. Every visit is a battle, but in the end what the movie gives us is a chance to look at these battles not in terms of winners and losers, but in terms of America. This is our dream, sure (classic American nicknames included)—but most of all this is life.

1 HOW TO FOLLOW A LEAD (AND WIN)
ALL THE PRESIDENT'S MEN
ADAPTED BY WILLIAM GOLDMAN FROM THE BOOK BY CARL BERNSTEIN AND BOB WOODWARD (1976)

So the thing about procedures is they're inherently kind of stuffy. I mean, for good or ill, you are watching people doing what they're supposed to be doing according to a set of pre-established rules. You are watching people do things by the book. This is not a sexy way of doing things. Most procedurals get around this by placing their attention on the thing the routine is responding to, rather than the process itself; on the crime, rather than the law. In *All the President's Men*, even that option is stripped; instead, we have to watch as two intrepid young journalists (the now legendary Woodward and Bernstein, by name) literally wait outside government offices, review account ledgers, and interview source after source after source, in an attempt to figure out what exactly happened at the Watergate Hotel. Since even they don't know who the villain is, we can't really be titillated by the big reveal! It sounds extremely prosaic (and it is) but the pacing, the performances, and the sheer immersiveness of the experience make every second tense and every revelation . . . well, revelatory.

In the end it turns out that you uncover American political corruption the same way you sell a Bible in Florida: You just. Keep. Working.

STAND ON THE SHOULDERS OF GIANTS
GENIUSES WILLING TO TALK TO NON-GENIUSES

Being a genius seems like a pretty hard job. On the one hand, you get to make a difference in the world and laugh at all us non-geniuses as we burn the roofs of our mouths, time and time again, on our morning coffees; but on the other hand, you have this enormous sense of self-worth that seems to drive you ever onward, never giving you a moment's rest. It seems so exhausting. And then, when you have actually done the thing you set out to do—like cure a disease, or explain the universe, or warn humanity about the coming apocalypse, or whatever—then the rest of humanity is like, "Oh, yeah, the polio vaccine, that was great. I'm so glad I don't have polio now." And then we change the channel and watch another episode of *Keeping Up with the Kardashians*. We get all of the benefit with none of the burden! But that's life, I guess.

Nonetheless, as non-geniuses—as mouth-burners and Kardashian addicts—it's the least we can do to heed these geniuses when they are trying to tell us something. With that in mind, here are ten geniuses that not only made an enormous contribution to our world, but also took time out to tell us what they were up to and why it mattered.

10 RICHARD FEYNMAN, PHYSICIST (1918-1988)
FOR AN INTRODUCTION TRY:

"SURELY YOU'RE JOKING, MR. FEYNMAN!": ADVENTURES OF A CURIOUS CHARACTER (1985)

Richard Feynman was a Nobel Prize–winning physicist and one of the most impressive theoretical thinkers of the twentieth century, but to stop there would be almost an insult. He was also a talented safecracker and lock-picker, a passionate percussionist, and an all-around talented and adventurous guy. He was much beloved as a teacher as well, and his books on physics are still widely read today, but it's his less serious books that show Feynman at his charismatic best. In *Surely You're Joking*, he recounts some of the more incredible episodes from his life, but also manages to convey a sense of scientific values and recent scientific history.

9 JAMES BALDWIN, NOVELIST (1924-1987)
FOR AN INTRODUCTION TRY:

"NOTES OF A NATIVE SON" (1955)

James Baldwin was the author of such novels as *Go Tell It on the Mountain*, *Giovanni's Room*, and the essay "Notes of a Native Son." All of the aforementioned titles achieved significant attention and praise when they were originally published, and they remain widely read today (which wouldn't be especially surprising were it not for the fact that Baldwin was gay and black and that his identity played a large and explicit role in his writings). Despite the fact that prejudice was widespread and that any kind of advocacy for either blacks or for homosexuals was a deadly line of work at the time, Baldwin's voice could not be silenced. The power of that voice is undeniable, and although it's certainly present in his novels, his personal essays are where it really comes alive. "Notes of a Native Son" provides an account of Baldwin's relationship with and feelings toward his father, but also paints a vivid picture of both Greenwich Village in the 1950s (a pretty interesting place in its own right) and of race relations in America at the time.

8 OLIVER SACKS, NEUROLOGIST (1933–) FOR AN INTRODUCTION TRY:

THE MAN WHO MISTOOK HIS WIFE FOR A HAT AND OTHER CLINICAL TALES (1985)

It's easy to take our brains for granted. After all, we humans do a lot of our best work when our brains are switched off. We dance best when we stop thinking, and our foreign language skills are clearly never better than after we've had a few drinks. But when the brain malfunctions, then we get a chance to see just how incredible—and just how diverse—the brain's body of work really is. Dr. Oliver Sacks first made his name with *Awakenings*, a nonfiction account of how his prescription of the drug L-DOPA was successful in "awakening" a group of patients suffering from sleeping sickness. In *The Man Who Mistook His Wife for a Hat*, he confronts a broader range of neurological conditions, but the end result is similar: We get to see just how important our brains are in determining not only who we are, but in how we perceive the world around us. To put it another way: Brains is crazy.

7 TINA FEY, COMEDIAN (1970–) FOR AN INTRODUCTION TRY:

BOSSYPANTS (2011)

The phrase "comic genius" is perhaps overused. In most other fields—in physics, economics, literature, or math, for instance—there is no simple metric by which to judge the achievement of "genius"; but in comedy, there is such a metric: Can you make a person (someone of able bladder and able mind, of course) make water by mistake? To put that another way: Can you turn a nice new pair of Levi's into piss-jeans? And for Tina Fey the answer is yes, several times over. (Don't ask me how I know or when I found this out.) In addition to writing the cable staple *Mean Girls*, Fey was the head writer for *SNL* during its renaissance in the early 2000s and is currently the driving force behind *30 Rock*'s success. In *Bossypants*, she takes time out from her comedy writing responsibilities to . . . write some more about writing comedy, and the result is hilarious (definitely piss-jeans worthy), illuminating (because it is kind of weird to think about how comedy gets made), and kind of thrilling. Even if you're not interested in developing a cocaine addiction or drinking yourself to death, behind the scenes at *SNL* is a pretty great place to be.

6 STEVE JOBS, ENTREPRENEUR (1955-2011)
FOR AN INTRODUCTION TRY:
THE LAUNCH OF THE FIRST IPHONE [You Tube]

After cofounding Apple with Steve Wozniak in the late 1970s, Steve Jobs returned in 1996 to take the company from near bankruptcy to its current position as one of the most valuable publicly traded companies in the world. So, he was good at business. But before he helped Apple market and sell these products, he also oversaw their genesis, helming the company as it developed, among other things, the personal computer, the iPod, the iPhone, and the tablet computer. He's the reason why our phones are so much smarter than us now. And for this reason it's hard to watch his launch of the first iPhone and not think about how much sense it would make as the opening scene for a dystopian sci-fi movie. Because what he's talking about, compared to what was available at the time, is just about as crazy as an army of sleek, hyper-intelligent spheres running wild over the planet and killing humans willy-nilly because they are "just too inefficient for words—and too ugly" (which is what this hypothetical dystopian sci-fi movie is almost certainly about).

5 WILL EISNER, GRAPHIC NOVELIST (1917-2005)
FOR AN INTRODUCTION TRY:
COMICS AND SEQUENTIAL ART (1985)

Will Eisner is the reason why we even talk about "graphic novels" today. In fact, he was the one who coined the term (when he was hoping to get his now legendary *A Contract with God* accepted by a publisher who he knew would balk at the idea of publishing a comic book for adults). His genius didn't lie just in producing iconic and hugely influential comics, but also in realizing what the medium was capable of, and then working to make that potential a reality. As a result, we now have comics like *The Spirit* (which Eisner created), which are more than just comic relief for newspapers; comics like *The Plot* (which Eisner wrote and illustrated), which provide education even as they entertain; comics like *Fun Home* and *Maus* and *Jimmy Corrigan*,' which are able to compete for literature's highest honors despite being told mainly in pictures; and even things like silent panels, which were unheard of before Eisner began including them in the hopes of appealing to adult readers.

In *Comics and Sequential Art*, Eisner—who was always available to talk about what he was up to and where he thought comics as a genre were going—outlines his views on how words and images intermingle to tell a story that (unlike movies) not only demands audience participation, but benefits from it. Eisner said that all of his innovations were the result of either "desperation or an attempt to solve a problem," but that doesn't make them any less impressive; it just makes him more charming. Smarts never came in a less pretentious package. (Smarties, however, did.)

4 ANNA WINTOUR, TASTEMAKER (1949–)
FOR AN INTRODUCTION TRY:

THE SEPTEMBER ISSUE 🎞️

One person's "fashion genius" is another person's "bag lady gone rogue"—but for that very reason, it's all the more important to cast your lot for the fashion genius who also happens to be the person in charge. And that person, now and for as long as Anna Wintour has anything to say about it, is Anna Wintour—*Vogue's* editor-in-chief. She was, as you may have heard, the inspiration for the titular "devil" in *The Devil Wears Prada*, and in *The September Issue,* we get a chance to see where the movie took advantage of some poetic license and where it pretty much got the story right. In terms of decisiveness, influence, and stone-cold independence, both films are in agreement. And in terms of devilishness—well, that's up to the viewer to judge.

3 AI WEIWEI, CONTEMPORARY ARTIST (1957–)
FOR AN INTRODUCTION TRY:

AI WEIWEI: NEVER SORRY (2012) 🎞️

Alison Klayman first traveled to China with the general intention of learning a new language and maybe getting some work as a journalist. On those counts she definitely succeeded, but the trip turned out to be much more important than she was first expecting. Because when she was hired to shoot some footage of Ai Weiwei as a supplement to a gallery exhibit, she decided to keep shooting after the filming was supposed to end, and as a result, when she returned to America she had a feature-length documentary.

Under normal circumstances you can't reasonably expect to win a Special Jury Prize at Sundance as a result of following someone around and talking to them, but Ai Weiwei isn't a normal person, and Alison Klayman didn't arrive in China in an ordinary time. Ai had already made a career out of provoking the Chinese government, but in the course of Klayman's film, things come to a head and begin to get out of hand. Ai is beaten in his apartment, detained by the authorities, and eventually released again, but throughout his travails he remains courageous, curious, and charming. Whether he's making sculptures, designing installations, tweeting, or just answering questions in an interview, "everything he does is a performance piece." His life is his art, and vice versa.

2 NEIL DEGRASSE TYSON, ASTROPHYSICIST (1958-)
FOR AN INTRODUCTION TRY:

@NEILTYSON NEIL DEGRASSE TYSON'S TWITTER FEED

One thing that's kind of annoying about space is how it is always blowing human minds. I mean, how are we supposed to deal with something that is bigger than the biggest thing we can imagine, but which is also shrinking? And how are we supposed to talk about a field that takes concepts like space and time—things that are already pretty much impossible to come to grips with—and then combines them, as though that is a useful thing? It seems safe to assume, then, that anyone who works in this field is either a genius or a charlatan. Neil deGrasse Tyson's calm demeanor offers strong evidence that he is not a charlatan; therefore, he is a genius. And for a genius, he is remarkably pleasant to be around. Whether he's fighting to strip Pluto of its status as a planet, or tweeting about his favorite television show, or talking about politics with Stephen Colbert, he is always clear, always open, and always entertaining.

1 BENJAMIN FRANKLIN, AMERICAN (1706-1790)
FOR AN INTRODUCTION TRY:

THE AUTOBIOGRAPHY OF BENJAMIN FRANKLIN (1793)

When he wasn't inventing bifocals, working to promote American self-government, writing bestselling books, establishing libraries and fire departments, or investigating the properties of electricity, Benjamin Franklin loved to talk. Luckily, as a result of his curiosity, ambition, and (self-) education, there were few topics on which he wasn't an expert. In his autobiography, Franklin explains how he achieved wealth and fame despite often coming into conflict with the authority figures that surrounded him (including, among others, his brother James and the British Empire as a whole) and why he was drawn into the various enterprises that occupied his life. The one thing he doesn't explain is how he was able to do all that he did—where he got the energy and how he had the mental capacity to absorb so very much. Some mysteries, however, are better left unsolved. It's thrilling enough just to hear him account for himself, the unaccountable man—"the first American."

CHEAT ON YOUR HOMEWORK
ESSENTIAL LITERARY ADAPTATIONS— FOR BOTH INFORMATION AND INSPIRATION

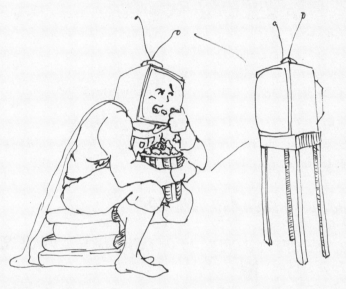

Here are some things that help with homework: a computer, caffeine, and a mind. Here are some things that don't help: a computer, nice weather, and being a human being. And this isn't just about homework at school, either. Even after reading assignments have stopped being assigned, there are still a bunch of cultural landmarks that we know we ought to read and somehow just can't. Because after all, we're only human, and most humans are never far away from either a TV, a computer, or a bed. So there it is: We need help. This list is here to provide that help. Here you'll find movies that will help you read a book without reading it, comics that will help you learn something while enjoying it, and songs that will inspire you to turn off the TV, flip on the desk lamp, and get down to work! So get to it!

10 HENRY V
DIRECTED BY KENNETH BRANAGH (1989)
BASED ON THE PLAY *HENRY V*
WRITTEN BY WILLIAM SHAKESPEARE

First up: a time-saver. Before Kenneth Branagh became Will.i.am Shakespeare 2.0, he really was an artist. Nay. Une artiste. His adaptations of *Henry V*, *Hamlet*, and even *Love's Labours Lost* are faithful, funny, and just really good. And here the casting of Branagh (aka "Me, the director, the one in charge, the boss") in the lead role really does makes sense, because at the time, Branagh, like Prince Harry, was brash, young, and ambitious. Here he stakes his claim to importance, and you can feel his enthusiasm. The speeches and the lines ("Once more into the breach" … "We few, we happy few, we band of brothers") roll off like reveille and wake us to the thrill of fighting for something we believe in (and something to believe in, too). It's great.

Cheater Rating: 10/10

It's got all the major speeches mostly where they belong, so if you need to read a play and don't want to read a play, this is the way to go.

9 TRISTRAM SHANDY: A COCK AND BULL STORY
DIRECTED BY MICHAEL WINTERBOTTOM (2005)
BASED ON THE NOVEL *THE LIFE AND OPINIONS OF TRISTRAM SHANDY, GENTLEMAN*
WRITTEN BY LAURENCE STERNE

It's hard to explain what Michael Winterbottom's *Tristram Shandy* does in just a few words. So here are just a few words about what Michael Winterbottom's *Tristram Shandy* does: (1) it allows two of Britain's funniest and most charmingly repellent comedians (Steve Coogan and Rob Brydon, both playing off of their public personas) to do their own respective brands of comedy in a setting that makes sense of both of them; (2) it uses the first postmodern novel (written "before there was even a postmodernism to speak of") as a launching pad for an investigation of postmodern film, involving references to (a) *Barry Lyndon*, (b) 8½, and (c) Steve Coogan's several hits and several more misses; and (3) it ends on a series of Al Pacino imitations which (x) take your breath away, (y) give you pause, and (z) provide a brilliant coda to the film's obsessions with identity, fame, and novelty. It is tough, coherent, great, and true to the source material to the utmost degree. Which means that its relationship to the source material is tenuous at best, and dubious at worst. So ha-ha, and good luck.

Cheater Rating: 6/10

The movie will make you want to read the book, but if you watch the movie instead of reading the book, you stand an equal chance of either (a) sounding like a pithy genius or (b) looking like a pretentious asshole. So best of one world, worst of the other.

8 THE BOOK OF GENESIS
ILLUSTRATED BY ROBERT CRUMB (2009) 💬
BASED ON THE BOOK OF GENESIS 📖

Words that are often used to describe the work of R. Crumb: "pornographic," "psychedelic," and "Fritz-the-Cat-ty." Words that are not often used in this context: "holy," "respectful," and "religious." So it was a surprise when word came out that Crumb's next book was going to be *The Book of Genesis Illustrated*—and that Crumb was taking it on as a "straight illustration job." But then the book actually happened, and upon reflection, yeah, it kind of makes sense. *The Book of Genesis* (unillustrated) is full of sex, violence, surreality, and very big personalities. And as it happens, so is the work of Crumb. What he wound up creating is a surprisingly straightforward, but also incredibly fresh and strange, adaptation. Humans imagine some pretty weird things. And God, for his part, is a pretty weird dude.

Cheater Rating: 9/10

Almost all of the original language is there, and the illustrations simply aid in the consumption. That being said, the illustrations do present their own version (and vision) of the biblical events, so it all has to be taken with a grain of salt.

7 "WUTHERING HEIGHTS"
WRITTEN AND PERFORMED BY KATE BUSH (1978) 🎵
BASED ON THE NOVEL WUTHERING HEIGHTS
WRITTEN BY EMILY BRONTË 📖

There's a pretty standard recipe for pop songs. This recipe includes, in broad strokes, sex appeal, a guitar solo, major chords, and a little bit of edge. Kate Bush was still a teenager when she wrote "Wuthering Heights," and it fails on almost all of these counts, but succeeds in every other way possible. Kate Bush sings like a muppet (but any sane lover would die for that muppet). The lyrics make obscure references to a nineteenth-century classic from English literature (but any sane reader would die for those moors). And in the music video, Kate Bush dances like she's performing in an *SNL* skit about "modern dance" (but so does Robyn). But it works. Jarring rhythms: check. Minor chords: check. Loopy dances: check. It's all here, it's all crazy, it's all beautiful. This truly is "Wuthering Heights."

Cheater Rating: 2/10

The song conveys a great sense of mood and beauty, but little sense of little else. If you were to try to derive a plot summary of the book based on the song, it would go something like this: Cathy is a ghost and she lives outside Heathcliff's window. The end.

6 ANNA KARENINA
WRITTEN BY TOM STOPPARD (2012)
BASED ON THE NOVEL ANNA KARENINA
WRITTEN BY LEO TOLSTOY

It's hard to update a truly classic piece of literature. If you stay too close to the original script, then people will say they've seen this one before; and if you go too far, then people will say that you were unfaithful to the original story. So in the end, when it comes to classics, you're damned if you adapt, and you're damned if you don't. And *Anna Karenina* is nothing if not a classic. From the opening line ("All unhappy families are alike; each unhappy family is unhappy in its own way") to the closing image, from its Russianness to its worldliness, it is BIG. And when things are big, they do not readily lend themselves to the big screen.

Maybe it was that very problem that inspired Joe Wright to make a movie that looked like a play where the background props could never quite get out of the way. It works. In adapting a book that, inasmuch as it's about anything, is about the way our world hems us in, the decision to put on display the showiness of everything was, at the very least, a wise one, and at the very most, a Tolstoyan insight. Big insights through prosaic means. Done.

Cheater Rating: 6/10
Anna Karenina is a very long book, and this adaptation hits almost all of the major plot points. That alone is worthy of commendation in a movie that devotes so much energy to conveying the spirit of a global icon.

5 SITA SINGS THE BLUES
WRITTEN, DIRECTED, PRODUCED, AND ANIMATED BY NINA PALEY (2008)
BASED ON SELECTIONS FROM THE RAMAYANA

Nina Paley did a bold and somewhat crazy thing. As a white woman living in the San Francisco Bay Area, she decided that she wanted to tell the story of both her own life and the Hindu classic *The Ramayana* by blending literary adaptation, literary criticism, personal memoir, and musical elements. She also wanted to make a movie that she could produce entirely on her own, using public domain materials (including most notably some early twentieth-century jazz songs performed by Annette Hanshaw) and basic animation soft-ware. Then she wanted to sell it for no dollars to whoever wanted it, and make it available for free distribution as well.

As a business plan, this would not have many takers. As a movie, it at least had the support of the one person who mattered most: Nina Paley. The film eventually built up a sizable audience, and by generating a share of controversy (as cultural critics both in the US and in India felt the entire film betrayed a neocolonialist attitude), it came to the attention of mainstream film critics like Roger Ebert, who have been almost universal in their acclaim. That is not unsurprising, because, at the outset you have to wonder what Hindu gods could have in common with contemporary American citizens, or why an icon of Hindu literature would be singing jazz songs. It's weird, it's beautiful, it's free, and, maybe most impressive of all, it makes a lot of sense.

Cheater Rating: 6/10
Even though the story of *The Ramayana* gets chopped up, remixed, and blended in this adaptation, the streamlined plotting of the actual story is a pretty handy guide, and the commentary really helps to give a sense of how many possible meanings are present in each individual scene. It's a loose adaptation, but it does pack a substantial punch.

4 *CLUELESS*
WRITTEN AND DIRECTED BY AMY HECKERLING (1995)
BASED ON THE NOVEL EMMA
WRITTEN BY JANE AUSTEN

The mid-1990s were a very good time for Jane Austen adaptations: In addition to *Clueless*, you also had Gwyneth Paltrow starring in *Emma*, and Ang Lee hauling in one thousand Oscars for his by-the-book (but still beautiful) version of *Sense and Sensibility*. All of these adaptations had a lasting impact, but *Clueless* is the one that still stands out today. It paved the way for the *Bridget Jones* franchise of the 2000s and played a pivotal role in turning the '90s into the '90s as we know them today—with knee-high socks, baby backpacks, "going postal," "getting snaps," slacker Paul Rudd, and Contempo Casuals all very much included. And in addition to being both funny and romantic (not an easy feat for romantic comedies as a genre), it did provide at least one insight into its source material: namely, that Emma, in addition to being an iconic character from English literature, is also, essentially, just a spoiled, popular teenager at heart.

Cheater Rating: 1/10
Yeah, this movie is pretty worthless as far as cheating on your homework goes. But if you really do want to get the story without reading the book, that's easier done than said when it comes to Jane Austen.

3 THE GREAT GATSBY NES VIDEO GAME
CREATED BY CHARLIE HOEY AND PETE SMITH (2011)
BASED ON THE NOVEL *THE GREAT GATSBY*
WRITTEN BY F. SCOTT FITZGERALD

Although Hollywood continues to profit by adapting literature into movie form, video game developers have stuck mainly to doing movie adaptations. That strange fact seems even stranger when you consider that the recent video game adaptation of *The Great Gatsby* was modeled after a game created for an essentially defunct system (the NES), with little effort and almost no capital, and yet became an internet sensation in 2011. Although it does an amazing job of setting the scene for each level, the levels themselves consist mainly of hyper-aggressive Jazz Age types, including tuxedoed waiters, drunken revelers, Charleston dancers, and gangsters. It's hard to find fault with any game, however, that ends with Fitzgerald's ending: "So we beat on, boats against the current, borne back ceaselessly into the past." Hoo-boy, old Fitzy could write some words! That line is almost always apt, but it works especially well here—in a game that points a new potential direction for video games on a system from the early 1980s.

Cheater Rating: 3/10
If nothing else, you'll learn some key lines from the novel and gain some help in identifying central metaphors.

2 TIME REGAINED
DIRECTED BY RAÚL RUIZ (1999)
BASED ON THE NOVEL *TIME REGAINED*
WRITTEN BY MARCEL PROUST

Marcel Proust's *In Search of Lost Time* is widely hailed as one of the all-time great accomplishments of not only modernism but also of world literature as a whole—but greatness doesn't always translate across media. His seven-volume novel is especially difficult on account of its length (4,000+ pages, usually), its complexity (most of Proust's sentences have more clauses in them than the average newspaper article), and its extraordinarily broad set of themes and interests (including, among other things, memory, identity, sexuality, class, race, religion, language, architecture, opera, death, metaphor, and human experience writ large). Most adaptations to date have stuck to just one of Proust's volumes, as Raúl Ruiz did here—but by picking the novel's last volume, he also forced himself to consider the meaning of Proust's work as a whole. *Time Regained* attempts to put Proust's point into cinematic form, and stunningly enough, it succeeds. What is it about? Watch the movie.

Cheater Rating: 8/10
There's no way of really cheating on Proust without cheating yourself, but this comes pretty close to pulling off that impossible trick.

1 THE AGE OF BRONZE SERIES, ILLUSTRATED BY ERIC SHANOWER (2001-) BASED ON HOMER'S *ILIAD*

The Iliad is an old story, and a long story, and a story that remains, in many ways, quite foreign to us today. It took place in the Bronze Age—that is, the age when bronze was a state-of-the-art technology. Today we live in the digital age, and we laugh at the fact that people used to have to take "film" to Walgreens in order to see what the pictures they took actually looked like. Times have changed, a lot. But in his *Age of Bronze* series, Eric Shanower trusted the things we have in common, and instead of updating the story of the Trojan War, his adaptation attempted to be even more faithful to the culture and customs of the ancient Greeks. He worked with scholars in order to render the dress of his characters in a realistic fashion—and thus manages to show us what Homer took for granted. And instead of shortening this epic for modern audiences, Shanower began his book far before *The Iliad* actually begins. These decisions sound risky in principle, but the story is so compelling, the drama is so real, and the conflicts are so enduring, that it all just adds up to even more entertainment.

Cheater Rating: 8/10
It tells the story of *The Iliad* (as well as the stories—the myths—that helped inform *The Iliad*), but its poetry lies in images, rather that in words. So in order to get the impact of the repetitions, the metaphors, and the austerity of the original, you really do have to go back to the original. But if you want to know what happens, this is the better option.

GAIN EMOTIONAL INTELLIGENCE
BECAUSE SOMETIMES IQ JUST ISN'T ENOUGH

If you get to the final in an international chess tournament, but then, upon winning, grab the checkmated king and scream, "Chess this out, your Excellency!!" before dropkicking him into the audience, it's likely that you have a high IQ—but it's unlikely you'll go on many dates the next weekend (or the next decade). So not a great arrangement, overall. Emotional intelligence, as a component of overall intelligence, isn't something that was taken very seriously until recently, but that doesn't mean that help is hard to find. From the sitcom (which is predicated on social errors and miscommunication) to pop music (and its obsession with failed relationships) to emotional flame-outs (the source of a thousand memes), pop culture runs on bad behavior. Sometimes it just mocks the problem, other times it offers real solutions, but either way it offers a great point of entry for identifying the problems that human beings encounter in dealing with our collective nemesis: other human beings.

10 SEINFELD
CREATED BY JERRY SEINFELD AND LARRY DAVID (1989-1998) 📺

Emotions are complex; the thing we are feeling is rarely just one thing. This is important to bear in mind when considering *Seinfeld*, because even though Jerry, Elaine, George, and Kramer are almost always at fault, that doesn't mean that they aren't also often right. It is really annoying when people invade your personal space (to take one example), but that doesn't mean you should forever shun any and all "close-talkers." And it does seem ridiculous that many offices support the exchange of gifts around the holidays, but that doesn't justify the creation of a fake nonprofit ("the human fund") for the purpose of deceiving your peers. Even so, despite the fact that the characters never benefit from their experiences and never, ever learn their lesson, that doesn't mean that we can't benefit from their insights. A little cynicism goes a long way—but too much makes you Larry David.

Most useful for: Those who struggle to break up with people they know they really ought to break up with.

9 FUN HOME: A FAMILY TRAGICOMIC
WRITTEN AND ILLUSTRATED BY ALISON BECHDEL (2006) 💬

Fun Home's title is derived from the funeral home where Alison Bechdel's father, Bruce Bechdel, grew up and later served as director. It is also an ironic commentary on the fact that the home where Alison was raised was not at all a pleasant place to be. Alison's father was profoundly at odds with his own sexuality, and this tension makes itself apparent in a number of very not-fun ways—including a very short fuse, a very distant demeanor, and a string of self-destructive acts that ultimately culminated in his apparent suicide. Alison's account of growing up, figuring out her own sexual identity, coping with her father's death, and teasing out the ways that everyone in the family interacted and influenced one another is as compelling as it is complex. Every panel in the book moves the story forward and casts the reader's mind back to previous panels and previous events, so if you want to know where to start, I'd recommend the last page. (I'd also recommend setting aside the next three hours, because then you'll have to read the whole book at once.)

Most useful for: Anyone who thinks self-reflection is a waste of time.

8 LIVE
PERFORMED BY TIG NOTARO (2012)

Speaking of "tragicomedy," this now legendary set by stand-up comedian Tig Notaro would make a great stand-in entry if dictionaries ever happen to run out of words. In her roughly 30-minute set, Tig discusses her mother's death, the dissolution of a long-standing relationship, and her recent diagnosis of cancer soon after surviving a life-threatening case of pneumonia. It sounds dark, and it is, but it's also full of laughs that hit like punches (because it's hard to laugh when it's hard to breathe, and it's hard to breathe when someone is dealing so immediately with danger, disappointment, and death). The performance was a spur-of-the-moment affair, but another comedian recorded it, and after Louis C.K. made it available on his website, it became a sensation. Hype has the unfortunate quality of damning perfectly good artwork, but this is a case where it's almost impossible to overstate the merits of the performance.

Most useful for: Perspective when things are good, and inspiration when things are bad.

7 MY BEAUTIFUL DARK TWISTED FANTASY
WRITTEN BY KANYE WEST (2010)

Kanye West wears his heart on his sleeve, and that's kind of a problem, because his sleeves are kind of very famous. His parts are not private, and his emotions are broadcast live (and turned into memes afterward). It can be embarrassing, and it would be embarrassing if he were just another celebrity; but as it happens he's famous because he's also a really talented, really original music-maker. And in his actual music, he's able to transform his insecurities into art. That's not especially surprising in and of itself—Weezer did something similar in rock, and Hemingway did something similar with his novels—but it's especially poignant when the art in question is hip-hop.

My Beautiful Dark Twisted Fantasy sounds great even at the very first listen (always a good sign for an album), but the more you listen to it, the more you lose yourself in his transparency. Normally that word would be used as an insult, but his walls and evasions and bluffs, like his musical production work, are so complicated that even when you see through him, you still don't know who he is. There's a lesson in that.

Most useful for: People who can't get over their own insecurities.

6 THIRTEEN REASONS WHY
WRITTEN BY JAY ASHER (2007)

Young adult novels are no longer just for young adults. *Twilight, The Hunger Games*, and *Harry Potter* have all provided ample evidence of that. But at the same time, there are also real points of distinction. For instance: novels for "young adults" still provide morals, and novels for "adults" don't. And *13 Reasons Why* provides a great advertisement for the value of morals—morals in every sense—whoever your audience may be. After high school student Hannah commits suicide, a package of audiotapes begins circulating. These thirteen tapes provide a person-by-person account of how negligence can lead to trauma. And through Clay, the narrator of the story and the ninth recipient of the tapes, we are forced to question how well we know the people that we think we know, and how well we have to gain by thinking just a little bit more about them.

Most useful for: People who have a little growing up to do (aka "everyone").

5 MODERN FAMILY
CREATED BY STEVEN LEVITAN AND CHRISTOPHER LLOYD (2009–)

Growing up is hard to do. *Modern Family* takes that cynical truism and makes it palatable without making it feel watered down. So the question then is, *how*? How do you provide a steady hand and a moral compass and not sound like the Cleavers? *Modern Family* makes it work because it's clear that the laughs always come first—not at the expense of character or plot, but it's clear that the show's top priority is always to keep the audience laughing. It succeeds. There are three sets of parents, and they are very clearly diverse. No longer is every wife white; and in this show there are husbands to husbands, as well as husbands to wives. But that's not really the point. The point is watching physical comedy be comedic again and seeing how teens, when at their worst, are still actually pretty okay. Laugh and learn.

Most useful for: Anyone in need of a little guidance (and a lot of laughs).

4 THE HAPPINESS PROJECT: OR, WHY I SPENT A YEAR TRYING TO SING IN THE MORNING, CLEAN MY CLOSETS, FIGHT RIGHT, READ ARISTOTLE, AND GENERALLY HAVE MORE FUN
BY GRETCHEN RUBIN (2009)

Ignorance is bliss (we're told), and happiness is a warm gun (some sing), but bliss is happines by definition, so does that then mean that ignorance is a warm gun? What does that even mean? Maybe happiness just isn't suited to metaphors. Maybe it's too big a concept for even the loosest of definitions. Instead, let's downgrade to analogies and just agree that happiness is like nothing so much as a heavily pomaded alligator. It's a great idea, but it's dangerous and very hard to wrangle. Gretchen Rubin saw the futility of wrestling with concepts that are like unto greasy swamplings, and instead of trying to be happy, she attempted, first in her blog and later in this book, to bring just a little more happiness into her life. Using contemporary research, pop-cultural insights, and long-standing theories and principles, she tries to understand how happiness works and how it can be cultivated in the life that she was already in the midst of living.

Most useful for: People who have the tendency to miss the forest for the trees.

3 PARTY OF FIVE
CREATED BY CHRISTOPHER KEYSER AND AMY LIPPMAN (1994-2000)

The 1990s, as an epoch, is now widely mocked for its heart-on-its-sleeves-iness. And that is fair. It wore thousands upon thousands of hearts on its sleeve. Grunge rock happened. *Dawson's Creek* happened. (And Barney the friendly purple dinosaur watched over it all, like the king that he was, nodding and saying, "Yes, more hugs. More hugs.") It all seems so ridiculous to us now, and we are right, because it was—but it was also kind of great. We felt feelings then as we feel feelings now, but then we had to dress like we felt them, and cry when we felt them, and talk about them with our friends. *Party of Five*, for its part, certainly adhered to these rigorous standards. The characters on the show, orphaned in the first episode, deal with all the issues of the day (and a sad day it was) and then some, but each episode ends on a largely harmonious note because, when it really comes down to it, they're all family. They share a common purpose, and that essential optimism is what always kept this show from descending into melodrama. Sometimes, of course, it did so descend, and that was all right, too. It was the '90s, after all!

Most useful for: Pessimists who doubt they'll ever find a port in the storm, and optimists who think that nothing bad could ever happen to them.

2 SAVAGE LOVE
HOSTED BY DAN SAVAGE (2006)

Sex is life. It's what makes humans happen, and it also happens to be a major part of what makes humans happy. But acknowledging that central fact doesn't detract from the reality that sex is also often messy, awkward, and, um, provocative. It stirs up a serious stew of trouble. And Dan Savage is here to help. His sex advice podcast, like his column, reveals itself almost immediately to be about much more than sex: It usually opens with a political diatribe; occasionally it's supplemented with proposals for new words (like) to add to the dictionary; and before he answers any caller's question, Savage never fails to offer qualifications about how much he knows, how much he doesn't know, and just how much the caller's call leaves open to question—especially when it comes to motives. He is not afraid to call an asshole an asshole (both literally and metaphorically). Hence, one of his key neologisms: "DTMFA." (Look it up.)

Most useful for: People who need to DTMFA. And for MF'ers who need to be D'd. If you have doubts about your behavior, or doubts about your doubts, Dan Savage is the man who can, at the very least, clarify your plight. (He also has a pretty solid set of rules for moral living and moral sexing, if you go in for that kind of thing.)

1 THE MISS MANNERS COLUMN
WRITTEN BY JUDITH MARTIN (1978-)

It is, without a doubt, a very bad idea indeed to blow your nose with your elbows on the table while playing footsie with the host. But even short of that trifecta, there is little to be gained from accidental slights and a lot to benefit in paying attention to how you interact with the world around you. Miss Manners knows this, and Miss Manners is here to help. Miss Manners is also, more properly, Judith Martin, and since 1978, she's been dispensing pithy, astute advice to people in need of proper perspective, a little common sense, and a little help with a slightly annoying neighbor. She is the state of the art for behavioral advice. Manners matter. Go to her.

Most useful for: People who want to make sure they don't offend via negligence. Oh, and sociopaths.

THE SMARTEST INANIMATE OBJECTS IN THE HISTORY OF POP CULTURE

10.
The monolith
from *2001: A Space Odyssey*

Because it knows that in a world where apes, humans, and computers are united in their thirst for blood, the best thing to be is a rock. And if you're a God-rock, so much the better, I guess. I don't know though. I'm not an obelisk. (PS: What is an obelisk?)

9.
Garden gnomes
from American lawns

Because they clearly know how to travel on the cheap, and that takes some doing. (Especially when you look as ripe for a con as those guys do.)

8.
The ring
from *Lord of the Rings*

Because if I were a ring, I would also definitely want to go hang out with some new people and stop plodding around with the boring old hobbits.

7.
The leg lamp
from *A Christmas Story*

Because surely, when leg lamp got up that morning and put that outfit on, it knew what it was doing. It had a goal—get some attention—and it achieved that goal. That's smarts, and nothing but.

6.
The tuxedo
in *The Tuxedo*

Because how often do pieces of formal wear manage to get themselves cast in a lead role!

5.
Couches
from American living rooms

Because they know how much our happiness depends on them, and who makes a better living doing less? They just sit there, day after day, and pocket that change, pocket that change, pocket that change . . .

4.
Dr. Pepper

Because how does something that goes flat in like two minutes manage to complete so much schooling? (By the way, I have a theory about how Dr. Pepper and his seemingly endless progeny are responsible for the student loan bubble, if you're interested . . .)

3.
Ken Jennings
from *Jeopardy!*

Because no human being can possibly know that much.

2.
Watson
from IBM (and *Jeopardy!*)

Because he beat the Ken Jennings.

1.
Google's self-driving cars

Google's cars are already being test-driven (by themselves!) on America's streets. It seems fair to deduce from this fact that the United States of America is now, in fact, Soviet Russia—because only in Soviet Russia do cars drive you.

PART III

STOP DOING IT WRONG

DROP THE FACADE
SONGS GUARANTEED TO MELT YOUR FROZEN HEART

Frozen hearts are like snowflakes: They're all utterly unique. And as a result, people need to find their own way back to emotional life. No single prescription will work for everyone, but the common ingredient in this list is emotion—pure and raw emotion. This is no place for irony. This is a time for tears. So let's cry it out together. And then, when people ask us what's the matter, we won't make excuses about dust in our eyes. "No," we'll say, "we're crying because someone, somewhere, is chopping a giant onion, and we have very sensitive eyes."

10 *"HALLELUJAH"*
WRITTEN BY LEONARD COHEN (1984), PERFORMED BY JEFF BUCKLEY (1994)

Leonard Cohen's lyrics and Jeff Buckley's voice go together like oatmeal and raisins. They blend into each other so naturally that it even makes sense when Buckley sings about the time "she tied you to a kitchen chair" and "broke your throne, and she cut your hair." That line, on its own, sounds like a lazy dream. Even when Leonard Cohen sings the line it sounds, at the very least, "poetic." But here it's just a fact. With Jeff Buckley on hand, the entire song becomes one huge, sorrowful, beautiful fact—akin to the fact of a raisin. Like the raisin, it just exists . . . and hallelujah for that.

9 *"FAITHFULLY"*
BY JOURNEY (1983)

If you've been living among strangers for months, then "Faithfully" provides a balm for your homesick soul; but if you've just gotten home from the party of the decade, this song is also just the thing. It's unaccountable, but it's true. Whatever the problem is, or however problem-free your life, "Faithfully" will speak to you and make things better. So while "Don't Stop Believin'" may be the proper response to the eternal question, "Karaoke?," "Faithfully" remains the answer to a different kind of question, namely: "How fast should we be swaying our heads right now?" This fast, friends. This fast.

8 *"UNCHAINED MELODY"*
WRITTEN BY HY ZANET AND ALEX NORTH (1955), PERFORMED BY THE RIGHTEOUS BROTHERS (1965)

"Unchained Melody" is like a crash course in human relationships. It starts out with a teen-age love affair ("LONE-ly times"), moves on to a mature, dynamic partnership ("I . . . need your love"), and concludes with the poignant, devastated reflections of old age ("Time . . . can do . . . so much . . ."). And then, after three minutes and thirty-six seconds spent hurtling through time and space, you open your eyes (your blurry, reddened, grief-stricken eyes) and realize you've just mourned the loss of an imaginary lover who would now be roughly 72 years old. The universe is cruel, and so is this song. The price of admission is all of the tears in your heart. Welcome.

PS: It's also worth noting that "Unchained Melody" basically starred, alongside Demi Moore, Patrick Swayze, and clay, in the '80s classic *Ghost*. (Proof that immortality happens when you least expect it.)

7 "LANDSLIDE"
BY FLEETWOOD MAC (1975) 🎵

For a while it seemed like Fleetwood Mac had a monopoly on both heartache and heartlessness. Everyone in the group was in love, everybody was cheating, and nobody cared what happened next. It was a confusing period for the band. "Landslide," however, is as simple as can be. It's beautiful and quiet and sad, and despite its heartfelt lyrics, it still feels right at home today—even making an appearance on *Glee* in 2011. No self-respecting breakup playlist would be complete without it.

6 "HOME"
BY EDWARD SHARPE AND THE MAGNETIC ZEROES (2009) 🎵

It's hard to project our minds back to a time when hippies were avant-garde, relevant, and cool. There are advantages and disadvantages to this state of affairs, but I think we can all agree that those hippies had an emotional intensity that we're missing out on today. Luckily, Alex Ebert (the band's robe-swaddled front man) seems determined to bring some of that intensity back. In a recent interview, he used the word "transcendent" to describe the magic of live shows, and that adjective certainly applies to "Home" as well. Wherever this song goes, it leaves jimmy-jangling fans in its wake. It has solved the problem of sadness. Next items on the agenda: tie-dyed raindrops and world peace.

5 "FAIRYTALE OF NEW YORK"
BY THE POGUES (1987) 🎵

"Fairytale" is a sentimental, obscenity-laced ode to New York that was written and performed by a Cetlic punk band, and it's as heartwarming as a teddy bear in socks. It's a legitimate miracle, and somewhere, pigs are flying. (Let's just hope that the Pogues aren't throwing them.)

4 "SOMEONE LIKE YOU"
WRITTEN BY ADELE AND DAN WILSON, PERFORMED BY ADELE (2011) 🎵

Everyone knows this song, everyone pretty much loves it, and everyone's heard it a billion times. But still, it just won't go away—and good thing, too, because how else would we explain to our pets what "lovesick" means? It's a big concept, and pets are generally quite poor at English. But now we can just play this song, and the problem is solved. How can we be sure that the animals really understand? Because how could they not!? It's Adele! Plus, my pet Gila monster doesn't normally sob like this.

3 "TIME TO SAY GOODBYE"
WRITTEN BY FRANCESCO SARTORI AND LUCIO QUARANTOTTO (1995), PERFORMED BY ANDREA BOCELLI AND SARAH BRIGHTMAN (1997) ♫

Super Bowl attendees and theatergoers alike swoon before the power of the Boch (Andrea Bocelli) and his rendition of "Time to Say Goodbye." This song offers irrefutable proof that the heart wants what it wants—full stop. (PS: The heart wants this song, sung this way.) I assume that this song is about saying good-bye to someone, but whether this good-bye is taking place literally or metaphorically, in Italy or in outer space, for a minute or for all time— there, I have no idea. I don't think anyone does, because as Bocelli and Sarah Brightman (another opera star at the time this song was recorded) belt this thing out, all anyone can hear is the sound of two people just loving each other. Just sweet-loving each other forever, with no jokes, no irony, no insults—just mutual respect and everlasting admiration.

2 "ROMEO AND JULIET"
WRITTEN BY MARK KNOPFLER (1980), PERFORMED BY THE KILLERS (2007) ♫

This song is as earnest as a nickel, crazy as a codpiece, and pretty as a peach. But you know what, so is love! (And so, for that matter, are the Killers.) "Romeo and Juliet" has a sweetness that's almost impossible to deny, and once you've opened your heart to the song's simple pleasures, then you're susceptible to the huge burden of melancholy that has somehow been smuggled in under wraps. Then you look up, and all you can see is mood. This mood is super weird. But it's only by virtue of that overall effect that lines like "when we made love, you used to cry" work so well. This song will not stop making love to us, and we cannot stop crying.

1 "WHATEVER YOU LIKE"
WRITTEN BY T.I., JAMES SCHEFFER, AND DAVID SIEGEL, PERFORMED BY T.I. (2008) ♫

Sweet melody? Check. Lyrics that appear to be lifted from a hyper-obscene Valentine's Day card? Check. Vows, compliments, promises? Check, check, checkmate. Some songs demand grand gestures. This is one of those songs. Or, in the tender words of T.I., "My chick could have what she want/And go in every store for any bag she want." Any bag. This is love. Go get it.

STOP TALKING BAD
MODELS OF SOULFUL, INCISIVE, HARD-HITTING DIALOGUE

You not good talker? Why is it!? Hey? So change then why not? Stop talking so bad with funtimes help from movies and books and things. Everyone says how fun it is of course. Then you learn and your mouth stops making all the dumbo mistakes like usual, stupid. And then when you do storytime, then new friends hug you for how good you do it. So do it then why not! Borrow help from jabber genius! I think so! A lot!

[Editor's note: The preceding paragraph was the author's original draft, before he had actually partaken of any of the entertainments mentioned below. Things, of course, improved afterward, but we thought it best to retain that original draft to show how effective this program really was.]

10 MY DINNER WITH ANDRÉ
WRITTEN BY WALLACE SHAWN AND ANDRÉ GREGORY (1981) 🎞️

So first of all you should know that *My Dinner with André* is a movie, but it will maybe change your life. It shows one man going to dinner, two men having a conversation over dinner, and one man going home from dinner; but in the course of this movie, we are forced to consider what it means to be successful, to be yourself, to be ambitious, and to maybe accept some measure of ambiguity in our lives and in ourselves . . . oh, and also blah blah blah.

On an unrelated note, can I just point out how ridiculous "trust falls" are? It's on my mind right now because trust falls is a thing that is still happening in the world. That seems kind of weird. Trust falls is that thing where one person walks off a plank backwards and "TRUSTS" that his coworkers (who presumably do not want to be prosecuted for manslaughter) will catch him. I would allege, however, that this is not the way one achieves trust. We trust the people we trust, and the people we trust are the people we know, and the more we know them, the more we trust them. It sounds like a complicated idea (and it is, next to trust falls), but when you see two old friends—two real old friends, like Shawn (who should be familiar to fans of *The Princess Bride*) and Gregory (who at this point should really only be familiar to fans of this movie, sadly)—getting together to make a movie about a fictional dinner where they talk like their actual selves and consider their actual lives (fictionally), you remember what it's like to believe in people. And you learn to trust that even when old friends lie to you (or fib, or fudge), they still can't help but tell the truth. In that spirit, let me now say to André, my new old friend: André, you crazy.

9 *WHEN HARRY MET SALLY . . .*
WRITTEN BY NORA EPHRON (1989)

When Harry Met Sally . . . is a movie that we kind of take for granted now. Everyone knows the "I'll have what she's having" scene, and a lot of people even know that director Rob Reiner's mom was the woman who delivered that very same line, but what gets lost in the film's luster is the fact that it created the romantic comedy as we know it today. Not in terms of the formula (which goes back to Jane Austen, if not earlier), but in terms of the themes, the terms, and even the conversations. It was the movie that gave us the "men and women can't be friends" speech in its modern form; the archetypal "women fake it" monologue; the idea of being a "high-maintenance" person; and the possibility of just having a "transitional" sig-oth (oh, and also, the Harry Connick Jr.-soaked '90s rom-com soundtrack). But it didn't establish all these new tropes because it was intent on doing something new, but rather because it was intent on doing something that was familiar enough to be pleasant and still good enough to be true. And now, like all classics, it feels like it's been around forever—and it sort of has.

8 *THE PHILADELPHIA STORY*
DIRECTED BY GEORGE CUKOR (1940)

The Philadelphia Story is the impossibly charming film adaptation of a stage play by Philip Barry. It takes place at a Philadelphia country estate, where three people love Tracy Lord (played by Katharine Hepburn), but only one can marry her. Two of those people are Cary Grant and Jimmy Stewart, and the third person is engaged to Mrs. Lord, so that is a problem. That problem is what drives the plot. But it's the lines that make the movie.

Philip Barry, the playwright, is now largely forgotten, but that's too bad because his play is just about the best thing ever. The lines he wrote were lovely, and the characters were deep. Luckily, though, in the film adaptation those lines were, if anything, improved by the performances of Cary Grant, Katharine Hepburn, Ruth Hussey, and James Stewart, who—I swear to

James Stewart—turns each and every one of his lines into music. The movie as a whole sticks in your ear like a pop song, but this is not a guilty pleasure. There is so much happening in each line of dialogue, that when someone finally does say something direct and simple—something like "You're wonderful," for instance—it sounds like "I love you" is supposed to sound. It sounds like it matters. Watch it and learn what love sounds like. (But watch out: You won't know what Tracy Lord's true love looks like until the end.)

7 OUT OF SIGHT
DIRECTED BY STEVEN SODERBERGH (1998)

In an early scene from *Out of Sight*, federal marshal Karen Sisco (Jennifer Lopez) stumbles across Jack Foley (George Clooney) and a couple of his pals during a jail break, and when the getaway car arrives she and Clooney eventually wind up in the trunk together (that is not a euphemism). Normally that would be the end of that—cut to the next scene; but in *Out of Sight* what follows is nearly three minutes of what very quickly becomes almost pillow talk: Karen explains why she's not acting afraid; Jack butchers a line from the movie *Network*, "I'm mad as hell and I'm not gonna take—I'm not gonna take any more of your shit!" and struggles to grasp a reference to Clyde Barrow; and right before the trunk opens, they seem to find a common ground in *Three Days of the Condor* ("the one with Robert Redford when he was young.") *Out of Sight*, for its part, is the one with George Clooney before he was a film star and Jennifer Lopez before she was J-Lo. Detroit has never looked better (or bluer), Miami has never looked hotter (or redder), and Elmore Leonard's dialogue has never sounded smarter or sexier than it does here, under Steven Soderbergh's direction. "Cool" looked pretty weird in the '90s, but here '90s cool actually makes some sense.

Oh, also, keep an eye out for Don Cheadle. (Because he'll keep an eye out for you.)

6 JAY-Z VS. NAS
WRITTEN BY SHAWN CARTER (IN THIS CORNER) AND NASIR BIN OLU DARA JONES (IN THE FAR CORNER), RESPECTIVELY (2001-2005)

I suppose it's a little strange to think of a rap battle as being a kind of long-form "conversation," but at the same time, if you have two people who are listening closely to each other and responding at length with not only words, but also music, what is that if not conversation-plus? And in the case of Jay-Z vs. Nas, this was not just a matter of name-calling. It began after the death of the Notorious B.I.G.—who both men knew, and who had previously been regarded as the best rapper alive—with a bunch of vague allusions and perceived insults, but by the time Nas released "Ether" in response to Jay-Z's "Takeover," pretty much all of the cards were all on the table. The rivalry was obscene and at times vicious, so it may not have been the most functional or the most productive conversation in the end, but it concluded with everyone friends again (and now business partners as well) and with New York once again at the center of the hip-hop world.

5 MILLER'S CROSSING
WRITTEN AND DIRECTED BY JOEL AND ETHAN COEN (1990)

The Coen brothers have always known how to write some of that sweet dialogue. Whether they're writing for mild-mannered Minnesotans (as in *Fargo*) or Wild Westerners (*True Grit*) or casual Californians (*The Big Lebowski*), these two bros never fail to account for the little tics that separate the dude-ers from the dontchaknow-ists. Their dialogue is also famous for its hiccups—its "ums" and "likes" and pauses, and in both instances their affinity for realism really does help to show us something that a lot of movies fail to identify: namely, the influence of where we come from, in both what we say and who we are. Those little verbal gestures are a lot more than simple background noise; instead, they show us as we are when we're not paying attention.

But the little differences that separate region from region and personality from personality have nothing on the separation between the slang of today and the slang of yesterday; so it's not surprising that the past is where the Coen brothers find their ripest terrain. In *Miller's Crossing*, they borrow heavily from the Jazz Age, but which is also thoroughly modern, and what they come up with is a movie that is not a period piece, not a mystery, and not a noir, but is instead a movie that—like all of their best films—reflects on the ways that our language affects our behavior. A movie about our "etics," in other words.

4 BRIDESMAIDS
WRITTEN BY KRISTEN WIIG AND ANNIE MUMOLO (2011)

Bridesmaids is a movie that contains multitudes. Some of its scenes are straight out of *SNL* (where Kristen Wiig had made her name), others were plugged in for their gross-out comedy factor, and as the movie nears its end, a smallish subplot takes over and resolves the movie as though it had been a romantic comedy all along. But it all kind of works because even though Kristen Wiig's character is hilariously inept at coping with her friend's upcoming marriage, the movie as a whole is, like a good (and more stable) friend, incredibly open to whatever its characters want to do—or simply can't help themselves from doing. That spirit of generosity pervades the movie, and it's never more apparent than in the opening conversation between real-life friends Kristen Wiig and Maya Rudolph. It sounds like real human friends, but it takes place in a movie, and it stars women. And it has perhaps the best penis impression ever committed to film. It is a Hollywood miracle.

3 THE BRIEF WONDROUS LIFE OF OSCAR WAO
WRITTEN BY JUNOT DÍAZ (2007)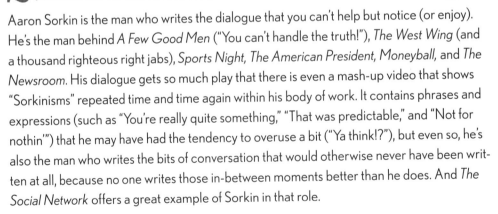

With the exception of its quotes from comic books (*The Fantastic Four* and *Watchmen*, most notably), there's hardly a single set of quotation marks in all of *Oscar Wao*. This isn't that exceptional—James Joyce used dashes and italics because he abhorred inverted commas, and lots of other authors have found their way around them, too—but in this case the decision to avoid them is especially poignant. Oscar, the character at the center of the novel, is a character who is surrounded by words. Everyone else is always talking, telling stories, and their conversations inform his life. But he finds himself more and more closed off as he grows up and appears to us from a distance, reading, thinking, pining away, and making plans. When Oscar does act though, he has an impact. His actions led, ostensibly, to the novel, after all. And that's the risk and promise that our actions carry: They can turn back into words, and carry on.

2 THE SOCIAL NETWORK
SCREENPLAY BY AARON SORKIN, DIRECTED BY DAVID FINCHER (2010)

Aaron Sorkin is the man who writes the dialogue that you can't help but notice (or enjoy). He's the man behind *A Few Good Men* ("You can't handle the truth!"), *The West Wing* (and a thousand righteous right jabs), *Sports Night, The American President, Moneyball,* and *The Newsroom.* His dialogue gets so much play that there is even a mash-up video that shows "Sorkinisms" repeated time and time again within his body of work. It contains phrases and expressions (such as "You're really quite something," "That was predictable," and "Not for nothin'") that he may have had the tendency to overuse a bit ("Ya think!?"), but even so, he's also the man who writes the bits of conversation that would otherwise never have been written at all, because no one writes those in-between moments better than he does. And *The Social Network* offers a great example of Sorkin in that role.

David Fincher's movie is about Facebook and the consequences of greed, ambition, and power. But since it involves a lot of young people, and since young people talk a lot, Aaron Sorkin was hired to inject some life into the script. That "life" is evident—as is "that Sorkin"—from the very first scene, where Rooney Mara, as Mark Zuckerberg/Jesse Eisenberg's soon-to-be-ex-girlfriend, keeps pace with him on several different conversational tracks at the same time. They all matter, and they're all juvenile, and they're all totally compelling. And sometimes that's the whole idea. When people talk, you want to make the audience care. That's what Sorkin does.

1 DEATH PROOF
WRITTEN AND DIRECTED BY QUENTIN TARANTINO (2007)

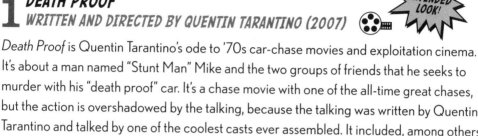

Death Proof is Quentin Tarantino's ode to '70s car-chase movies and exploitation cinema. It's about a man named "Stunt Man" Mike and the two groups of friends that he seeks to murder with his "death proof" car. It's a chase movie with one of the all-time great chases, but the action is overshadowed by the talking, because the talking was written by Quentin Tarantino and talked by one of the coolest casts ever assembled. It included, among others, Sydney Tamiia Poitier (aka "a girl named Sydney Poitier"), Tracie Thoms (Tracie Thoms!), Rosario Dawson (who grew up in a Lower East Side tenement building and today works with the Lower East Side Girls Club), and Zoe Bell (a real-life stunt woman and, I think, a human cat).

The film is split into two parts: In the first part, three young female friends (Arlene, Shanna, and "Jungle" Julia—a local DJ) drive around Austin, talking; talk and drink at a local bar; and then drive home, talking and listening to music—at which point "Stunt Man" Mike plows into them at high velocity and kills them all, but is himself mostly unharmed. In the second half of the movie, three young female friends (Abernathy, Kim, and Lee) drive around Tennessee, talking; pick up their friend Zoe; take an iconic car out for a "test drive," and then engage in an epic off-road chase with "Stunt Man" Mike, which ends with Mike being beaten to a pulp in the middle of the road.

The chase and the action at the end of the movie give the film its raison d'être, but they are not the point. The point is that Jungle Julia wants to hear "Hold Tight," by Dave, Dee, Dozy, Beaky, Mick, and Tich, when she rides home from the bar; the point is that Arlene didn't do "the thing," and that Zoe fell into the ditch that Kim had told her about, but that even so, she "practically landed on her feet." The point is that they are alive, and the way they speak to each other shows who they are and what they believe—which is why the movie, as a chase movie, is so good. If you don't really want to hear what someone has to say when they get out of a car, it doesn't matter as much whether or not they ever do get out. And if you do care, it does matter. A lot. We root for these ladies to win their fight against "Stunt Man" Mike not just because he is an evil murderer and they are some awesome friends, but also because we want to hear them finish their stories. (And finish Mike's, too.)

GAIN SOME PERSPECTIVE
READ A BOOK AND TRY ON ANOTHER HUMAN BEING

The earth may revolve around the sun, and we Earth-dwellers may very well revolve along with it (except, of course, for polar Santa Claus, who sits, unmoving, upon his throne of gilded children), but every human being also resides at the center of his or her own universe. This is true at all times, but it's especially true when we're stuck in traffic and late for an event. Then it is us vs. the world—with us in the role of hero, and every-one else in the role of villain (aka "that a**hole"). But if we stop to think about it, this is not the happiest of all possible attitudes; in fact, it's the time-honored recipe for good old-fashioned road rage. So before we all Mad Max each other to our graves, it's worth remembering that there are 6 billion other "I's" on the planet. So step back, take a deep breath, check out these books, and find the "I" that works for you.

10 THE CATCHER IN THE RYE
WRITTEN BY J.D. SALINGER (1951)

The Catcher in the Rye is the book that made teenage consciousness a thing in American pop culture. It took the insecurities and pretensions and confusions of youth and made them not just interesting, but also appealing. Holden Caulfield—the "I" of this iconic novel (and the prototype for almost every teenage hero ever since)—has been expelled from Pencey Prep and, instead of going home, decides to take his principled, anti-phony outlook to the streets of New York. What happens on those streets—and in those bars, and at those houses, and at the zoo—is also somewhat indistinguishable from what goes on inside Holden's head. But in either case, they're nice places to spend a few days, and there's no better tour guide either. Plus, midcentury teenage slang! Wuddya think!

9 THE CURIOUS INCIDENT OF THE DOG IN THE NIGHT-TIME
WRITTEN BY MARK HADDON (2003)

For almost as long as there's been a mystery genre to speak of, there have been mysteries written from a child's point of view. Even William Faulkner tried his hand at it (in *Intruders in the Dust*)! And that makes sense: having a child narrator just doubles down on the mystery element—because now, instead of just having to figure out "who did it," your lead investigator also has to figure out the world (and there's no mystery deeper than that). In *The Curious Incident of the Dog in the Night-Time*, author Mark Haddon takes that conceit and ups the ante yet again by making his narrator a teenager who appears to be living on the autism spectrum. When a large black poodle is killed, Christopher John Francis Boone wants answers, but he can't investigate without encountering a much larger and more complex world than he had formerly known. He does eventually solve the case, but it is the other mysteries—how can he get to London? why aren't his parents still together? and what are the neighbors like?—that are the most interesting. Christopher has his own way of solving problems, but his outlook on life and the dawning world in front of him are inspirational for those of us with less unique perspectives, too.

8 I CAPTURE THE CASTLE
WRITTEN BY DODIE SMITH (1948)

Dodie Smith isn't a household name anymore, but households are making a big mistake because, first of all, we should all be naming our daughters "Dodie" (how could they fail to be intelligent yet wildly eccentric when they grow up!), and second of all, because Dodie Smith wrote two of the all-time great books for children and young adults: *The Hundred and*

One Dalmatians and *I Capture the Castle*. And whether she's writing from the point of view of dalmatians or teenage girls, Smith gets inside her characters' heads like few other writers can. From the first words ("I write this sitting in the kitchen sink") to the last ("I love you, I love you, I love you"), we live inside Cassandra Mortmain's notebooks and get an intimate and incredibly poignant look at what it's like to grow up inside "the castle"—the grandiose but dilapidated home of the Mortmain clan—and some of the most eccentric characters English literature has to offer.

7 THE ABSOLUTELY TRUE DIARY OF A PART-TIME INDIAN
WRITTEN BY SHERMAN ALEXIE, WITH ART BY ELLEN FORNEY (2007)

It's easy to forget sometimes, but the life of a teenager, for a teenager, is pretty all consuming. Questions about what we should wear, how to get the things we want but can't afford, and who we are vs. who we want to be, are all matters of life and death—not literally, but also yeah, pretty much. As a nonteenager, the importance of those questions tends to wane somewhat, but Sherman Alexie's book reminds us of what it feels like to actually be a teenager. The "part-time Indian" in question is one Junior Spirit, and Junior has a lot on his mind. More than the average teen, it's safe to say—because every teen has to struggle with questions relating to their identity, but not every teen is pulled in two by the twin struggles of both fitting into reservation life and also finding a way to escape. That's Junior's plight. But it's also the thing that gives this book the heft to match the easy appeal of Junior's personality, voice, and art.

6 ROOM
WRITTEN BY EMMA DONOGHUE (2010)

It's hard to write about this novel because it's just so unspeakably upsetting. The set-up is brutal (a mother and her five-year-old son, Jack, are held captive by a character known as Old Nick); the slow reveal—provided in Jack's voice and according to his own limited understanding—is so heartbreaking; and the dream of eventual escape is so agonizingly far-fetched, that it's difficult to endorse the novel without also damning it. ("Dude, you should totally check out this book about rape and kidnapping told from a toddler's point of view! You'll love it!") But if you just pick it up, rest assured, you will not put it down again. Despite the harsh reality of the novel, the book is also really, really enjoyable to read. Jack's world and worldview are profoundly limited, but with those limited resources, Jack and his mother (and Donoghue, of course) have built their own real world. The more you understand, the worse things get, and then you get to the climax. Remember to breathe.

5 THE SILENT HISTORY
CREATED BY ELI HOROWITZ, KEVIN MOFFETT, MATTHEW DERBY, AND RUSSELL QUINN (2012-)

The Silent History is a big project in a small package. In the most general terms, it is an app that attempts to tell the science-fictional story of a world essentially parallel to our own, where an increasing number of children are born without the ability to process language. Testimonials—which offer accounts from the people whose lives have been affected by the disease—are published on a regular basis and are supplemented by field reports that only become available when you are in the exact same geographic location that the field report concerns. So the story finds a lot of ways to get into your head and change the way you look at the world around you. Sometimes the results are poignant, sometimes profound, and sometimes deeply haunting. There are a lot of ideas out there now about what the future of the book looks like. It generally seems safe to say that there are a lot of futures out there—but this one is definitely worth paying attention to.

4 PERSEPOLIS
WRITTEN AND ILLUSTRATED BY MARJANE SATRAPI (2000)

In *Persepolis*, Marjane Satrapi (aka "Marji") manages the neat trick of being both very Iranian and still very recognizable to American audiences. Marji's a cool, ambitious, artistic kid, and her dreams are the standard American dreams: She wants to do what she wants to do, rather than what other people want her to want to do. But as the political climate in Iran becomes more and more heated, the tension between what she wants and what others want for her— as a girl, as an Iranian, and as an Arab—becomes more and more problematic. And after the revolution, it becomes downright dangerous. To see someone who seems so much like us, and someone who lives in a culture so much like ours, suffer—and watch others suffer—at the hands of religious extremism and totalitarianism, offers a rude awakening to the dangers that endure in the world that surrounds us, in the world that we all share.

3 INVISIBLE MAN
WRITTEN BY RALPH ELLISON (1952) 📖

The Invisible Man is about a man who is literally invisible. It was also, once upon a time, a movie starring ("starring") Chevy Chase (the man, not the Maryland). *Invisible Man*, on the other hand, is about a man who is figuratively invisible—a black man living underground in New York City at the middle of the last century. In addition to being one of America's most celebrated authors, Ellison was an immensely talented jazz musician, and in keeping with that tradition, he drew heavily from the literary past in the construction and style of his novel, but he also created something entirely new. His invisible man, for his part, has a past, but he has given up on the future. What he is left with is a story and a voice. That voice is what keeps us reading even when the story becomes unbearable—during the battle royal scene, for instance, or in any of the book's numberless betrayals. We travel with the *Invisible Man* deep into the bowels of American life, and because his voice is so vivid, it's hard to resist seeing his world, even when we look out at our own today. Throughout his life, Ellison was badgered about the production of a new literary work to match *Invisible Man*; but maybe that's because his work was already done.

2 CLOUD ATLAS
WRITTEN BY DAVID MITCHELL (2004) 📖

Each of *Cloud Atlas*'s six different story lines comes to us via a different narrator, writing in a different time and working within a different literary genre (spanning from dystopian sci-fi to conspiracy thrillers to literary fiction); but the worlds that David Mitchell builds up out of these different moods are so complete that it doesn't really matter where the story goes (although the story's fun, too). When you're in an eighteenth-century seafaring vessel, you feel like you're in the eighteenth century—and manners may be your only way out (until there's another way). And when you're in the distant, distant future, and blood-soaked barbarians are attacking you from every side, you feel like anarchy is the only real option (until it's not). It keeps you reading because you always want to know what happens next—but in the end, ironically, it's not the plot that matters; it's the people . . . and the words . . . and the worlds. It's fun to be there, because it's fun to be these people. It's fun to be them even though they are, in sequence, poisoned, manipulated, assassinated, falsely imprisoned, mock-trial'd, and hunted for sport. But whatevs. Humans are a tough bunch, y'all!

1 I AM LEGEND
WRITTEN BY RICHARD MATHESON (1954)

Things that are hard to imagine: black holes, a trustworthy scorpion, an internet without advertisements, and a world without other people in it. *I Am Legend* doesn't concern itself with most of those items, but it certainly takes up the challenge of imagining the last item on the list, painting a vivid picture of Robert Neville's life on Earth now that all the other people are gone. It is a lonely life, and one sequence where he attempts to get a stray dog ("stray" is a little superfluous at this point, I guess) to trust him is particularly affecting—especially since every time the dog wanders off, Neville imagines that he's going to be eaten by the vampires.

Oh yeah, the vampires. Did I neglect to mention that? The humans are gone because the vampires (vampire-zombie hybrids, really) have completely taken over. Neville is the last man standing, and because he needs something to do besides drink and barricade himself inside his house, he attempts to figure out how the vampire-zombie disease works, how the vampire-zombies can be defeated, and how he, on his own, can actually defeat them. The Will Smith movie adaptation did a great job of portraying the loneliness and isolation of the book, but the procedural survival aspect was lost, as was the amazing conclusion, where you realize that—well, suffice it to say that there's something especially impressive about a final twist that doesn't rely on any new information or events. Check it out.

BE MORE RESPONSIBLE
ESSENTIAL REMINDERS THAT IF YOU DON'T DO IT, NO ONE WILL

It isn't very sexy to "be responsible," but man alive, is it a good thing to be. Responsible people are excellent at not leaving the stove on, and they thrive in "don't forget to lock the door" scenarios (which, it's worth noting, are frequent if you frequently leave your house). And if you accrue trash, as humans do, and have a raccoon for a pet, you definitely need to have someone responsible around to help you remember to take out the trash and take out the raccoon. (Also, responsible people are probably great at dissuading others from adopting feral pets.)

So yeah, obviously: It's better to be responsible. But it's also very hard. It takes a lot of work, and there are other things to do, like . . . wait, what? Sorry I was just watching a raccoon do a little dance—maybe a mating dance?—on this pile of unopened mail over here. Man is that guy (girl?) cute. Anyway. Like I was saying, sometimes it's worth considering what the world would look like if all of us paid no attention to due dates and deadlines and dancing raccoons. That world, as it happens, is a very scary place. So scare yourself straight—and then pay your rent, you derelict. Oh, and also maybe open my mail, because speaking of scary: that pile.

10 FIELD OF DREAMS
BASED ON THE BOOK BY W.P. KINSELLA (1989)

In addition to containing one of the most ridiculous premises ever, *Field of Dreams* is also one of the all-time great non-baseball-oriented baseball movies. And like all great non-baseball-oriented baseball movies, it begins when a whispering spirit (literally) tells a Kevin Costner, made of wood (metaphorically), that "if you build it, they will come." They being Shoeless Joe Jackson's "Black Sox" of the 1919 baseball season, who allegedly threw the World Series for a gambling pay-off. Costner then builds it, they then come, and at that point grab your handkerchiefs and mufflers, because things are about to get sobby. For me, the best sobs occur when the voice of Darth Vader (aka James Earl Jones), here playing a withdrawn, embittered writer, slowly gets on board with Kevin Costner's absolutely nut-balls project: to follow the voice wherever it leads. And in the process everyone learns lessons about learning to forgive the past, I guess? I don't know. Ask the whispering voice in the cornfield. (Is that you, Batman?)

Essential for when: You think maybe someone else will build it? (They won't. You have to, or he won't come.)

9 ALIEN
DIRECTED BY RIDLEY SCOTT (1979)

You know what's a bad idea? Swimming too soon after eating, that's what! What a bellyache that is! Oh, and also going into outer space. That too. It has no oxygen in it for breathing!— and also, Lord only knows what it does have! Probably your worst nightmares. And definitely H.R. Giger's worst nightmares, because he designed the alien in *Alien*, and man is his nightmare-alien awful. Unlike other special effects from the late 1970s (I'm looking at you, *Star Wars*) *Alien* looks like it could have been shot yesterday. It knew the limits of the time; it knew exactly how far it could go and how much it could get away with. How much, you ask? The answer to that question is exactly how much pants you have left after it has scared 99 percent of the pants off of you all these many years later. So listen, if you do encounter an alien, just please, please let there be no survivors, because seriously, alien babies, though somewhat cute, are the absolute worst.

Essential for when: You're tempted to just ignore that queasy rumbling in your tum-tum. (Don't. Explode yourself immediately.)

8 TELL NO ONE
DIRECTED BY GUILLAUME CANET (2006)

Tell No One is a Netflix miracle. It's the movie you put on because it just keeps popping up. So you know: Netflix wants you to watch this movie, and eventually you do. The first scene has you at hello: It opens with a charmingly mature French dinner party. You want to hang out with these people. And then these people go home, and hey, what's that noise? Oh, it's MURDER. And MYSTERY. And CONSPIRACY. And CHAOS. And then this guy is running through the streets of Paris and getting help from charming gangsters and the soundtrack is all of a sudden the most romantic and evocative piece of American soul you could ever hope to encounter on the slow-mo streets of Paris and then—well, that's the point where the plot kicks into high gear. You know, with horses and horse trainers and such. Does that make sense? Of course not. But trust in this: You will love it, so just give it a chance. Oh, and also: Do not trust anyone, anywhere, except your one true love. (PS: When I say "you" I definitely mean "me," but I also definitely mean "you" because *Tell No One* tells everyone the same story, and it is, in a word, totally, beautifully walnuts.)

Essential for when: You think maybe the police will figure out what happened to your wife. (They won't. They will charge you with murder. Run.)

7 THE HOST
DIRECTED BY JOON-HO BONG (2006)

So first of all it's worth noting that this movie is an inspiration for all the lazy boys out there—for the people who have a hard time imagining themselves as heroes in cases where a hero is called for (especially if the heroism in question requires confronting a mucous-y monstrosity from Industrial Light & Magic). It's also worth noting that this movie is crazy. It asks the question: How would a normally dysfunctional but still tightly knit family respond if one of its own was taken to an underground lair by a mutant sea creature? It also asks the question: What would that same family look like in a grief-stricken, slapsticky dog pile? And one final note worth noting: This movie is beautiful. Seriously. Even if you don't normally go in for South Korean action-adventure movies (which you really should), you have never seen such hypnotically beautiful and poignant slow-motion shots of mutant freaks in all your days, I promise. If you were ever tempted to turn your back on the freakish consequences of toxic pollution, this movie will turn your back around again. I promise.

Essential for when: You can't see how it can possibly be a bad idea to pour a bunch of toxic chemicals down the drain. (It can be a bad idea. And it can attack you. In terrifying slow-mo. Don't do it. Seriously.)

6 THE LORD OF THE RINGS TRILOGY
DIRECTED BY PETER JACKSON (2001–2003)

Forces of darkness getting you down? Oh, yeah, just let the Hobbits handle it, right? Right!? But here's the thing, you silly fool: The hobbits are us, and we are the hobbits!! Oh, you don't think so? You don't think your feet are as hairy as all that (point to you), and you don't think it's fun to jump on oversized mattresses like that? Okay, sure, fair enough; but what about metaphorically? No? Still no? Okay, then, fine—reset: You know what's hard to defeat? Evil. And evil is up to its usual tricks and unusually armed to the teeth in *The Lord of the Rings*. We normally imagine fantasy novels to be all pastels and ivy-colored castles, but, yikes, this is some World War II–style junk happening here. Men exist in this realm—and men are helpful, too—but in order to actually take back the world from the forces of darkness, you need to be a little less than human and a little more than that as well. Oh. Is that a riddle? Yeah, well, so are trees that have the wisdom of the ages and talk like dreary old humans (ent-nigmas?), so get on board or prepare to be Orc'd. Hobbit power!

Essential for when: You think you're too small to take on the eye of Sauron. (You probably are. But so is everyone. Just do it.)

5 BONE
WRITTEN AND ILLUSTRATED BY JEFF SMITH (1991–2004)

Speaking of unspeakable darkness, holy smokes. Rat creatures. The Lord of the Locusts. And even the good (or at least the goodish) guys, the cartoonish Bones, have the names of things that remain after we have perished and withered away to almost nothing. This is not a happy tale. But, man, it is fun. A thousand plus pages have never moved so fast. The three Bone cousins—Phoney Bone, Smiley Bone, and Fone Bone—have been expelled from Boneville (due to Foney Bone's perpetual foney-isms and scam-heartedness), and are, in quick succession, lost, attacked, and forced to try to save the world. Hilarity and adventure don't normally go well together, but here they make the perfect team. Stress never felt so good.

Essential for when: You think you're too small to have an impact on world-historical events. (You are. But still. You got to.)

4 13 ASSASSINS
DIRECTED BY TAKASHI MIIKE (2010)

There is a long and glorious tradition of underdog movies where half of the challenge is simply assembling a team of underdogs that's just big enough to be considered a team, but small enough to be considered a massive long shot. *Seven Samurai* was the prototype (and still probably the best in this mold), but there have been Western versions (*The Magnificent Seven* and *The Wild Bunch*), space-pocalypse versions (*Armageddon*), and even comedy versions (*The Three Amigos*)—but in order to find the state of the art for this mini-genre, you really have to go back to Japan.

As with *Seven Samurai* (both the film and the characters), *13 Assassins* takes advantage of everything that appears to work against it. It spends time with its numerous protagonists and allows you some insights into their individual natures and personalities; and instead of allowing the action to fracture into as many different fights as there are fighters, it paints a very clear picture of the geography and of the strategic opportunities that surround them. But none of this would matter if we didn't care about the outcome of this fight. Luckily, of course, we do, because few villains have ever been as sadistic or as compelling as Lord Naritsugu. Thirteen is usually a lot of assassins, but sometimes it is just enough.

Essential for when: You think you don't have enough people on your side. (Too bad. The time is now!)

3 CONTAGION
DIRECTED BY STEVEN SODERBERGH (2011)

You know a disease is serious when it kills Gwyneth Paltrow. That has to be like item #2 in the pathologist's playbook. And when Gwyneth Paltrow is patient zero, then you know that you're dealing with a seriously ambitious virus. Some may call that a spoiler, but it's not revealing much, because *Contagion* is much more about *how* than it is about what and why. It's a procedural in the most literal sense, but its fidelity to what epidemiologists now know about the spread of disease is what's really terrifying. Finding the cause of a disease and ceasing its spread is like racing backward in time; it's impossible under normal conditions and even more impossible in our now impossibly rapid world. So in conclusion: Ack!

Essential for when: You're tempted to breathe the air that everyone else on the planet does. (Don't! It's poison!)

2 THE HUNGER GAMES
WRITTEN BY SUZANNE COLLINS (2008)

Times are tough in the twelve districts of Panem, and as a result, there are lots of opportunities for young people to display the virtues of reliability and self-reliance. Katniss Everdeen has both in spades: With her father dead and her mother still living her life in apparent shock, she is the rock that her mother and sister rely on. And because food is hard to come by, she has found some innovative (and, as it happens, illegal) means of increasing their supply. Unfortunately, being the most responsible member of your family also makes you the most likely to be arrested, killed, or selected to participate in the murder festival known throughout Panem as simply "The Hunger Games."

That's certainly the way it goes with Katniss. Before you can say "Gale or Peeta," she has volunteered (in place of her sister) for the games, proved herself to the judges, avoided wholesale slaughter in the opening melee, and headed out for the wilderness. Because when the world is out to get you, paranoid is a pretty good thing to be. Until it's not. (Cue the romance, and the sequels.)

Essential for when: You think there's no way that things can really be as bad as they look. (They are. Those aren't Cracker Jacks in your pocket; they're . . . TRACKER JACKERS!!!)

1 HOME ALONE
WRITTEN BY JOHN HUGHES (1990)

John Hughes is most famous now for having directed some of the best teenage comedies of the 1980s, including *Sixteen Candles*, *The Breakfast Club*, *Weird Science*, and *Ferris Bueller's Day Off*, to name a few. But that wasn't all he did. He also produced, acted (playing a girl with a bag over "her" head in *Class Reunion*), and, most importantly, wrote. His writing credits are extensive, but *Home Alone* stands out as the John Hughesiest of the bunch. It's got a lot of language that seems raunchy but really just amounts to vague threats about doing poops (both literal and metaphorical) on or near other people, a whole lot of mugging for the camera, several primal screams, one wise old man, a morbidly cute but somehow much abused Macaulay Culkin in the leading role, and a whole lotta heart throughout. Everyone gets what they deserve, everyone learns a lot in the process, and, of course, everybody screams. (But Daniel Stern's anti-tarantula howl is the winner.)

Essential for when: You think that you have hit Joe Pesci hard enough in the nuts to stop him from pursuing revenge. (You haven't. Joe Pesci doesn't know the meaning of "hit hard enough in the nuts.")

EAT BETTER
WHERE TO FIND YOUR CULINARY INSPIRATION

Eating well is hard to do because there are a lot of ways that foods can be bad for you. Macaroni and cheese, at one end of the spectrum, does a great job of combining easy to make with delicious to eat/gorge upon, but there's a reason it never winds up as the centerpiece of a diet plan; and fresh-caught fish with a side of farm-fresh vegetables is a great idea, but it's neither cheap nor especially quick to the table. Humans have come a long way since we first chased down a wild animal in the field. Our phones can talk to us, so why can't we make raw almonds taste like roasted salted almonds? Just spitballing, but yeah, why can't we make grass taste like spinach, and make pizza healthy . . . like spinach? Where is our real-life Willy Wonka?! We need answers to these questions, but until those answers and Wonkas arrive, it's up to us to get inspired to not just make good food, but to also make it well.

10 BABETTE'S FEAST
BASED ON THE NOVEL BY KAREN BLIXEN, AKA ISAK DINESEN (1987)

Babette, a French refugee in nineteenth-century Denmark, has served for fourteen years as the cook and housekeeper for two kind elderly women. Since their father's death, these two women have been the de facto leaders of a small Christian sect, which their father founded many years ago. And thus, when Babette wins a large sum of money in a French lottery, she decides to help her employers celebrate what would have been their father's 100th birthday with the meal of a lifetime. It is to be a dinner for twelve, and most of the remaining members of this small Christian sect are invited, along with one of the sister's old admirers. That's pretty much the whole movie.

The vigilantly pious Danes don't want to be seduced away from their religious observations through the luxury of Babette's feast, but in the end they are, with ironically transcendent results. Babette also has a secret—which I won't spoil—but to see her put together this world-class meal and awe her profoundly skeptical dinner guests is to be awed yourself. It is a beautiful portrait of a beautiful meal, and it makes you wonder how come no one ever makes you any "Blinis Demidoff."

9 JIRO DREAMS OF SUSHI
DIRECTED BY DAVID GELB (2011)

Does Jiro enjoy sushi? That is not clear. Does he make the best sushi on the planet, and does he make said sushi in a metro station in Tokyo? Yes, most people agree that that is the case. How this is possible is the implicit subject of *Jiro Dreams of Sushi*, which is much more occupied with questions of happiness, quality, process, prestige, family, and history, than it is with the question of what it means to make a sublime shrimp roll. Jiro is an inspiration because Jiro cares about doing things well. Very, very well. And the fact that he has turned his humble restaurant into one of the most famous locations on the planet is a testament to either his profound acting skills or his profound dedication. Either way: Wow. (Also worthy of that exclamation: the cost of a meal at Jiro's table. Put it on the [other person's] card.)

8 BLOOD, BONES & BUTTER: THE INADVERTENT EDUCATION OF A RELUCTANT CHEF
WRITTEN BY GABRIELLE HAMILTON (2012)

There are few things better than a great family dinner—especially when the definition of "family" is expanded from the people that you sometimes love and sometimes hate but always know, to include everyone in the small town where you grew up. That's where Gabrielle Hamilton's story begins, and in a way, that's where it ends as well: reimagined as her East Village restaurant Prune, which serves up hot plates of rustic, memory-soaked, new (and old) American cuisine. But it's the in-between that gets to the heart of the matter, when as teenagers, Gabrielle and her brother were left to their own devices at her newly fractured family's country home and forced to fend for themselves. They scrounged, they cooked, and they learned. (Oh, and they also stole and did some serious drugs. Cooks are crazy!) And although not all of her lessons are always useful—after all, when are you planning your next blow-out lamb roast party—they're definitely always relevant, so long as you care about what makes up a human being. (Trapped! You can't say no to that one!)

7 EAT DRINK MAN WOMAN
DIRECTED BY ANG LEE (1994)

A lot of recent Hollywood success stories—especially in directing circles—tend to have the same basic trajectory: A promising upstart has a promising start, and then he struggles a little bit, and then he becomes monstrously famous and insanely wealthy. It seems like a miracle because it is a miracle that anyone becomes well known in a world that is as full of people (there are several billions of us!) as Los Angeles is full of Oscars. Ang Lee's story, however, really is kind of magical: It's true that he went to NYU's Tisch School of the Arts and worked on a student film with Spike Lee, but it's also true that Lee was unemployed for more than several years and that his wife supported him while he submitted screenplay after screenplay to the decision-makers in China. Eventually, of course, he did make it, but *Eat Drink Man Woman* was the film that announced his arrival in America.

Like *The Ice Storm*, *Sense and Sensibility*, and *Brokeback Mountain*, *Eat Drink Man Woman* is a movie that is very much about something, but which is also, much more importantly, about the ways that close-knit people interact when they are together. It is a domestic drama in the best possible sense. Our lives *are* domestic dramas, after all, unless we are the Hulk (not Ang Lee's best work) or a crouching tiger, hidden dragon. This is a movie about a family, the food they eat, and the way they eat it—and although it doesn't sound like much, sometimes that is the recipe for pure genius. Just leave it to the chef.

6 THE FAMILY MEAL: HOME COOKING WITH FERRAN ADRIÀ
WRITTEN BY FERRAN ADRIÁ (2011)

There are a lot of cookbooks out there, and a lot of food magazines, and a lot of food blogs, vlogs, and clog-logs (a meatloaf-style dish that is served out of traditional Scandinavian footwear, if you must know), but in terms of sheer inspiration, there is nothing that gets the wheels churning (the cheese wheels, I mean) like a photo-heavy primer for three-course meals designed by the man currently lauded as "the best chef on the planet"—Ferran Adrià. Is there anything else that needs to be said? Oh, yes. Only a few of the meals require a blowtorch, and for the most part, even the most idiotic amateur can at least hope to serve, roughly, what the author has described. And if, like most people, you have never served an elegant three-course meal to a party of six, serving what the author has described stands as a real accomplishment.

5 TOP CHEF, LAS VEGAS
HOSTED BY PADMA LAKSHMI (2009)

So okay, sure: Reality television isn't real. That's fine; it can still be entertainment. But compensating for the lack of real events and realistic dialogue with even more "reality" (in the form of screaming matches, hostile cocktail sessions, and superfluous backstabs) can often overwhelm even the most inspired reality show concept. *Top Chef* has, for the most part, avoided this pitfall of hyper-drama by keeping the focus where it belongs: on the competition. And Season 6 (in Las Vegas) stands above the rest of the series for the quality of the contestants and the likability of its central character, Kevin. It's hard to think of a reality show that doesn't benefit from having at least one character who comes across as a nonmalicious, non-fame-hungry, non-nonhuman type. Kevin Gillespie is ideal in this respect. He's a talented chef and a genuinely nice guy who never wilted (or deformed) under the nuclear heat lamps of the *Top Chef* kitchen. That's a guy worth rooting for. And having a guy worth rooting for means that, when the audience's expectations are bucked, the feelings of shock, horror, and righteous indignation reach their highest pitches—and that's what reality entertainment, in the end, is all about: being pissed and loving it.

4 THE JULIA CHILD PBS REMIX
CREATED BY JOHN BOSWELL, AKA MELODYSHEEP (2012)

Julia Child was a truly amazing woman, and if you want to engage with her legacy there are many ways to do so. There are many books, many articles, many recipes, and at least one movie that bears her name. But sometimes the internet really does know best. Child remains best known for her iconic cookbook and for the equally iconic television show that arose as a result of the book's success, but in this brief mash-up video you get to see what really made her special—her sincerity, her enthusiasm, and her ebullience—all set to haunting techno music. And all produced by PBS!!!

3 THE TRIP
DIRECTED BY MICHAEL WINTERBOTTOM (2010)

The Trip is not a documentary. That fact can be confusing at first, because Michael Winterbottom likes to blur the line between reality and entertainment in much the same way that his actors do—except for the overall polish of the thing. The actors never look at the camera, but the actors are also in almost every other respect playing themselves. And that's the whole movie in a nutshell. Steve Coogan is the slightly more attractive and slightly more well-known comedian who is asked to go on a food tour of northern England with his girlfriend, and when his girlfriend begins to back out of the project (and the relationship, maybe?) Coogan's friend (fremesis?) Rob Brydon is invited to sign up instead. The results are, in a few words, the most tense and hilarious thing ever. Did you know that an imitation of Michael Caine can show you what it means to be human? Well, it appears that it can. Did you also know what a tiny man in a box sounds like? No? Well, you should.

And there's a lot of really futuristic food that looks pretty cool and interesting. And subtlety. A lot of that, too.

2 RATATOUILLE
WRITTEN AND DIRECTED BY BRAD BIRD (2007)

Since Pixar first released *Toy Story* in 1995, the studio has made a very good living showing very familiar things (toys, bugs, cars, fish, dogs) behaving very unfamiliarly. And that's all well and good, because children's stories have always played on the possibility that the world that we can see hides a world that we can't. And again, no problem there. But then Pixar said, "Hey, you know what we can see? Rats. [Heads nod.] And you know what it would be weird for rats to do? Work in a kitchen—that's what! . . . Cooking human food!" (At which point a Hawaiian-shirted John Lasseter barrels into the room screaming, "MAKE THAT MOVIE MAKE THAT MOVIE NOW!!")

That could have been the point where Pixar went too far, but fortunately for rats, and unfortunately for everyone else hoping to win Best Animated Feature at the Oscars that year, they actually succeed in making us believe in their contrariness. We root for Remy— the story's main rodent, and a very gifted chef to boot—because he's charming, yes, but also because he cares about food. His passion is as human as his body is ratty. And because we have the chance to see the functional but uninspired kitchen of Gusteau's before Remy makes his presence felt, it just becomes that much more magical when the titular dish comes out at the end and sends us all spiraling back to the memories of our first memorable meal. If tears were a delicious dessert, every *Ratatouille* viewing would end with a delicious dessert. Oh, rats . . .

1 ANTHONY BOURDAIN: NO RESERVATIONS
HOSTED BY ANTHONY BOURDAIN (2005-2012) 🖥

Anthony Bourdain is a little bit impossible to hate—and please trust me when I say that I, for one, have made an honest attempt to hate this wildly successful, somewhat smug, pretentiously "real," and ostentatiously "no-good/very bad" food celebrity. But then, on the other hand, he really does appear to be a passionate and hardworking fan of good food. And his show operates as both the best of all possible travel shows and the best of all possible food programs, because it never tries to be one or the other and always succeeds at being both. And what matters more when we travel than who we're with, where we are, and what we eat? This show has its priorities very much in order. So if you don't know where to go when you're in Barcelona, he's got the answers, and if you don't know what to do on a Thursday night, this is a great place to go.

GET MOTIVATED
SONGS GUARANTEED TO GET YOU PUMPED

*I*f you are an active, sociable, and hardworking person, those traits are probably going to help you stay in shape, meet new people, and find an interesting job. That is on the one hand. On the other hand, there is the profound pleasure that is located in a bowl of ramen, a comfortable couch, and an endless succession of BBC miniseries. Hmmmm . . .

In the unlikely event that someone were to put a gun to our heads and demand that we choose between these two lifestyles (which personally I prefer to imagine as a kind of bandit-leprechaun, riding upon a unicorn), the choice is obvious: We go couch. It is hard—*very* hard—to overcome the lure of a familiar seat, a familiar show, and a hot meal. But these ten songs offer an antidote to that seductive fantasy. These are the songs that have the power to get us up in the morning and keep us going at night.

10 "THE FINAL COUNTDOWN" BY EUROPE (1986) ♫

There are a lot of places that it is cool for a band or an artist to be named after: Beirut, for instance, or Calexico, or even Cypress Hill. "Europe," however, does not quite manage the trick. Europe, the place, is such a broad, familiar, and long-standing concept that the name manages to evoke almost nothing at all. It is as bland as milk (which would have been a much better band name, when it comes down to it). But it's at least fitting, since Europe, the band, is ostentatiously uncool. "The Final Countdown" was initially conceived as an introductory hype song for use at concerts, but it became a hit in its own right and lives on as the anthem for a number of professional sports teams and as GOB's signature song when performing acts of illusion (on *Arrested Development*). But no matter how ridiculous it may be (and for proof of its ridiculousness, just try and imagine a righteous army marching to the beat), it's hard to resist those epic blasts from the synth-trumpet section.

9 FEED THE ANIMALS
BY GIRL TALK (2008) 🎵

Girl Talk is Gregg Gillis, a former biomedical engineer who also has a special knack for converting the best, the worst, and the most interesting samples from pop music into something breathlessly energetic, hyper-entertaining, and entirely new. *Feed the Animals* was his fourth album, and although it contains bits and pieces from over 300 different songs, the result is less a collection of different tracks than it is one enormous, complex, but totally self-contained and coherent song. If you're sitting down, it will get you up; if you're walking, it will make you run; if you're working, it will make you want to party; and if you're partying, it will make you want to party forever and sweat out all the sweat that your body can possibly sweat. It is the answer to apathy.

8 "SEARCH AND DESTROY"
BY IGGY POP AND THE STOOGES (1973) 🎵

Punk rock is a genre that's naturally conducive to self-motivation. It's got a ton of energy, a lot of emotion, and a general willingness to just keep on going. But even though Iggy Pop is frequently mentioned as one of the founding figures of punk rock, and although "Lust for Life" is certainly a great early punk song, many of his other recordings—"The Passenger," "Nightclubbing," and "Gimme Danger," for instance—bear little resemblance to punk rock as we know it today. Iggy's songs tend to be slow, long, ambient, and dark. They're not here to party; they're here to say something and get under your skin. "Search and Destroy" is one of the rare occasions when Iggy Pop and punk make sense. It's the perfect blend of energy, anger, and the kind of background melody that seems all the more incredible because it's really not the point. The point is the middle finger. The point is up yours. The point is a swift kick in the pants. "Search and Destroy" isn't always the right song to play (it's not the best first dance song, for instance), but when you need that kind of medicine it really does the trick.

7 "SINCE U BEEN GONE" BY KELLY CLARKSON (2004) ♫

There are a lot of great breakup songs. A lot. Some are best suited for dwelling on the good times ("Romeo and Juliet"); others are made for getting the anger out ("We Are Never Ever Getting Back Together"); others are designed to get the tears out ("Don't Think Twice," "Landslide"); and still others are intended to empower you and get you dating again ("I Will Survive"). But if you're actually going through a breakup, there's only one kind of song that is always right—and that's the kind of song that is so good it will make you forget about everything else. It will make you forget that you're even going through a breakup. And that's what Kelly Clarkson achieves with this break-up anthem. It's the kind of song that almost makes you want to breakup with someone, just so that you can put it on without having to come up with an excuse.

6 "LIVIN' ON A PRAYER" BY JON BON JOVI (1986) ♫

Obviously.

Whether you want to get a party started, keep a party going, or need to find a way to keep your good friends Tommy (Tommy from the docks, I mean) and Gina (diner Gina, not zookeeper Gina) from breaking up, "Livin' on a Prayer" is the correct answer. It's got lyrical screaming (which makes it a great karaoke song as well), wailing guitars, a thumping beat, dramatic key changes, and, in the video, flying humans to go along with all the naturally flying hair. This is all as it should be—this is the essence of the man, the miracle: Jon, and his merry band of Jovi's. The '80s are dead; long live the '80s.

5 "CALL YOUR GIRLFRIEND" BY ROBYN (2010) ♫

Speaking of music videos, this music video. The outfit, the hair, the lighting, the setting, the earnest expression, and oh my awkward Gumby, those dance moves. It is a pop culture gift that could not be more enjoyable despite the fact that none of its individual ingredients makes much sense at all. Why is Robyn dancing alone in a warehouse? Isn't it hard to move in those shoes? Why did you write such an inspiring song about such a sad subject? Why are you humping the floor like that, and why does that seem so cool all of a sudden? Can I do that? Why not?

There is no doubt that the song is inspiring, but due to its overwhelming strangeness, it's hard to know what to do with the energy it gives you. Unless, of course, you need to be inspired to put on platform shoes and paint-splattered pants and dance alone inside a giant gym to Robyn's "Call Your Girlfriend."

4 "BOHEMIAN RHAPSODY"
BY QUEEN (1975) ♫

On the one hand this is an obvious choice—a choice hallowed by Wayne's World and by the entire music-listening world, circa 1975; but on the other hand "Bohemian Rhapsody" occupies a space so far removed from what we normally think of as pop music that it's worth taking a moment to appreciate just how unlikely this song's impact really is. None of these points are new, but again, they're worth repeating: The song is called "Bohemian Rhapsody," when by all rights that should be the name of a failed operetta from nineteenth-century France; it was written and performed by an all-male band called Queen at a time when gayness was hardly sanctioned or supported by the culture at large; and it clocks in at nearly six minutes, despite the fact that it has no chorus. It is not what we expect to hear on the radio, and yet now it is a classic radio staple. Not only does it reinvigorate whoever listens to it, it also really serves as an inspiration for anyone who wants to try something really different or who wants to get a little weird.

3 "HUSTLIN'"
BY RICK ROSS (2006) ♫

Rick Ross is the boss. On that point he is adamant. As a matter of fact, he is adamant about pretty much everything. When he rhymes "hard" with "hard," it sounds like the most unexpected and innovative line in the world; and when he rhymes boss with Ross—as he does, often—he pronounces those words like they were handed down from heaven, like they were fated. Sometimes his lyrics are smart, funny, and full of meaning; other times it sounds like he knows four words that rhyme and just wants to stick with those. But either way his songs always sound right. And his confidence is infectious. After all, it's hard not to believe in a man who has succeeded in turning his last name into a synonym for "the leader." And luckily, when we hear Rick Ross, it's hard not to feel a little bosser ourselves. The Boss rubs off.

2 "WE FOUND LOVE"
BY RIHANNA, FT. CALVIN HARRIS (2011) ♫

Do you remember Big Mouth Billy? The animatronic fish that would sing to you if you disrupted its motion sensors at a Walgreens store, circa 1998? Well, the director of the "We Found Love" video certainly does, and he put him in the video—and if that's not inspirational then I don't know what it is. Billy's been stapled to a board for almost fifteen years now, but that doesn't stop him from singing, oh no. That scaly old grump just refuses to die.

Like Big Mouth Billy, Rihanna isn't especially happy or hopeful in "We Found Love," but man if she won't get in your head and refuse to leave and make you want to make some really bad life decisions. Drinking, smoking, fighting, donutting, skateboarding, running with fireworks, heroin-y eyeballs, and abusive relationships all get a real PR boost in the video. But you don't have to be on board with the self-destructive element to just get really pumped.

1 "BORN IN THE U.S.A."
BY BRUCE SPRINGSTEEN (1984) ♫

Inspiration is cheap if it doesn't account for the possibility of failure; then it's just a lot of happy noise. "Born in the U.S.A." is not happy, and it is not noise. It's simple, hopeful, fervent, and built on the idea that you can be proud of yourself even when life has beaten you down to nothing. If you need a reason to pump your fist, this song is here to help. And if you're not quite sure when to pump your fist, please consult the video. And then get to pumpin'.

STOP BEING SUCH A PHILISTINE
EASY ACCESS POINTS TO THE WORLD OF HIGH ART

The world of high art is a pretty obnoxious place, says everyone. (And everyone agrees that everyone has a point.) But even so, it feels pretty good to dip your toes into that world every once in a while, even if only to show up some loud talker at your local museum. ("Sir, I must respectfully disagree: Although the work of de Kooning certainly participates in the modern economy of art, that doesn't preclude it from also being art. After all, did not the Renaissance masters also paint for a profit? . . . And please, do keep your voice down.") Whatever your motive, if you do want to beef up your knowledge of capital-A Art, there's no need to go in with your nose plugged; there are lots of easy, pleasant, popular points of access that can help put even the most unpretentious plumber at his ease. Even at the opera, if it comes to that. Even at the ballet.

10 BEYONCÉ'S *"COUNTDOWN"* VIDEO
DIRECTED BY ADRIA PETTY (2011) 🖥

What it provides: Contemporary dance moves in a form that's as easy to consume as it is impossible to forget.

Beyoncé has done a lot of dancing over the course of her career, so it should come as no surprise that she has, on occasion, been accused of replicating other people's dance moves. Whether such replication represents a tribute or an act of theft, of course, remains open to interpretation, but there is something odd about the "Countdown" video. On the one hand, it highlights the debt it owes to Belgian choreographer Anne Teresa de Keersmaeker by filming de Keersmaeker's moves in a setting and a style that mimicked her original production, but also fails to acknowledge that debt in any more explicit terms. Leaving the legality (and the propriety) of that omission aside for a moment, there is something pretty exciting about seeing one of the world's most famous people—the mother of Blue Ivy, for goodness sake!—taking her cues from the super weird world of contemporary dance. And it is worth noting that the result is, of course, amazing. Smooth and herky-jerky go together on the dance floor like sweet and savory go together in a jar of peanut butter: They go together well.

9 *MATCH POINT*
DIRECTED BY WOODY ALLEN (2005) 🎞🎞

What it provides: A brief, tense defense of operatic arias (and a white-knuckle thriller to boot).

Woody Allen has made a lot of movies. A lot. Most prolific directors tend to work in, if not one genre, then at least one fairly specific style: Hitchcock made suspense movies; Cronenberg makes movies about bodies; Tarantino makes movies that are heavy on dialogue, violence, and obscure pop references; and Tim Burton, of course, makes Johnny Depp movies. But Woody Allen has made movies that seem to be almost exactly as diverse (or as ephemeral) as his passions. He started out making parodies and straight comedies (*Bananas; Sleeper; What's Up, Tiger Lily?*), then moved on to more serious-minded comedies (*Annie Hall, Manhattan, Hannah and Her Sisters*), Ingmar Bergman–inspired domestic dramas (*Interiors, Husbands and Wives*), light comedies (*Manhattan Murder Mystery, Mighty Aphrodite*), and, most recently, London-based dramas (*Match Point, You Will Meet a Tall Dark Stranger*). He has made great films in all of these moods, but because of his broad sphere of interests, influences, and styles, each film can wind up feeling like a bit of a crapshoot. You never know how everything will combine. But in the case of *Match Point*, it all worked out . . . The end.

No, sorry, here is the point: *Match Point* borrows its themes (guilt, moral responsibility, justice) from *Crime and Punishment*, its plot from *A Place in the Sun* (a man kills his lover in an attempt to maintain the financial benefits of his married life), and its music from Italian opera—but the result of this combination is something that is so coherent, it almost feels like truth. That is vague, so here's something more specific: At one point Chris (played by Jonathan Rhys Meyers) tells his mistress Nola (played by Scarlett Johansson) that tenor Enrico Caruso's voice "expresses everything that's tragic about life." That comment on its own sounds pretty trite, but when you consider it in light of the fact that so much of the movie's soundtrack is provided by the arias sung by Caruso, it becomes profound. It is beautiful, sorrowful music, and it is a steady presence throughout the film, in both scenes that matter and scenes that kind of don't. It makes you feel the presence of death and potential throughout, and that's kind of amazing.

PS: We are all going to die!!!! But hey, that's life.

8 LEVI'S *"GO FORTH"* AD CAMPAIGN CREATED BY WIEDEN AND KENNEDY (2009-)

What it provides: A reminder that poetry is alive and well, even when it's old and craggly.

Under normal conditions, we prefer to have recordings that keep outside sound to a minimum. That makes sense. We want to hear what we want to hear and not what it sounds like when tape is rolled around plastic. But it's still pretty awesome that on the 1890 wax recording of Walt Whitman's poem "America" (as read by the author himself, it is believed), the background noise sounds a lot like train cars in motion (presumably churning across this great nation of ours). In this series of Levi's ads, you see healthy bodies running, healthy bodies running with fireworks, American flags, optimism, flips, and a whole lot of Levi's. And that's okay! It makes a lot of sense! America is a lot of things, as Walt Whitman himself noted frequently, and America is not afraid to sell a little product to make a little money. (And it is even less afraid to sell a lot.) Walt Whitman makes Levi's sound authentic; and Levi's makes Walt Whitman sound cool. Even Steven—No Fault Walt.

7 BARRY LYNDON
DIRECTED BY STANLEY KUBRICK (1975)

What it provides: The best music videos that classical music has ever received, and the best painted pictures that moving pictures ever replicated.

Do you like beautiful pictures and beautiful music? Of course you do! Do you like them enough to spend one hundred and eighty-four minutes watching a movie shot entirely in natural light? That is less likely, in all likelihood—but when it comes to *Barry Lyndon*, you should. Patience is necessary if you want to see paintings come to life. Almost every scene begins with a shot that looks like it was pulled off a wall at the Metropolitan Museum of Art, but then, time and time again, something stirs—something comes to life, almost grudgingly—and then, after an uncanny pause, a conversation starts. This is the rhythm of the movie: so slow that it's painterly, but so gripping that it really does feel like fine art is somehow animating itself.

The fact that the movie's story (based on the novel by William Makepeace Thackeray) takes place in Europe in the eighteenth century also allows Kubrick to supplement his gorgeous visuals with music to match. Bach, Handel, and Vivaldi could not have found a better music video director if they tried (not least because no one at the time would have any idea what they were talking about). If you weren't a fan of classical music before, you will be after this.

6 BILL CUNNINGHAM NEW YORK
DIRECTED BY RICHARD PRESS (2010)

What it provides: An unpretentious look at the most unpretentious man in fashion—*New York Times* photographer Bill Cunningham.

Bill Cunningham is a very nice older gentleman who wears the same thing every day, eats the same lunch, and works, works, works. His job, which exists because he created it, is to take pictures of people wearing interesting clothes, wherever and whoever they are. He attends many high society events and takes pictures there, but he also bikes all around the city (even now, when he's in his 80s), capturing a new look here, a trend there, and an old staple reimagined somewhere else. This documentary is relatively straightforward: It shows Bill Cunningham doing his job and it shows how completely his life is that job. But it isn't simple. There's something startling and profound about Cunningham's purpose and accomplishments, and as a side note, it's pretty exciting to suddenly see fashion as a democratic concept—as a project in which everyone has a voice.

5 BLACK SWAN
DIRECTED BY DARREN ARONOFSKY (2010)

What it provides: A terrifying introduction to ballet.

A crazy little bird once told me that ballet and soccer are, in fact, long-lost second cousins. At the time I told that crazy little bird that he was crazy, but now I think he may have had a point. Both were born in Europe, both rely primarily on feet (which is weird because of how bad toes are at pretty much everything, save stubbing), and both are as popular with American kids as they are unpopular with American adults. Luckily, soccer now has MLS and ESPN, but ballet's not likely to sign any big-time TV deals next year—so can ballet be revived as a big-time entertainment?

Black Swan is about a lot of other things besides ballet (including art, mothers, madness, beauty, and ambition), but ballet is central to the movie's spirit and aesthetic. It is grand, gestural, expressive, fraught, and, in the eyes of some critics, even campy. But it is also definitely captivating. The movie follows ballerina Nina Sayers (Natalie Portman) as she desperately fights to become the black swan/white swan at the center of Tchaikovsky's *Swan Lake*. Nina has a controlling and abusive mother and a controlling and manipulative director, and she is rapidly losing control. The dividing lines between life and art, sanity and madness, and self and other are never stable, and as a result the movie is deeply disorienting and creepy, but it is also fantastically beautiful as a result of both Tchaikovsky's music and Benjamin Millepied's choreography. If you want to love ballet more than you loved it after watching *The Company* or want to cultivate an irrepressible fear of the art form to exceed that which you achieved after watching *The Red Shoes*, this is the place to go.

4 ANTONIO GAUDÍ
DIRECTED BY HIROSHI TESHIGAHARA (1984)

What it provides: Immersion into some of the strangest and most beautiful structures ever produced.

Although most of us try, at some point, to learn a musical instrument, or paint a painting, or write a poem, or dance a dance, or take a picture, not many of us can honestly say we had the chance to draft and build a building. As a result, architecture, as an art form, appears more than usually distant. Most of us wouldn't know a flying buttress if it flew (or buttressed) us right in the face. (And Lord knows what we would do/where we would run if we ever encountered a groin vault!) But some architects transcend our ignorance.

Antonio Gaudí is one such architect, but since he did most of his work in Barcelona, and since architectural works are notoriously resistant to world tours, many of us will never have the chance to see what Sagrada Familia (his iconic cathedral, still under construction) looks like from below, or feels like when atop one of the spires, or feels like in the nave. Here, foundational columns become trees; trees become branches; and everything solid eventually gives way, yet nothing falls down. These are architectural mysteries that go beyond sight. But luckily for us, Hiroshi Teshigahara wants to bring us into these mysteries: He shows us the enduring power of these structures by giving us the chance to be in them and move around in them. And despite these revelations he remains confident in the endurance of these mysteries, because, for him, there is always another angle.

3 BURDEN OF DREAMS
DIRECTED BY LES BLANK (1982)

BURDEN OF DREAMS

What it provides: The chance to see what it costs (in terms of soul dollars) to make an art-house film.

Movies are now an established presence in American life and culture, but it wasn't always that way. When they first arrived on the scene in the late nineteenth century, they had to fight the same fight that comic books and video games would fight in the late twentieth century: They had to convince people that they were not going to corrupt the children and ruin America forever—turning us all into lollygaggers, ne'er-do-wells, and no-goodnicks! Now that the brouhaha has subsided, movies (aka film) have climbed, rung by rung, up the social ladder, and sit now alongside painting, photography, and other nonmoving arts that possess the ability to make people feel not up to the task. They have, in other words, made it.

Burden of Dreams follows German filmmaker Werner Herzog's attempt to make *Fitzcarraldo*—a movie about an impossible man attempting to do an impossible thing: namely, build an opera house in the bowels of the Amazon jungle. Most people (slash everyone else on Earth except for perhaps two native bug species) would shoot such a movie on a set; but Herzog not only decided to film on location, but also attempted to haul a real, actual steamship up a real, actual hillside (not made of water, in case that wasn't clear) using only the most rudimentary tools. That was difficult, but so were the warring Amazonian tribes, the bugs, the diseases, the cast changes, the heat, the near-insanity, the actual insanity, and the director himself, who is at the center of everything. This is his dream, after all. Not every art-house film costs this much, of course, but as a metaphor for artistic ambition and its cost, it is just about perfect.

2 AMADEUS
DIRECTED BY MILOŠ FORMAN, BASED ON PLAY BY PETER SHAFFER (1984) 🎞️

What it provides: An incredibly poignant introduction to Mozart as both a composer and as a human being.

Most bio-pics fail because they rarely look away from their subjects—because everything else in the film becomes subservient to the idea of the person, and the person, as a result, withers. If they're famous, we already know their stories, so for a biography to work it has to show us something not just new, but rather something else. In Peter Shaffer's play (which draws heavily from the historical record), Mozart appears to us through the eyes of his chief competitor, court composer Antonio Salieri. Salieri, as he himself acknowledges, is a mediocrity, and he cannot bear to see such genius bestowed on such an ungrateful, impious, and obscene "creature" as Mozart appears to him to be (and apparently kind of was). Mozart's behavior and bearing injure him profoundly, but those injuries make the indisputable, ineffable beauty of his music seem all the more sublime. If it were Mozart telling you, "No, I'm serious, this aria really is quite innovative and beautiful," then that would be a hard truth to hear, but in Salieri's tortured words, that truth becomes almost poetry.

1 EXIT THROUGH THE GIFT SHOP
DIRECTED BY BANKSY (2010) 🎞️

What it provides: Direct/indirect access to Banksy, one of the world's most famous and least recognizable contemporary artists.

If the art world is hard to penetrate (and having made no effort, I can personally confirm that it is at least not easy, because I am still not an insider), that goes double for the street art world, which is now not only one of the hottest areas of contemporary art, but also peopled by individuals who could very well be prosecuted for their body of work. Banksy is perhaps the most famous living street artist, but we don't know what he looks like, what his real name is, or even which works are definitely his. He is famous, but he is unknown. *Exit Through the Gift Shop* attempts to get around that problem (the problem of featuring someone who prefers to remain faceless and nameless) without really changing anything about that situation, and the miracle is that it succeeds. Banksy tells his own story by taking the camera away from his self-appointed documentarian—one Thierry Guetta—and turning the camera around on the man. The resulting film offers a hilarious critique of art, celebrity, and authenticity, while at the same time presenting a thrilling, inside look at the actual creation of street art.

STOP BEING SUCH A SNOB
LOWBROW ENTERTAINMENT THAT PUTS THE HIGH-MINDED STUFF TO SHAME

Boredom is easy; entertainment is hard. That basic fact holds true whether you're talking about a Renaissance painting or a performance artist or a Hollywood blockbuster. Whatever adjectives we use to describe these things in retrospect—whether we call them "revealing," "insightful," "provocative," or "dumb"—they all ask of us the very same question: Are we not entertained? And if the answer is "yes, and do it again," then we should call these entertainments good. And that should be the end of it. Conscience be damned (because conscience be boring).

This list contains the very best of the things that we call "good" despite the fact we know they're bad.

10 ARMAGEDDON
DIRECTED BY MICHAEL BAY (1998) 🎞️

Armageddon is a derivative, unbelievable, bombastic, and poorly cast blockbuster about a team of non-astronauts who venture into space to drill down into an asteroid and detonate an atomic bomb in order to save the earth. Much like the Aerosmith song that punctuates the film and highlights the soundtrack ("I Don't Want to Miss a Thing"), it sounds terrible, but it is not. Michael Bay never attempted to make this film into anything other than what it always was: a bombastic action movie that turns ordinary men into heroes. The characters (aka the men) are two-dimensional, sure—but who ever said that two-dimensions were a bad thing?! Lines are great! And a straight line is especially great for when you want to get to the point (one-dimensional! also great!).

Everything moves fast here, but everything makes its own kind of sense as well: People of the earth have to do something because a killer asteroid is going to blow the planet up; if you need to detonate an atomic bomb inside a killer asteroid, you had better hire some really good drillers; really good drillers are probably going to be some crazy-ass dudes, but let's get those dudes up in space now and worry about the rest later! Shuttle crashes! Aerosmith sings! Things blow up! Sacrifices are made! Everyone cries! Everyone exults! This is what movies are all about. And although this is recipe is old, this recipe is good. [PS: ALL-CAPS EXPLOSIONS!!!]

9 *"DON'T STOP BELIEVIN'"*
PERFORMED BY JOURNEY (1981) 🎵

Karaoke-ability is a pretty good marker for the quality of a song. I mean, if you can get a bunch of strangers in a room to support you even while you (metaphorically) hit their eardrums with tiny fiery hell-hammers, then hey, okay, that song's got something. "Don't Stop Believin'" was a hit when it came out (when just the band believed), and then a hit again when *Monster* came out (because serial killers also believe?), and then a hit again when the White Sox used it as their anthem (fans definitely believe), then a hit again when it was featured in the *Sopranos* series finale, and then a hit again when it was *Glee*'d. When the song is heard, its virtues are recognized, and its faults are forgotten. It is obvious, heavy-handed, over-the-top, and made of pure sonic gold. And no one has, nor ever will, pronounce "boulevard" the same way again. (By the way, traffic is pretty bad on the BOO-LEE-vard right now, so I'd recommend that you take the highway instead.)

8 *WIPEOUT*
HOSTED BY JOHN HENSON, JOHN ANDERSON, AND JILL WAGNER (2008-) 🖥️

Wipeout is a show about how people can get hit by things and then fall down and then hit something else again . . . HARD—and often with their faces or groins. Sometimes it sort of seems like it must really hurt. But no matter what happens to the contestants on the show, we laugh. But the competitors are right to compete (because there is money at stake, and we must compete for riches), and we are right to laugh (because down-falling is hilarious, especially when we do contortions), and in the end, everybody wins. This is *America's Funniest Home Videos*, but without all the unwitting ball-shots. Everyone who gets hit in the balls here knows exactly what's coming to them: giant foamy flapping knocker-beams and foam fluster knobbers. Watch it, and be glad.

7 STEP UP 2: THE STREETS
DIRECTED BY JON M. CHU (2008)

To explain the plots of any of the first *Step Up* movies would be to miss the point. These are not movies about people, or art schools, or the streets, or Baltimore: These are movies about crazy dance moves and pulsating music and poor set-ups and incredibly stilted dialogue. These are movies in which forced slang ("They just hatin' on you cause you dope"; "Yo, why my crib smell like Funyuns?") and intensely awkward social interactions set the stage for mind-blowing, rain-coated dance-offs where nothing else matters but WHAT THE EFF DID HE JUST DO WITH HIS SHIRT ON THAT HOOK! IS THAT REALLY POSSIBLE? WAS THAT A LEG? WHICH HUMAN IS THE CGI ONE!? It is dance pornography—bad acting and poor script included—and it is irresistible. If more people could dance like this, I think Dance Armies (that is, armies full of dancers that attack other countries with the force of their dance) would be a real thing. Probably.

6 THE REAL HOUSEWIVES OF NEW YORK CITY, SEASON 1,
STARRING LUANN, RAMONA, ALEX, JILL, KELLY, AND BETHENNY (2008)

Reality television rose to prominence because it was cheap to make and it made good money. The fact that it was not conceived through a glorious union of lofty ideals and high ambition is not news to anyone—least of all to critics, who often punctuate their reviews with adjectives like "cheap" (which is true for the producers, but not for the advertisers) and "trash" (which is, it must be said, in the eye of the beholder—and, of course, in trash cans). *The Real Housewives of New York City* was intended to be cheap trash, but it achieved in its cheap and trashy purpose so completely, that those terms, in the end, seem glorified as a result. The formula—and even the people—have been repeated many times, but after that first season they broke the mold. It had everything, and it had it all in due proportion: outlandish purchases, outlandish parties, and outlandish outfits; confusing fights that result in confusing speeches; and bitter feuds that simmer and belch their bitter fumes at all of the most inopportune opportunities. It was glorious. None of it makes any of us want to move to New York or teaches any of us how to be a housewife, but all of it makes all of us just a little bit happier living in this cheap trash that we call life on Earth.

5 TOP GUN
DIRECTED BY TONY SCOTT (1986)

Decades ago (three decades ago, to be precise) there was a place called America, where people wore Levi's when they took it easy and long hair when they rocked. These people left their shoes untied to show how much they didn't care, and yet they still made time to strive for riches and for international hockey titles in equal measure. It was a great time to be alive. The king of this time was a man named "President Reagan," but the symbol of this decade was a fighter pilot known simply as "Maverick." President Reagan presided over the fall of communism, but Maverick stole the show in the greatest beach volleyball contest the world has ever seen in slow motion; he overcame the death of his prized Goose; and when he flew, he soared.

Maverick was Tom Cruise, and Tom Cruise was Maverick, but when it was all over, both of them were more. They were American heroes. Some say, "Put on the brakes, and he'll fly right by," but this is a film that never puts on the brakes and always flies stubbornly on ahead, into the danger zone. This is a film that is not afraid to bounce some ego checks. It is not afraid of greatness, nor of rebukes. And in the end, it truly is the toppest gun of all.

4 "TRAPPED IN THE CLOSET"
BY R. KELLY (2005–)

The "Trapped in the Closet" series now includes 33 songs (with attendant videos) that range from two to eight minutes in length and tell the story of Sylvester (played by R. Kelly), his wife Gwendolyn, his lover, her lover, and an ever-increasing number of their lovers as the series steadily unravels. There are apparently plans for 85 new episodes. But if R. Kelly announced plans to produce "infinity plus one" new episodes, even that wouldn't seem out of the question, because infidelity and betrayal are never in short supply—especially in R. Kelly's world.

The music remains constant throughout the series, but the sense of fun that pervades the songs and videos means that they really never get old. You can watch the videos time and again, and the new songs always reveal new layers (if not always new depths). It is soap-operatic in the extreme, campy in the extreme, and R. Kelly-y in the most extreme way possible, but that's not always a bad thing (although sometimes it certainly is). And if this is not what music videos were made for, then it begs the question: What were music videos made for? (R. Kelly's answer being, in all probability: "For Sexosauruses. Let me give you that beep! Beep!" And he is right. Once again, he is right.)

3 ANGRY BIRDS
CREATED BY ROVIO ENTERTAINMENT (2009)

"Simple" and "mindless" are relative terms. When it comes to mathematical proofs, "simple" is synonymous with "elegant" and "beautiful"; and what higher praise can we give to an athlete than to say that she is "in the zone"—that is, playing her sport at a level that is, essentially "mindless." So let us not cast scorn upon *Angry Birds* for the simple reason that it is simple and mindless. It is also profoundly entertaining. The pigs want to steal the eggs of the birds, the birds want to carry out a four-star punishment campaign upon the pigs, and we, the humans, desperately want to help them. For level after level, for month after month, for angry bird iteration after angry bird iteration, we fight the good fight because we literally cannot help it. It is just too fun. It's also an essential reminder that even though we now have games like *Assassin's Creed III* and *BioShock*, our puny human minds haven't really gotten all that far away from *Pong*.

2 THE NOTEBOOK
DIRECTED BY NICK CASSAVETES,
BASED ON BOOK BY NICHOLAS SPARKS (2004)

The Notebook is ridiculous. It contains Ryan Gosling before he learned to control his full Gosling; he simply cannot stop winking, smiling, and desperately seducing everything that comes in range. He sort of succeeds, but that's even worse—it is rude and distracting. But he was young then and lacked the scorpion jackets of his later years, so he must be forgiven. The movie is also manipulative in the extreme. It does not believe in crying; it seeks repayment exclusively in sobs, convulsions, and snotty weeping. When the two young lovers (poor Noah, played by Gosling, and rich Allie, played by Rachel McAdams) just aren't suffering enough, the movie flashes forward to the same lovers in their old age, when Noah is caring for Allie in her final days. WHAT ARE WE SUPPOSED TO DO THEN!? ARE YOU KIDDING ME?! We are out of tears, you saltwater thieves!

But still, the movie is addictive. These are the kind of tears we feed on; the kind that make us whole, even while they flee with everything we formerly had inside ourselves. I think this must be what a cleanse feels like—but luckily, in this cleanse, popcorn still plays a critical role.

1 "HAPPY LITTLE CLOUDS," THE BOB ROSS PBS REMIX
CREATED BY JOHN BOSWELL, AKA MELODYSHEEP (2012) 🖥

Bob Ross is the ultimate in lowbrow art. For years he hosted a painting show on PBS in which he operated as a one-man art factory. He made insipid landscape after insipid landscape, and he wanted to teach us to do the same. To grow up while his show was on was to dread PBS in daylight hours. But distance reveals truths that we often miss from up close—and remixes, as the proverb goes, make all public television programs a billion times better.

In this three-and-a-half minute video, Bob Ross's kindly, gentle spirit, and kindly, gentle art are transformed from something lukewarm and watered-down into something sublime and transcendent. Ross himself was a man who had spent time in the armed services, and after his retirement, he sought a job where he would never have to scream or berate others ever again. He found his dream job and lived his dream life. He painted "happy little trees" and "happy little clouds," and although it sounds silly, this remix shows he had a real kind of grace.

This is our world. We're the creators. Let's do it! Let's find freedom on this canvas! [Sigh.]

HOW TO FIX POP CULTURE

10.
PROBLEM:
"Reality television isn't real at all!"

SOLUTION:
Invest in the coming hit-pocalypse: real-life hunger games.

9.
PROBLEM:
"Romantic comedies have nothing whatsoever to do with real-life romance!"

SOLUTION:
Rom-coms aren't going to change, so let's meet these movies halfway and try to end every relationship with a footrace to the airport and a proposal of marriage.

8.
PROBLEM:
"All the great movie franchises are dead. *Harry Potter* is over, *Twilight* is over, nothing is left!"

SOLUTION:
Once upon a time, people said that the *Alien* and *Predator* franchises had run out of gas. But then somebody (I assume Albert Einstein?) came up with the idea of *Alien* versing *Predator*, and with that both series were revitalized. The same remedy can be applied here, in the form of Harry Potter vs. Edward (vs. Jacob). There. Done and dusted.

7.
PROBLEM:
"There are too many sequels for everything!"

SOLUTION:
Make more prequels to balance things out. (Because you're right: If we can have Muppet Babies why can't we get a Baby Batman? Where's toddler-butler Alfred?!)

6.

PROBLEM:
"CGI technology still looks horrible."

SOLUTION:
Force the CGI developers to work as humans-inside-monster suits until they get the technology up to snuff.

5.

PROBLEM:
"Everything is for kids, but I am not a kid anymore."

SOLUTION:
Get the hell offa the lawn, old man.

4.

PROBLEM:
"The Super Bowl halftime show is super weird."

SOLUTION:
Instead of relying on musical medleys from musical icons, let's fight fire with fire and get even weirder: Let's force the NFL to offer its fans a series of puppet medleys from the world's premier puppeteers. I can't wait to see what Hans Speckl is going to do with "Lambo at the pasture down at Lambeau."

3.

PROBLEM:
"Video games are too violent!"

SOLUTION:
You get punched. Punched for dumbs.

2.

PROBLEM:
"Action movies don't even try to make sense. Everyone is always outrunning explosions and dodging bullets, but these things are clearly impossible."

SOLUTION:
Make the explosions more explosive and less outrunnable; make the bullets faster and less dodge-able; account for shorter running times.

1.

PROBLEM:
"Tom Cruise keeps popping up, but I no longer feel comfortable in his presence."

SOLUTION:
Stop fighting it and get on board.

ACHIEVE MINDFULNESS
MOVIES THAT WILL SHOW YOU THE WAY
(WITH WISE ELDERS NOW INCLUDED!)

WANNA GET LATTES AFTER THIS?

Unlike intelligence (which we all have at least some share of), wisdom does not operate on a continuum. You cannot be "wise about geese" but "unwise about mongeese." You either are wise, or you are not. Old people, as a rule, are wise; but movies—whatever their age—are not. As a result, blockbuster movies with old people in them have the dual benefit of being, on the one hand, enjoyable (hence their ability to bust the block so much), and on the other hand, edifying (because of all the sage advice and anecdotes). It is a wise recipe, and as with all great recipes, it tastes even better when someone else cooks it. In (unwise) conclusion: Let's eat!

10 THE EMPIRE STRIKES BACK
STORY BY GEORGE LUCAS (1980)

Wise elder: Yoda (voiced by Frank Oz)

Yoda does not speak English wisely; he speaks it mysteriously, with the words all jumbled and the pronouncements all vague—but hey, that's Yoda! And anyway, Yoda is also the thing (the vegetable? the runt? the stool?) that teaches young and budding Jedi knights which way is up and which way is Vader, when it comes to the Force. He helps to point us on our way, and in a story that can hardly resist rushing forward, he is the sole voice urging us to stop. Without his sage warnings (sage because he says them sagely), the anxiety we feel in Luke's departure at the end would be nowhere near as intense. More than even Darth Vader and the Emperor, Yoda makes us face up to the fact that things may not turn out as we want them to, even if we do have the good sweet magic on our side. Yoda's wisdom lies in contradictions and paradoxes; it forces us to choose. (Also: Work we must, to understand the words of Yoda.)

Words to live by: "Do, or do not. There is no try."

9 CITY SLICKERS
DIRECTED BY RON UNDERWOOD (1991)

Wise elder: Curly (played by Jack Palance)

Aside from *Deliverance*, *Wild Hogs*, and *The Shining* (which are all terrifying), there aren't that many movies really about midlife crises. That's kind of surprising. *City Slickers* begins, like *Deliverance*, with a few middle-aged dudes trying to figure out what to do together. They have no answer to this question, and as a result, they wind up on a dude ranch with a truly bizarre parody of Ben & Jerry, some drunken cow-hands (not to be taken literally), and Jack Palance, aka "Curly." Jack Palance, in case you were not aware, was A MAN by profession. To put that another way: He was terrifying. Always. But especially on a dude ranch. That makes his wisdom, when he somehow spits it out between his grizzled pair of (presumably leather?) old-man lips, all the more poignant and touching. He tells us a story, as old men do. And then we learn from it and think things might be better now. Oh, but then the movie resumes and Curly dies and the dudes are on their own. Good luck, dudes! Definitely try and use that wisdom when threatened at gunpoint and/or drowning!

Words to live by: "Do you know what the secret of life is? . . . One thing. Just one thing. You stick to that and the rest don't mean shit."

8 FRIED GREEN TOMATOES
WRITTEN BY FANNIE FLAGG AND CAROL SOBIESKI (1991)

Wise elder: Ninny Threadgoode (played by Jessica Tandy)

If you are named "Ninny Threadgoode," there are basically two paths open to you in life: You can either be an animated mouse and play a charming character in a charming cartoon about charming mice (called "Threadgoode Theater," most likely), or you can live a quiet life, age gracefully, and eventually dispense wisdom and anecdotes in a Southern nursing home. The Ninny Threadgoode of *Fried Green Tomatoes* chose the latter course, thankfully (since it would have been awkward to have to shoehorn some rodent characters into this otherwise very human drama). As the film's narrator, Ninny is able to tell her story about life and death at the Whistle Stop Cafe in terms that will resonate with her audience (a dissatisfied, middle-aged housewife) but also give her time to reflect on those past events with the kind of perspective and insight that anyone can appreciate.

Words to live by: "A heart can be broken, but it will keep beating just the same."

7 SEVEN SAMURAI
DIRECTED AKIRA KUROSAWA (1954)

Wise elder: Kambei Shimada (played by Takashi Shimura)

Is there anything more charming than an elderly man who kicks ass? Magic Eight Ball says: "Very doubtful." Kambei Shimada is the first of the titular seven samurai in Akira Kurosawa's hugely influential (and hugely entertaining) film, and he remains the spiritual center throughout. The basic plot of the film is simple: Farmers who have grown tired of annual attacks from marauding bandits decide to hire a team of samurai to help in their effort to fight back. They send several young men out into a neighboring city to recruit the necessary samurai (and thus created the template for all of the super-team recruitment montages that followed in its wake), but since the villagers' only form of payment is food, it is not an easy task. But then the villagers come across the rescue of a hostage child by a canny old man—Kambei—and after he agrees to sign on, things take a turn for the much, much better.

Kambei is clearly a man who has lived a lot of life—and by the end of his first scene, we know him as a man who has also killed at least one human being. His approach to both life and death is clear-eyed in the extreme, and it is that quality—rather than his honor or valor, for instance—that makes him so admirable. He is the rare moral hero who isn't boring or flat, and he is at the center of everything in *Seven Samurai*. He is the one who determines who the fated seven will be; he is the one who comes up with the plan of battle (a plan which is thrillingly reliant on the geographical reality of the village itself), and although he is not afraid to change his mind about things, he is the one whose decisions have to be either accepted or challenged. He is the key to the movie, and he's the reason that *Seven Samurai* is so much more than just an action movie.

Words to live by: "A good fort needs a gap. The enemy must be lured in. So we can attack them. If we only defend, we lose the war."

6 THE SILENCE OF THE LAMBS
DIRECTED BY JONATHAN DEMME (1991)

Wise elder: Hannibal Lecter (played by Sir Anthony Hopkins)

For the purposes of this entry, let's momentarily modify our definition of wisdom. For the purposes of this entry, let's say that wisdom is the ability to teach someone to fish at a time when fish don't even exist. It is the ability to talk about things that are not seen by others, in such a way that they can not only understand those invisible truths, but also act upon them.

There. Now we can call a homicidal cannibal "wise" without feeling like a murderer ourselves. Hannibal Lecter is a reprehensible thing in a cage. Yes. (And please, stay there.) But he is terrifying because he is smart, and when Clarice Starling (Jodie Foster) goes to him for help in tracking down the similarly inclined murderer "Buffalo Bill," he is helpful because he allows her to "see" this criminal, in a sense, before she comes anywhere near him. When she does, the lights go out, and oh my god change the channel please and erase my mind. [Cue lifelong moth nightmares.] Apparently there is a rule that in return for talking seriously about "flesh suits" and making adults sob in terror, a film is to be granted "all the Oscars," and as a result *The Silence of the Lambs* won Oscars in all the top categories.

Words to live by: "Of each particular thing ask: What is it in itself? What is its nature? What does he do, this man you seek?"

5 THE BIG LEBOWSKI
WRITTEN AND DIRECTED BY JOEL AND ETHAN COEN (1998)

Wise elder: The Dude (played by Jeff Bridges)

Wisdom generally arrives on the scene looking fairly dignified, but there are times when wisdom really needs to put on a different outfit (shorts, a milk-stained shirt, and a comfortable pair of jellies, for instance) if it really wants to make a difference in the world. Jeffrey "the Dude" Lebowski's world is a Los Angeles out of time—a Los Angeles whose cowboys, nihilists, and pornographers (not to mention marmots) feel as comfortable borrowing language from the 1880s and the 1930s as they do from the 1960s and 1990s. Johnsons are threatened, rugs are micturated upon, and through it all, the Dude (an old soul if ever there was one) abides.

The Dude is wise like language is wise, like water is wise: He is wise because he is one with the wave. He is wise because no matter which way the tide turns, he flows along with it. And without such a character as Dude at its core, there is no way that a movie like this—a movie wherein a nymphomaniacal wife forces her wealthy husband to hire two thugs to pee on a rug that belongs to a slacker who loves smoking drugs to . . . yeah, etc.—could have ever made sense. Let alone so much sense as to inspire everyday fans and professors of philosophy alike to emulate the ways of this beloved spaceman bowler detective.

Words to live by: "The Dude abides."

4 THE MATRIX
DIRECTED BY LARRY (LANA) AND ANDY WACHOWSKI (1999)

Wise elder: Morpheus (played by Laurence Fishburne)

If you want to make a wise movie, it's not a bad idea to base your screenplay on the wisdom of one of the wisest philosophers of all time: Plato. In Plato's parable of the cave (from *The Republic*), humanity lives out its days in almost total darkness, watching nothing but shadows as they flicker on the walls around them. Only the philosopher, the lover of wisdom, is capable of recognizing this ruse for what it is and turning around, climbing out, and bathing in the true light of reality. When *The Matrix* begins, Neo is living his life in a cave, but this time the metaphor is also literally true. Humanity has been enslaved by the machines, and the matrix is being utilized to keep humans docile as their bodies are used as fuel for the generation of ever more machines. Morpheus (aka the philosopher) has awoken from his slumber, and now he seeks to return (as Plato himself instructed) to wake others. Neo may be "the one," but Morpheus is the original philosopher, and he deserves some credit, too.

Words to live by: "The Matrix is everywhere . . . It is the world that has been pulled over your eyes to blind you from the truth."

3 THE HARRY POTTER SERIES
BASED ON THE NOVELS BY J.K. ROWLING (2001-2011)

Wise elder: Albus Dumbledore (played by Richard Harris and Michael Gambon)

Speaking of "the one," now we have another one: Harry Potter. But unlike Neo or Frodo, Harry Potter's "one-ness" seems less about destiny than it is about courage. In both the books and the films, it is always clear that Harry is destined for something great, but in the course of his journey that fate relies much less on his innate abilities than it does on his will to do the thing that no one else will do—to do the thing that no one's even asking for. And it's that quality that makes Harry unique among his peers. He isn't the only one who could do what he does; he's the only one who tries. To take that idea one step further, his courage isn't the result of his will alone; rather, it is something that his mentors cultivate in him, no one more so than Professor Albus Dumbledore—aka "The Potter-Trainer." (Would that we were all so well Potter-trained.)

Words to live by: "It is our choices . . . that show what we truly are, far more than our abilities."

2 LITTLE MISS SUNSHINE
WRITTEN BY MICHAEL ARNDT (2006)

Wise elder: Grandpa Edwin Hoover (played by Alan Arkin)

Little Miss Sunshine is the Platonic form of the contemporary independent movie. Excuse me. Film. It's got a brightly colored automobile, a silent teenager, an irrepressible child, a quirky family mission, and an equal ratio of depression to jokes. It is pretty much perfect. But then at some point they also added Alan Arkin, and thus did the movie become not just perfect, but also good. Arkin plays the heroin-loving grandfather of this dysfunctional clan, and through his jaded eyes we're able to see the optimistic hues of the movie for the jaundiced yellows they also kind of are. Sometimes wisdom is just the ability to see the truth and then see past it! By calling things the way he sees them (and then moving on), he enables the movie and the people around him to just kind of be—and that makes all the difference. (Abigail Breslin's triumphant dance routine to "Superfreak" doesn't hurt much either though. It's hard to think of a better tribute.)

Words to live by: "Losers are people who are so afraid of not winning, they don't even try."

1 THE KARATE KID
DIRECTED JOHN G. AVILDSEN (1984)

Wise elder: Mr. Miyagi (played by Pat Morita)

Mr. Miyagi wasn't written to be an especially deep character (even if Pat Morita managed to turn him into one), but he was definitely intended to be wise. Normally that's just not enough, and normally it would result in a pretty bland character. I mean, Yoda is interesting because, in addition to being wise, he is two feet tall, and a Yoda; and Dumbledore is interesting because, when he's not providing empathy and advice, he's out of the office and frying bigger fish. They are more than just wise words. Mr. Miyagi, it must be said, is not; but the nature of his wise words is different, and it's this difference that makes him special. His wisdom begins with the body before it enters the mind (first you learn to wax a car, and then you learn that how you wax a car is also how you repel an attack), and that's the way we as viewers experience it as well. First we wax the movie on, and then we wax the movie off, and then we CRANE KICK YOU IN THE FACE. [Bows (with eyes always on opponent). Steps back (eyes remain). Departs (still staring).]

Words to live by: "Wax on, wax off."

SLEEP WITH THE FISHES
THE TEN BEST PLACES TO FIND YOUR SPIRIT ANIMAL

It is a truth universally acknowledged that no human being is complete without his or her spirit animal. Abraham Lincoln was just "that rather tall and serious-looking man over there" before he met Oswald the Chipmunk (a charming and perceptive animal whom our history textbooks have sadly neglected). And without her rambunctious parakeet Hernan (later known as "Bags"), Lady Gaga was just Stefani Germanotta. The precedent has therefore been set: You need to find your spirit animal, and you need to find it now. So take a breath, take your time, and choose wisely—because spirit animals, like face tattoos, are forever.

10 HIS DARK MATERIALS
WRITTEN BY PHILIP PULLMAN (1995-2000)

Many people have noted the ways in which Pullman's trilogy—which includes *The Golden Compass, The Subtle Knife*, and *The Amber Spyglass*—resembles C.S. Lewis's *The Chronicles of Narnia* (both stories originate in a wardrobe, for instance), but Pullman has always been very critical of Lewis, and the contrast between the two authors is obvious when you look at the animals they celebrate: In *The Chronicles of Narnia* there's really only one, Aslan, whereas in *The Golden Compass*, each human character gets her own "dæmon," which doesn't take on a fixed form until the character becomes an adult. Pullman's trilogy also includes armored polar bears (which is rad), and overall, it represents the state of the art in spirit animalia.

9 F U, PENGUIN: TELLING CUTE ANIMALS WHAT'S WHAT
WRITTEN BY MATTHEW GASTEIER (2009)

This book, based on the hugely popular blog of the same name, is probably the only reason why anyone in America knows what a nudibranch looks like or why a silky hen is hilarious (the answer is because it looks like "David Bowie meets Tim Burton meets Colonel Sanders," and because "CHICKENS ARE NOT SUPPOSED TO DO COCAINE"). It is essential for anyone who loves or despises animals, and for the Tibetan fox, who would otherwise have no idea how very superior he looks. Sometimes you need to look in the mirror, Tibetan fox. Sometimes we all do.

8 BABE: PIG IN THE CITY
DIRECTED BY GEORGE MILLER (1998)

The first *Babe* was simple, sweet-hearted, and magical. It was about a "sheep-pig" who won a sheep-herding competition and saved his owner's farm. This sequel is profound, sad, chaotic, and beautiful. It has almost nothing to do with the original, but it does have: two of the most poignant slow-motion scenes you'll ever see (one of which involves Mickey Rooney in a clown suit), a dog in a wheel chair, singing mice, the best animal performances on this side of Meerkat Manor, profound mediations on life, death, and an animal's "nature," and, once again, the immortal phrase "That'll do, Pig." Excuse me for saying so, but if you are looking for a spirit animal with real heart, this movie'll do, Pig; this movie'll do.

7 THE WIND IN THE WILLOWS
WRITTEN BY KENNETH GRAHAME (1908)

Are you more than casually interested in sensitive and articulate British animals? Of course you are! And lucky for you, between sensitive moles, paternal badgers, reckless toads, and a wide assortment of weasels, ferrets, and stoats, author Kenneth Grahame captured a sizable chunk of human nature. Most of the animals are rodents, so that may be a problem for some, but for normal people with normal problems who aren't afraid of the occasional weasel, these animals have a lot to offer. They also wear very handsome tweed clothes.

6 WATERSHIP DOWN
WRITTEN BY RICHARD ADAMS (1972)

So if you're not interested in having a rabbit for your spirit animal then you should skip ahead right now, because *Watership Down* is rabbits and nothing but (one seagull aside). That being said, these rabbits are also deeply human: They've got a language and a culture all their own, and when their survival is threatened, they dig deep (sometimes literally). The book's publishing history is almost as charming as the book itself. Author Richard Adams came up with the idea after his daughters begged him to tell a story on a long car ride, and it was turned down by 13 publishers before it was finally published and became a huge international bestseller.

5 THE WESTMINSTER DOG SHOW
HOSTED BY THE WESTMINSTER KENNEL CLUB (1877-)

Things that dogs can do: herd sheep, detect hypoglycemia in humans, dance a mean salsa (thanks, internet), and parade majestically around the Westminster Dog Show, despite having names like "Rumpus Bumpus" and "Lafford Fly Me Too Farleysbane" (aka "Dave"). Things that dogs cannot do: say no to butts and stop charming humans. So why fight it? I mean, they may all be part of the same species, but you're still spoiled for choice. Chihuahuas star in poorly reviewed comedies and look down on the world from celebrity purses, whereas mastiffs were formerly war dogs. They were dogs that fought in human wars! If Rambo had a spirit animal, it would definitely be a mastiff. A mastiff named "Bullets" (because bullets is what Bullets eats). I say again: Mastiffs fought in wars, and they look like dinosaurs. Mastiffs for the win.

4 THE LAND BEFORE TIME XIII: THE WISDOM OF FRIENDS
DIRECTED BY JAMIE MITCHELL (2007)

And speaking of dinosaurs, are you kidding me?! This movie isn't actually very relevant to the spirit animal discussion, but man alive! They made 13 movies about the land before time? Was there ever a time before *The Land Before Time*? Also: If someone makes 13 *Land Before Time* movies, is that person $^{12}/_{13}$ths crazy, or $^{1}/_{13}$th dinosaur? I may not be able to answer these questions, but I do know this: If you do ever try to make 13 movies about a land before time, you will definitely go out of business. RIP: Universal Animation Studios.

3 FANTASTIC MR. FOX
DIRECTED BY WES ANDERSON (2009)

Whether he's making an American Express commercial or a feature film, Wes Anderson is always likely to include slow-motion tracking shots, British rock, and small but poignant gestures. He likes what he likes (the FUTURA font, for instance), and he is, above all else, in control. But people are notoriously hard to control, and that's why it made sense when, in 2009, Anderson made the move to animation. *The Life Aquatic* included some cartoon elements, but it was still a live-action, live-human movie, whereas *The Fantastic Mr. Fox* is entirely animated. There are no human beings left here, and thus Wes Anderson is now in total control of not only the music and the scene-setting and the art, but also every little gesture and tic. It might not be Anderson's best or deepest movie, but it's totally charming, and it even includes a climax where possums, foxes, otters, and badgers take advantage of their unique skills to overcome long odds (so in a way, it's a superhero movie). Also, how many inspirational speeches include a brief course in Latin?!

2 THE MUPPETS
WRITTEN BY JASON SEGEL (2011)

In this recent update of Jim Henson's profoundly charming franchise, the Muppets' spirit—which had gone wandering in recent years—has finally returned. So go ahead, press play on the "Rainbow Connection" scene, close your eyes, and by the time the song ends, I have little doubt that you'll have found your true self, your Muppet manifestation. (And if what you see when you open your eyes is a flashback to Doc Hopper—the villain from the original Muppet movie—then god help you, you horrible, Muppet-murdering monster. I will see you in Hell [and the Muppets most certainly will not].)

1 PLANET EARTH
PRODUCED BY BBC NATURAL HISTORY UNIT (2006) 🖥

If you want to make a really informed decision about your spirit animal, then this is the place to go. *Planet Earth* is our planet, Earth, but more so: with llamas that spit more spitefully, salmon that swim upstream more desperately, and birds of paradise that flaunt their plumage even more coquettishly. And that's without even mentioning the great white sharks. In *Planet Earth*, instead of just, like, hanging out at the top of the food chain, these toothy cannonballs go flying out of the ocean to catch whole seals in their mouths and then mug at the camera like, "What now, humanity!" before plunging back into the underwater melee.

So in choosing your spirit animal, you would do well to recall that if you're not the predator, then you're probably the prey. *Planet Earth* is out to kill, and cuteness is not a viable form of self-defense.

EAT, PRAY, LOVE, SPELUNK
TAG ALONG ON A LIFE-CHANGING VACATION

Tired jokes often have a grain of truth to them. "Not until I have my coffee!" is not funny, yet we say these words and laugh at them because otherwise we would be forced to have conversations that none of us could remember or enjoy. The same thing goes for "I need a vacation from my vacation." It is a joke because we laugh at it, but we don't laugh because it's funny. We laugh because what else would we say?

Vacations are a great and needful thing—after all, life is hard and worth escaping—but they're also hard to plan, hard to pay for, hard to get to, and hard to leave. That's as true for a weekend at the beach as it is for a hiking expedition. So all things being equal, we might as well take the vacation that has the potential to turn us into better, more interesting people, right? But then again, no one wants to be lost in the woods or attacked by bears while on holiday, so what I propose is the following: Take your vacation at the beach, but while you're there, go on vicarious vacations with the hard-core travelers of the world. And then when people ask you what you did, you can tell them about how incredible it feels to dodge a Pamplonan goring, while also benefitting from compliments about your newfound tan. There, problem(s) solved. Now get out of my way while I pour myself a cup of coffee. (I can't do anything before I have my morning joe HA HA HA.)

10 CLIMB A MOUNTAIN IN *TOUCHING THE VOID*
DIRECTED BY KEVIN MACDONALD (2003)

So to be clear, this is not a vacation anyone should ever actually go on (ever); but it is a vacation that, shockingly, two people—Joe Simpson and Simon Yates—actually did (or had done to them, rather). They attempted to climb Siula Grande—a previously unscaled peak in the Peruvian Alps—and after reaching the top, they hit some difficulties. Joe lost his footing and when he landed, the impact was so intense that some of the bones in his lower leg were driven up through his knee into some of the other bones in his upper leg, which is known in medical circles as an "oh my god please tell me this is not something that actually happened"; then Simon, in attempting to lower his friend down the mountain using basically his ropes and his hands (a feat that had to be accomplished very rapidly, since he had to brace himself on really nothing but snow), eventually wound up in the unfortunate position of having to either (a) cut the rope, or (b) tumble along with Joe into a crevasse hundreds of feet below. This is what is known as a "life or death decision."

Simon eventually cut the rope, and Joe fell into said crevasse (aka the scariest and loneliest place ever not filled with vampires, murderers, or rabid aliens); Simon eventually made his way down the mountain, enduring frostbite, horrible thirst, and tremendous guilt along the way; Joe eventually found the courage to somehow actually get out of his profoundly awful situation. Both men survived without any real outside help. So that was a fun little trip, I guess.

9 GO FROM HOT TO COLD IN *AN AFRICAN IN GREENLAND*
WRITTEN BY TÉTÉ-MICHEL KPOMASSIE (1981)

Like most stories written by people who grew up in midcentury Togo but wound up living in 1960s, Greenland, Tété-Michel Kpomassie's story begins with a python encounter on a palm tree. After said encounter, Kpomassie (the narrator and main character) does the only logical thing and plummets to the earth, injuring himself on impact. While recovering, he reads about the Arctic North and—in an unusual reaction to the prospect of eternal winter—vows to make his way there to live as a hunter. And despite being groomed as a future priest and beginning his mission with almost nothing, he eventually succeeds in his goal, albeit after a few extended (and revealing) layovers in France, Germany, and Denmark.

Because Kpomassie has no idea which people are privileged here, which values are sacrosanct, and which opinions are taboo, he is forced to report everything in the starkest possible terms. He has no frame of reference, and his objectivity is, as a result, actually pretty objective. This ideological outlook isn't very different from your standard anthropologist, but few anthropologists have ever found themselves in a stranger, more foreign, or more unmooring environment than Kpomassie does here. And that's the key difference. Kpomassie has to simply absorb the culture before he can begin to form opinions about it, and the open, honest testimony he provides is as charming as it is revealing. The two cultures at the center of his book could hardly be more different, but Kpomassie's journey toward understanding is something that here becomes simultaneously literal and metaphorical. It's the trip of a lifetime—of several, in fact. And it provides a great reminder that every vacation story is better when it begins at the top of a palm tree.

8 DRIVE A YUGO ACROSS THE FORMER YUGOSLAVIA IN THE VICE "GUIDE TO TRAVEL" SERIES PRODUCED BY VICE MEDIA (2006-)

So as far as great ideas go, the VICE guide to travel series is a pretty good one. The idea is as follows: VICE sends its various employees to various global hot spots and has them do the things that people do there when they are either young, adventurous, and not restricted by the law. So we get to watch as these vicious and intrepid journalists attempt to infiltrate North Korea, pay a visit to a Libyan heroin den, and sing traditional folk songs with fans of Tito's Yugolsavia at what has to be the weirdest amusement park in Europe—or anywhere. So if you're sort of curious about what a Libyan heroin den would be like, but you're not really that curious about what it would be like to die under mysterious circumstances, then you should check it out!

7 HUNT FOR A MYTHICAL MEXICAN BEACH IN Y TU MAMÁ TAMBIÉN DIRECTED BY ALFONSO CUARÓN (2001)

The thing about road movies is that they're always in danger of falling apart. Since the people are traveling from place to place, the genre tends to rely on a kind of episodic storytelling—which means that one bad pit stop can bring the entire movie to a halt. Director Alfonso Cuarón solves that problem by keeping his focus firmly on the people in the car and on the drama that they themselves contain (in spades). By taking his focus off the landscape, it becomes that much more poignant and eloquent. The members of the car in question are two very handsome students (Tenoch and Julio, played by Diego Luna and Gael García Bernal, respectively) and one very beautiful woman (Luisa, played by Maribel Verdú), and good luck keeping them apart for very long. The two students weren't planning on going on a road trip until Luisa took them up on a boastful offer they had made, but after they embark, you have the feeling that, whatever they're looking for, they're probably going to find it. Regardless of whether or not they want it found.

6 GO ON A CRUISE VIA "A SUPPOSEDLY FUN THING I'LL NEVER DO AGAIN"
ORIGINALLY PUBLISHED AS "SHIPPING OUT,"
WRITTEN BY DAVID FOSTER WALLACE (1996)

David Foster Wallace wrote one very big book with a very big reputation (*Infinite Jest*), but also a lot of much smaller, less footnoted essays that solidified his reputation without making anywhere near the same amount of noise. If you're looking to find a point of access to his body of work, this is a great place to start. The "supposedly fun thing" of the title is a ride on a cruise ship, and the "thing that [he'll] never do again" is ride on a cruise ship. In case that wasn't clear. The essay is hilarious but also really insightful, and if you've ever been profoundly miserable while engaged in something that was ostensibly "fun," you will find a deep well of insights here. Without overstating things, it could also be fairly said that this essay provides the answer to the question: "What is America?"

5 TAKE A TRAIN ACROSS INDIA IN **THE DARJEELING LIMITED**
DIRECTED BY WES ANDERSON (2007)

So let's talk about family vacations for a minute. They're a bad idea, and if you disagree, you are probably on a family vacation right now, and you are lying as an act of self-preservation. I don't think there's anything more to say on the matter. Did that take a minute? Either way, let's move on.

Wes Anderson did a neat trick in *Darjeeling*. After suffering from complaints of entitlement, coldness, and even racism in many of his earlier films, he decided to tackle these criticisms head-on by making a travel movie in India—the most dangerous place on Earth to make a travel movie, as a white director. But once there, he took his standard cast of main characters (white, moneyed, and dysfunctional, all) and made them external to the actual climax of the film: the drowning of a young boy in an isolated Indian village. The Whitman brothers (played by Adrien Brody, Owen Wilson, and Jason Schwartzman) are still the emotional core of the movie, but by displaying their collective egocentrism as a kind of frivolous background to the things that really happen, we get the chance to see how superficial their entire universe is. And that's not a bad thing. Whether we're talking about movies or books, there's a lot to be said for people who can convey a lot with a little, and *Darjeeling* deserves special praise on this account. Whether that praise outweighs the scorn it deserves for encouraging brothers to take vacations together—that is another matter entirely.

4 BURN THROUGH A MASSIVE BOOK ADVANCE IN *EAT, PRAY, LOVE: ONE WOMAN'S SEARCH FOR EVERYTHING ACROSS ITALY, INDIA AND INDONESIA*
WRITTEN BY ELIZABETH GILBERT (2006)

There are a lot of things to love about *Eat, Pray, Love* (the charming narrator, the high-minded mission, and the devotion to self-improvement, for example), but there are also a lot of things to loathe (including especially the title, which has since become, collectively, an equally despicable verb, as in "oh yeah, Shelly went eat-pray-loving in the Chilean Adirondacks this year"). But in the end, the book (and its empowering advance) exists because we want it to: We want to watch people discover themselves through exposure to new places, new people, new ideas, and new foods, because that's the way we want to discover ourselves. Unfortunately, however, most of us are not paid for that purpose; fortunately, however, Elizabeth Gilbert was. She took a fairly trite idea and ran with it, but she took the idea seriously, and she ran at the right times (although some reviewers noted that she might have fled a little sooner from the praying portion). As a personal memoir, it's pleasant, but as a vicarious vacation, it's pretty much the best. In conclusion, to paraphrase a never-before-seen (or produced) bumper sticker: Make eat-pray-love, not starve-curse-war.

3 DRIVE AROUND THE WORLD IN THE *LONG WAY ROUND*
STARRING EWAN MCGREGOR AND CHARLEY BOORMAN (2004-2005)

Technically speaking, it isn't possible to drive a motorcycle from London to New York; but just because something is impossible doesn't mean it's not worth attempting. After all, what would people have said to a young Ewan McGregor if he had told them that one day he would play Obi-Wan Kenobi? They would have said, "Over my dead body! That's Alec Guinness's role!" But still, he did it: He became Kenobi. (PS: Boo.)

In *The Long Way Round*, Ewan McGregor and his friend Charley Boorman take a minimum of shortcuts in riding their motorcycles from England to Manhattan, and suffer from many (many) hardships on the way. To repeat: Ewan McGregor, an actual movie star, here suffers from actual hardships. In a world where celebrities generally struggle to do anything on their own, that alone constitutes a minor miracle. The trip covered, in total, almost 20,000 miles, and included breakdowns, robberies, injuries, and accidents. But those obstacles were also always kind of the point. The point was just doing it and suffering for that decision accordingly. (Their pain is our gain.)

2 GO EVERYWHERE, VIA EVERYTHING, IN *THE AMAZING RACE* AUSTRALIA HOSTED BY GRANT BOWLER (2011-) 🖥

It's a shame that successful shows don't automatically get an Australian spin-off. *Seinfeld*, Australia, would have been huge, and there's a lot of pun potential with programs like the HBO prison classic *Oz* (aka Oz-stralia). But leaving aside these missed opportunities, *The Amazing Race Australia* really is a standout in the genre (of amazing races, not Australian spin-offs). It's got everything every other season of *The Amazing Race* had (exotic locations, absurdist competitions, and archetypal teams—including the cowboy team, the sexy team, and several super-villains), but for reasons that remain unclear, it also manages to feel kind of comfortable. The antic energy is still there, but there are also enough truly likable people (and truly enjoyable villainy) for the show to feel, for lack of a better world, relaxing. Plus, any show that has a soup-selling competition is all right by me.

1 TREK THROUGH THE AMAZON IN *THE LOST CITY OF Z: A TALE OF DEADLY OBSESSION IN THE AMAZON* WRITTEN BY DAVID GRANN (2009) 📖

There's an amazing moment in *The Lost City of Z* when reporter David Grann (an amazing storyteller obsessed with amazing stories) heads to an outdoor supplies store in order to prepare for his first trip into the Amazon. That's when you realize that David Grann isn't some kind of budding superhero: He's just a normal dude. He prepares for an expedition into the homicidal Amazon in the same way that we prepare for a weekend camping trip. In other words, HE IS CRAZY. But he's also just as inept as we are. It sort of makes you wonder why we aren't going into the Amazon to hunt for a lost civilization and solve the mystery of what happened to explorer Percy Fawcett in his attempt to discover Z. Then we remember it's because we don't want to be threatened by starvation, disease, hostile Indians, hostile animals, and hostile bugs. But still, it's good that David Grann isn't overly bothered by those horrors, because without him, we wouldn't have this story. This is a vacation only in the sense that David Grann vacated his faculty of common sense before he began—and it is not a vacation for the faint of heart.

GO WHERE EVERYBODY KNOWS YOUR NAME

THE BEST PLACES TO HANG OUT FOR AN HOUR

There are few things more heartwarming than the sight of familiar faces in familiar places, wearing familiar smiles. Wait—does that sound weird and terrifying? Please don't misunderstand. Obviously faces don't "wear smiles" the way people wear pants, so it's not like these people are just pasting fake smiles over their lips and then parading madly about the streets. Yeah, no, sorry. That phrase was intended metaphorically. The point is that friendly people are fun to hang out with, especially if they don't hate you (as sometimes happens in real life when you hang out with friendly people for too long), and even more especially if they have a cool place to hang out, like a bar or a rec room or a shire.

This list contains the people and the places that will always welcome us with open arms—because they have no choice: They are fictional and subject to the whims of our remote controls and emotional needs. But they have a real warmth. So let's get in there and get comfortable.

10 THE BAR IN *CHEERS*
CREATED BY JAMES BURROWS, GLEN CHARLES, AND LES CHARLES (1982-1993) 💻

People look down on sitcoms now because in many ways we have moved past them. We're done with laugh tracks, and it's hard to believe in characters that live on a set when HBO is flying actors to Mars for their latest "Gangsters in Space" series (not really but almost). But at the same time, if it makes us laugh, it makes us laugh, no matter how outdated it may be (search online for "falls on face" if you doubt this), and there's a real charm to familiar people doing familiar things in a familiar place. *Cheers* is noteworthy because it's really nothing special. It's a traditional sitcom that takes place almost entirely on set, employs a stable cast of characters, and relies on reliable storylines. But even so, almost every episode feels fresh. The characters, over time, became so fully realized that they really do appear to have a repartee that is organic and entirely their own. The laughs feel earned, and they feel good.

Oh, and also any place that cheerses a man (a Norm, more specifically) for the simple reason that he has entered a bar certainly can't be faulted for being overly critical or judgmental. So let's live there, maybe.

9 THE CAMPFIRE IN *POINT BREAK*
DIRECTED BY KATHRYN BIGELOW (1991) 🎞

If you are attempting to infiltrate a gang of bank robbers, then it makes sense to not be Keanu Reeves. Because pretty much any gang of bank robbers will ask (1) why is this movie star talking to us, and (2) why isn't this movie star moping on a park bench in La Jolla (and asking if, like, "La Jolla" is the Spanish word for bulldogs probably?). And those are both good questions. But luckily for Keanu, *Point Break* is not your (nor his) standard surfer-action-bank-robber-thriller. It is so un-standard, in fact, that Patrick Swayze (aka "Sex: E, Swayz: E") is the leader of this gang, and the only thing he wants more than big money is big waves. And really, that little bit of insanity is the only way this movie makes any sense at all.

Only Patrick Swayze is good-looking enough to think that Keanu Reeves is "just a normal surfer dude who wants to be my bro and maybe rob some banks while wearing presidential masks with me and my bros." And only thus are we able to enjoy the company of these xxx-treme dudes while they take a load off, relax, and sit around a beach campfire. And if there is anything that can rival the thrill of riding the big one, it is listening to two chill-ass bank-robbing bros just chilling the hell out in front of a fire.

8 THE THEME PARK IN *ADVENTURELAND*
WRITTEN AND DIRECTED BY GREG MOTTOLA (2009)

Summer jobs are the worst, but sometimes also the best. The confusion of that moment—when you simultaneously resent the hot-dog hat on your head but also crush heavily on the hot-dog-hat-wearing-employee beside you—is what makes high school movies so popular. Or it's at least what made them so popular before the 1980s ended and we forgot about them. *Adventureland* solved this problem by setting its action back in high school's prime: the late '80s, but it also approaches the material with a sensibility that is much less . . . pointed.

The characters here grow a little, and learn a little, and yeah, there's a little moral. But the movie itself is much more interested in just being there again. There, in this case, is a small Pittsburgh amusement park where Jesse Eisenberg winds up after his summer plans fall apart. His friends go on European tours, but he finds Kristen Stewart and realizes that, wherever you go when you're 18, you still have a long way to travel. Jesse Eisenberg also learns that it is better to punch others in the nuts than to be punched in the nuts yourself. (Literally, not metaphorically.) This is post–high school, pre-adulthood life par excellence . . . sans France, avec Ryan Reynolds.

7 THE MUSIC STORE IN *HIGH FIDELITY*
DIRECTED BY STEPHEN FREARS (2000)

The point of *High Fidelity* (based on the book by Nick Hornby) is that John Cusack is immature and only when he grows up can he recapture the heart of his beloved and achieve his dreams and blah blah blah etc. Those things all matter and are pleasant to watch and all, but really, the star of the show is John Cusack's record shop, its employees (played with atomic aplomb by Jack Black and Todd Louiso), and the soundtrack that it conveniently enables. In this record shop, dreams are forestalled, lists are made, and emotional tribulations are put to the side. And what more could any of us ask for, really?

6 BACKSTAGE WITH ALICE COOPER IN *WAYNE'S WORLD*
WRITTEN BY MIKE MYERS (1992)

It seems a little unfair that ostentatious rock stars are so intelligent. I mean, if you are stupid enough to play with guillotines, or pee on people in public, or eat bats or whatever, you should not be smart enough to explain what such an act "means" or why someone would want to do it. In fact, if you eat a bat, you should not be smart enough to explain what "bat" rhymes with. You should say that "bat rhymes with head." You should be Ozzy Osbourne. That seems only fair. So how can we account for Iggy Pop, or Marilyn Manson, or Alice Cooper—artists who not only do all manner of unaccountable things, but also provide incredibly insightful accounts of said things? There is no way to do this. The only thing to do is just accept that they are, for lack of a better word, penis-radical ("penis" because many of their antics revolve around penises [literally]; "radical" because many of their acts have a political component"). Alice Cooper is penis-radical and also really very polite. There is just nothing cooler than this. And if it's good enough for Wayne and Garth, it should be good enough for us. We are not worthy.

5 THE SHIRE IN **THE LORD OF THE RINGS** DIRECTED BY PETER JACKSON (2001-2003)

How fun would it be to just hang out in the shire and never have to go saving the world with a bunch of cos-play fantasy dorks?! Pretty fun, right? The shire has all the ingredients for a pretty great party: lots of ale, lots of hair, lots of whimsy, and lots of really tiny doors. That is a recipe for one million laughs tonight, and the same again tomorrow morning (when full-sized adults try to open the bathroom door and are clotheslined by low-lying beams). Seriously, if you were a Frodo, why would you ever try and save the world? If the world can't learn to live in Shire-ly peace, let the world burn. To you, Frodo Baggins. To you.

4 THE SNAKEHOLE LOUNGE IN **PARKS AND RECREATION** CREATED BY GREG DANIELS AND MICHAEL SCHUR (2009-)

Parks and Recreation is the rare sitcom that blends a maximum of jokes with a maximum of character. Like the aforementioned *Cheers*, or *Arrested Development*, or *Modern Family*, every joke here is built on character, and every character is built on laughs. Every character on the show is ridiculous, but together they operate as one big, ridiculous family—that seems just a little bit real. Tom Haverford (played by Aziz Ansari) is the most outrageous character on the show; he is the promoter of "Snake Juice," and apparently a frequent guest at the Snakehole Lounge. In these stark terms, it sounds crazy, but at the same time, if Tom Haverford asked any of us to come try his new drink tonight at the Snakehole Lounge, who among us could say no? The answer is none. None among us. (Note to self: Ask Tom Haverford if he's willing to serve as the front man for a new rap-metal band called "NONAMONGUS.")

3 THE EMPORIUM IN *DAZED AND CONFUSED*
WRITTEN AND DIRECTED BY RICHARD LINKLATER (1993)

The Emporium, in case you forgot, is the local drive-through joint in *Dazed and Confused* (Richard Linklater's ode/takedown of high school life and culture). It is also a place that everyone can recognize: It's the bleachers beside the football field or the lawn in front of the woodshop—it's the place that everyone in high school knows about and goes to in order to see what's going on with everyone else before everyone else breaks off and goes their separate ways. It's the gathering place. And even though it is realized in exceptionally vivid detail here (including an iconic appearance from Matthew McConaughey), it also remains archetypal. That's true of the movie as a whole as well. Even though it takes place over the course of a single day and night in 1970s Austin, this is the high school experience of America as a whole. It's got upperclassmen, underclassmen, bullies, bullied, nobodies, jocks, freaks, iconoclasts, dorks, and cheerleaders. We may not all be Texans, but everyone can find a place here.

2 THE KITCHEN IN *PARTY DOWN*
CREATED BY JOHN ENBOM, ROB THOMAS, DAN ETHERIDGE, AND PAUL RUDD (2009-2010)

Party Down is one of the great failures of modern television. "Great" because it was always funny, always poignant, always insightful, and mostly tasteful; and a "failure" because it failed to find an audience of alive human beings. But even though it didn't survive to a third year, it's still worth celebrating this upstairs/downstairs comedy/drama that never really had an upstairs to speak of, and it's also worth noting that since the show was cancelled, its cast has dominated pop culture: Jane Lynch now presides over *Glee*; Lizzy Caplan has first choice among all the finest indie films; Adam Scott is the man who would be Paul Rudd; and Martin Starr is that guy in the background of everything that's great that somebody's friend once told you about, you think. Maybe. And this makes sense, because they're all great, but they've never been better than they were on *Party Down*, when they were all adorable misfits wearing pink shirts and working in catering. If this is failure, then God bless failure. (And actually, God bless failure either way.)

1 THE *COMMUNITY* STUDY ROOM
CREATED BY DAN HARMON (2009-)

Everything is possible in the *Community* study room, and if something is possible at Greendale Community College, rest assured that it will be done. Abed (Danny Pudi) will have a mental breakdown and come to believe that his entire study group has turned into Claymation characters; Troy (Donald Glover) will be accepted into the prestigious "elite air conditioning repair program" and yet neglect to enlist; Pierce (Chevy Chase) will betray his friends at every opportunity; and Jeff (Joel McHale) and Annie (Alison Brie) will stubbornly refuse to fall in love. Expectations will be bucked, tropes will be subverted, in-jokes will be made, and nonetheless, it will all end in laughs and heartwarmth. That is the miracle of *Community*. It offers both the deconstruction of the sitcom and also the reinvigoration of the same.

LOSE YOURSELF IN A GOOD STORY
ESSENTIAL POTBOILERS

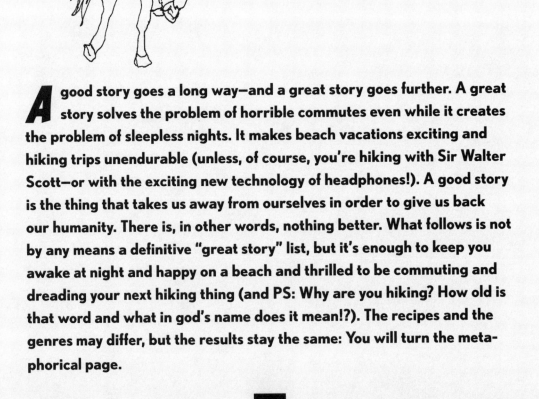

A good story goes a long way—and a great story goes further. A great story solves the problem of horrible commutes even while it creates the problem of sleepless nights. It makes beach vacations exciting and hiking trips unendurable (unless, of course, you're hiking with Sir Walter Scott—or with the exciting new technology of headphones!). A good story is the thing that takes us away from ourselves in order to give us back our humanity. There is, in other words, nothing better. What follows is not by any means a definitive "great story" list, but it's enough to keep you awake at night and happy on a beach and thrilled to be commuting and dreading your next hiking thing (and PS: Why are you hiking? How old is that word and what in god's name does it mean!?). The recipes and the genres may differ, but the results stay the same: You will turn the meta-phorical page.

10 *A TALE OF TWO CITIES*
WRITTEN BY CHARLES DICKENS (1859) 📖

Charles Dickens is the original master storyteller. Serialization worked to his advantage, as fans thronged around incoming ships demanding to know what was going to happen to the characters they had grown to love. But serialization also encouraged Dickens to keep stories going, and as a result, his enormous tales of injustice, cruelty, and retribution often have a tendency to go too far and last too long. But *A Tale of Two Cities* remains an immaculate work of plotting: Dickens knew where he was going (to the guillotine in Revolutionary France, if you must know), and he got there with a maximum of tension and a minimum of dross. It's a member of the establishment, definitely, but it deserves its place. It starts with a genius opening, it ends with a genius ending, and it ends when it ought to end. And what more can you really ask for?

9 *WATCHMEN*
WRITTEN BY ALAN MOORE (1986-1987) 💬

Watchmen was a revolution, but it's kind of hard to see that now. At this point, we've all seen Pixar's *The Incredibles* and Chris Nolan's *Dark Knight* trilogy, and we know that every comic book character worth his salt has an origin story first and foremost. But *Watchmen* is the true originator of the origin trend and a high point for the genre as well. Alan Moore's comic took the comic book—a medium that had grown tired and old—and he revitalized it completely by making it real. This is the innovation that continues to drive pretty much all of pop culture—from film to books to comics to television. They take what is outlandish (a man who dresses as a bat to stop villains; a human being who stays awake all night to fight crime) and make it real. In *Watchmen*, the plot matters, too (because it threatens the human race), but it is not the point. The point is that if there's a mask, there's also something behind that mask. And that's a thrilling thought.

Also, just something to bear in mind, whether or not you're a hero or a superhero or a cartoon mouse or a cartoon man: Please wear pants. It's just not cool to not wear pants. Even if you're a doctor from outer space. Even if you're blue. Just do it, old blue doctor: Just put on some pants.

8 DELIRIUM
WRITTEN BY LAUREN OLIVER (2011)

If you're looking for a gripping story, young adult novels are not a bad place to start. YA books, as a general rule, take it upon themselves to convince us at every page and in every chapter that the book in our hands is a book we actually want to be reading. And that's a mission that readers of all ages can appreciate. (Hence the enduring popularity of *The Perks of Being a Wallflower*, *The Outsiders*, *Harry Potter*, and *The Hunger Games*, among many others.) But at the same time, if a book is truly to benefit young adults, it has to find a way to edify them without also corrupting them. That's a tough balance. Lauren Oliver solves this by taking an essentially adolescent problem (namely, coming to grips with romantic feelings for other human beings) and addressing it with the intelligence of a fully formed adult.

Oliver's main character, Lena Haloway, is smart as a whip (although, come to think of it, whips don't seem that smart now that humans rarely whip other humans, and wounds hurt instead of smart, so maybe it's better to say that she's "much smarter than a whip"), but she's also come of age in a society that places more value on stability than it does on actual human emotion. It becomes apparent early on (almost as soon as another not-old human comes into view) that her initial answer is inadequate, but that still begs the question: What is she going to do about it?

7 THE HIDDEN FORTRESS
DIRECTED BY AKIRA KUROSAWA (1958)

Akira Kurosawa had two steady sources of inspiration for his films: William Shakespeare and Fyodor Dostoevsky. From Shakespeare he borrowed actual plots and characters (in *Ran* and *Throne of Blood*), but from Dostoevsky he borrowed themes and ideas in a much looser, more spiritual fashion (although he did directly adapt Dostoevsky's novel *The Idiot* in 1951). Both Shakespeare and Dostoevsky were experts in tailoring characters to plots and plots to ideas. And even though it wouldn't be fair to say that Kurosawa learned how to plot a movie by reading these authors, the fact is that whatever he did learn from them, he learned well. *The Hidden Fortress* is not Kurosawa's deepest or finest film, but it certainly is among his most entertaining.

The story concerns a general, a princess, and two poor peasants who are enlisted to help these luminaries make their way out of enemy territory. In writing the script, Kurosawa encouraged his fellow screenwriters to pose new obstacles wherever they felt they had solved an old problem. That process—and the film that resulted—can now be seen all over pop culture. George Lucas has acknowledged the influence that *The Hidden Fortress* had on *Star Wars* (in which the two peasants are transformed into droids), but you can also see its influence today on TV thrillers, action adventure films, and any number of other science fiction films. It takes place in feudal Japan, and its story, like almost all of Kurosawa's works, has deep resonances when considered in light of Japanese history and culture, but this is also a work out of time. It's a story first and foremost. The question is always simply: What happens next?

6 BRAID
DESIGNED BY JONATHAN BLOW (2008)

In an interview about *Braid* with the *A.V. Club*, game designer Jonathan Blow said, "I used to write fiction . . . and I kind of knew what I was doing when writing, and then the question was just, 'What do I write about now?' And I couldn't really find anything that I felt was important enough to write about. So I just kind of gave up." *Braid* is what happened next. Tim is the main character in the game ("hero" would be too suggestive a term), and you, as Tim, are trying to rescue your beloved (though little known) princess from a (also little observed) monster of some kind.

Gamers learn about Tim's life and past by manipulating time—in one level time can be rewound; in another, time moves in the same direction as Tim moves; and in the final level, time flows in reverse, in order to solve puzzles and obtain pieces of a jigsaw puzzle.

When the levels have been completed, the jigsaw puzzle opens up a new, even more meta set of mysteries, and turns the story that you thought you knew and the game you thought you were playing into something else entirely. If this was a movie or a book, we would call those moments "plot twists," but here that term is insufficient; these are twists that change the very idea of what "plot" is and does. Forget "is," "was," and "will be," because in all tenses and at all times, *Braid* = big. Each time you learn how to use time to solve a puzzle, it seems like one world has fallen away and a new one has arisen. The more you play, the more you learn, and the more you learn, the less you know. The game is also beautiful looking, beautiful sounding, and just beautiful. It is transformative.

5 CITY OF THIEVES
WRITTEN BY DAVID BENIOFF (2008)

Under most circumstances, "two young men go hunting for a dozen eggs" would not be a promising book idea. But under most circumstances, a dozen eggs doesn't make the difference between life and death. And Leningrad, under siege, at the end of World War II is not a place where normal circumstances much apply. Lev (an awkward Jewish teenager) and Kolya (a smooth-talking, good-looking soldier) have both found themselves in jail, and their only hope of escape is to find the eggs that a Soviet colonel needs for his daughter's wedding cake. Death is around every corner (and sometimes fates worse than death), but Benioff never overdoes the terror or the melodrama. The book is just as funny and just as sad as it needs to be. Like a great wedding cake, everything is in proportion—except, of course, the enjoyment it provides. It is a real human drama written by a real human author. But if there are flaws, it's hard to spot them.

4 RED RIDING
BASED ON THE NOVELS BY DAVID PEACE (2009)

Nothing keeps the pages turning like a good murder mystery, because few questions are more pressing than "Who did it?" In the profoundly depressing and yet deeply thrilling *Red Riding* trilogy, the answer to this essential question is: everyone—but that doesn't remove any of the suspense. In the course of these three films, three different directors show us how crime and corruption are covered, uncovered, suppressed, and revealed. The series as a whole is incredibly dark, but each episode sheds new light on its characters—some of whom begin in the background before taking center stage—and takes us deeper and deeper into the crimes and misdemeanors of the English north. It's a character portrait, a sociological study, a crime thriller, and straight-up un-put-downable. Watch it when it's raining, and then watch it again when it's pouring.

3 CRIME AND PUNISHMENT
WRITTEN BY FYODOR DOSTOEVSKY (1866)

Crime and Punishment is a novel whose reputation as "a classic" and as "serious literature" has a tendency to put people off. But despite Dostoevsky's deserved reputation as one of the world literature's greatest literary thinkers, he also wrote books that helped to pay his very real bills. And whether or not you read *Crime and Punishment* with an eye to its impact on detective novels, modern literature, or existentialism, the urgency of Raskolnikov's voice is hard to resist. Raskolnikov is a student who believes he has a special right, granted by virtue of his intelligence, to do as he wishes. He writes a paper expressing this view, but then he takes action as well, and tests his theory at its most extreme point: He kills and steals from an old pawnbroker, just to show that he could. This all takes place in the novel's opening pages; the rest of the book is occupied with the gradual solution of the crime by a surprisingly astute detective and the moral trials of the main character. *Crime and Punishment* was a meta-mystery before mysteries were even a genre to speak of, and it's a classic that remains a superlative form of entertainment.

2 PRIDE AND PREJUDICE
WRITTEN BY JANE AUSTEN (1813)

The claim that every great work of art either kills a genre or creates one has never found a better ally than *Pride and Prejudice*. Jane Austen's masterpiece functions as both the assassin of all romantic-comedic imitators and the staunch defendant of the romantic-comedic genre as a whole. Darcy and Elizabeth are bound to each other. We know that from the first. But we also know that they hate each other. They really do. The balance of that tension between those two essential facts—the fact that Elizabeth and Darcy must wind up together and the fact that they also don't really want to be anywhere near each other—is the fulcrum on which all romantic comedies lean. But this is the first and the best. There's really nothing else to say. Just light that fire and pour that bath and hand me that book and shut up forever.

1 THE FILMS OF ALFRED HITCHCOCK
DIRECTED BY ALFRED HITCHCOCK (1925-1976)

EXTENDED LOOK!

We often like to imagine that great storytellers are born, not made. The idea that Charles Dickens, Jane Austen, and Stephen King act as mediums for the stories that drop down, fully formed, from some great storytelling spirit in the sky lends an even greater sense of magic and necessity to their stories—but that idea is just not borne out by the facts. A great story requires much more than just the ability to put events into some kind of order: It takes character, structure, timing, and, if you're a film director, then you also need to possess technological know-how, an ear for sound, and an eye for the telling detail.

Alfred Hitchcock was possessed of almost all of these traits, but he was also savvy enough to involve artists like composer Bernard Hermann, designer Saul Bass, and writer/director

Alma Reville (his wife) to help out in the areas where he was lacking. The films that resulted (*The 39 Steps, The Lady Vanishes, Rebecca, Notorious, Rope, Dial M for Murder, Rear Window, North by Northwest, Pscyho, The Birds*, and on and on and on) were often adaptations, but they're all noteworthy for their lack of fidelity to the primary source. Because for Hitchcock, the point didn't lie in what happens, but rather in why it mattered. His films make us care about what happens next, and they make us care by any means necessary.

Hitchcock wasn't an easy person to work with, but he knew what he was doing, and he never stopped thinking about how to do things better. When it came to the question of how to tell a story, the central challenge for him (as he described it in a series of famous interviews with French director Francois Truffaut) was how to maintain suspense, rather than generate a sudden surprise. This seems like a minor insight at first, but if you think about his films in light of this idea, they are, above all else, suspenseful. They are a lot of other things, too, but that core emotion is what drives the interest and keeps us at the edge of our seats.

REST ASSURED
MOVIES WHERE PEOPLE GET EXACTLY WHAT THEY DESERVE

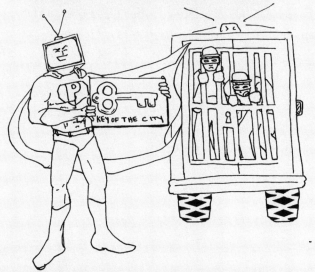

Life is unfair. On the one hand, this is an obvious truism. But on the other, more interesting hand (the foot-hand, perhaps?), it is deeply bogus, because as we all know, life really ought to be fair. This troubling contrast—between what ought to be and what is—is a constant thorn in our collective side; but it's also one of the primary sources of tension in our entertainment. Whether we're talking about courtroom thrillers or sci-fi space epics, Hollywood rom-coms or Korean revenge fantasies, we buy our movie tickets in the hope that things will turn out as they should in the end.

The movies included in this list are all gratifyingly conclusive, but the nature of the justice depends, of course, on the people involved. So pick the villain whose comeuppance you most want to see (if you've got the bile in you), or choose the hero whose victory you've been rooting for (if you're feeling whimsical), and then put your feet up, take off one shoe, and have any and all of your house pets put on their helmets, because sooner or later that other shoe is definitely going to drop.

10 12 ANGRY MEN
DIRECTED BY SIDNEY LUMET (1957)

Juries are like traffic lights: they're critical to the integrity of America as a nation, but they're also hugely annoying. Turn off the traffic lights, and America becomes one enormous and homicidal game of roller derby; turn off the juries, and America becomes Prisons Without Borders. So yeah, juries are made up of human beings, so juries are inherently flawed, but juries also kind of work. They're not impartial, they're not unbiased, but they're the best we've got. *12 Angry Men* is, in sum, an ode to the jury. True to its title, it shows us twelve angry men as they journey from a place of flawed individuality to something like collective genius. And even though we never leave the room, it's hard to find a more thrilling piece of entertainment—or a more inspiring testament to the power of civil discourse.

Best for when: You think jaded eyes are clearest.

9 THE FUGITIVE
DIRECTED BY ANDREW DAVIS (1993)

Sometimes it's enough to just know in your own heart that you are right, but in Dr. Richard Kimble's case, no, sorry that is not enough. His lawyer's inability to persuade a jury that Kimble is innocent of his wife's murder means that Kimble is headed to jail for a very long time. Until, that is, his prison bus flips over and our hero is given a new chance to clear his name and punish the wrongdoers. *The Fugitive* is, for the most part, a chase movie, but Richard Kimble is both hunter and game, for as he hunts the now proverbial "one-armed man" so also does deputy US marshal Samuel Gerard (Tommy Lee Jones) hunt him. As Gerard and Kimble come into closer and closer contact, the movie also becomes a demented kind of buddy movie, and without giving too much away, we can at least point out that the frenemies do wind up going home together. Kimble's hunt for justice, rather than revenge, also makes this a more-than-usually poignant tale of the good guy winning out in the end.

Best for when: You can't see the point of trying any more.

8 THE PRINCESS BRIDE
DIRECTED BY ROB REINER (1987)

The Princess Bride is that rare thing: a movie that has a plot we want (an adventure story with eels, super-villains, riddles, true love, and magic—at least, I think that's what America ordered in 1987, before sushi arrived on the scene), with the cast we want (including Wallace Shawn,

Peter Falk, baby Fred Savage, young Robin Wright Penn, and Andre the Giant), and the ending we want (with revenge and a kiss), but which doesn't fall to pieces under the weight of all its many attributes.

If anyone can resist the charm and pleasure of *The Princess Bride*, then that person is almost certainly an R.O.U.S. (a rodent of unusual size) and not a human being at all. (And if you are around such an R.O.U.S., it's probably time you moved out of the fire swamps.) *The Princess Bride* is a comedy, a romance, a fantasy tale, and a revenge story—but whichever aspect of the story most lights your particular fire (swamp), rest assured that the people you are rooting for will win, the people you are rooting against will lose, and you will want to hear the story again tomorrow.

Best for when: You think that simply knowing what's going to happen next means that you won't care. Revenge is a dish best served . . . unexpectedly.

7 JEAN DE FLORETTE AND MANON OF THE SPRING
DIRECTED BY CLAUDE BERRI (1986)

So to borrow a line from Woody Allen, "If you want to make God laugh, tell him about your plans." The ancient Greeks had an even simpler way of saying the same thing: with the single word "hubris." Hubris—a willful defiance of the gods—is at the heart of almost all Greek drama, and we retain it today in the dramatic idea of a "fatal flaw," and in all the tragedies that draw their inspiration from the tragedies of Aeschylus, Sophocles, and Euripides. Claude Berri's two films begin innocently enough (the most foreboding phrase of all) in the countryside of France, where Gérard Depardieu, a newcomer from the city, has inherited some land. He intends to teach himself all he needs to know about farming, raise rabbits, and live off the soil. Unfortunately, the neighbors (played by Yves Montand and Daniel Auteil) have their eyes on the newcomer's land and its hidden spring, and they plot together to take control of his property.

Manon of the Spring takes place many years later, but it is still very much the same sort of film. Manon is the young daughter of that same failed farmer, and she is living like a wild animal on the outskirts of the farming village. She still harbors a deep resentment about what happened to her father, and before long she is finding out much more than she ever wanted to know. As it happens, no one knows quite as much as they think they do, but when the truth comes out, everyone who's still alive has done the duty of the farmer and reaped what they have sown. Cue tears of humans/laughter of the gods.

Best for when: You want to see smiles wiped off of faces.

6 MY COUSIN VINNY
STARRING JOE PESCI AND MARISA TOMEI (1992)

So here's the set-up: Bill (the Karate Kid, Ralph Macchio) and his friend Stan have been imprisoned and charged with a murder they didn't commit, so Bill asks his family for help. They send cousin Vinny (played by Joe Pesci) down from Brooklyn. Vinny has not yet passed the bar in any state, let alone in Alabama, so he is not legally a lawyer, but he comes down anyway, and he brings with him his beautiful, if impatient, fiancée (played by Marisa Tomei) and enough attitude to fill an attitude bucket to the very brim. (Attitude buckets, in case you don't know, are those things that athletes turn upside down over coaches' heads when they win championships. Attitude!) This is, quite obviously, a ridiculous set-up for a ridiculous movie, but this is also a movie that made a relationship between short, irritable Joe Pesci, and charismatic, beautiful Marisa Tomei seem completely believable—so this is a movie that is not short on miracles. And when, against all odds, cousin Vinny does win his case and does free his cousin Billy (on the heels of Marisa Tomei's career-making testimony, I might add), it just feels so, so good.

Best for when: You doubt that your uncouth and relatively unlearned cousin will be able to forestall the machinations of American justice and save your skin. (But also, for the record, it's probably best not to call your cousin under those circumstances—unless, of course, your cousin really is a Vinny.)

5 DO THE RIGHT THING
DIRECTED BY SPIKE LEE (1989)

Do the Right Thing is a bit of an outlier here, because not only does it not end well, it ends very badly indeed. There's a riot, someone is murdered, something is destroyed, and all the people we thought we knew and liked have been compromised in some very serious ways. But there is a very real sense of justice here as well, despite the overwhelming injustice of the movie. And despite the fact that almost everyone winds up betrayed, and nearly everyone winds up playing the role of betrayer.

It is not right that a young man should be killed because he is black. There is no just recompense for murder, because lives can't be returned. But there can still be such a thing as a just portrait of a people in crisis, and at its core that's what *Do the Right Thing* is. The film itself provides the prescription for the malady that its characters face. It itself contains the empathy and understanding that its characters sometimes have and sometimes lack. And it shows, at one and the same time, the logic (on the one hand) and the superficiality (on the other) inherent in the concept of revenge. It doesn't pretend there are easy answers—and there's a real sense of justice in that answer.

Oh yeah and it's Spike Lee's breakout movie, and it takes place in '80s Brooklyn, and it came out the same year that *Driving Miss Daisy* won Best Picture, so if you haven't seen it yet, you should check it out.

Best for when: You think you've found the solution to a problem like race.

4 *SHAKESPEARE IN LOVE*
WRITTEN BY MARC NORMAN AND TOM STOPPARD (1998)

Human beings prefer good to evil and pleasure to pain, and we would rather see innocence rewarded with pleasure than we would see guilt punished with pain. The thing is though, it's not really that fun to watch good people get wealthy, get married, and have happy little bouncing babies—none of whom are murdered or robbed. There's just not a lot of suspense in that. And that's where the problem lies. Jane Austen solved that problem by allowing her shockingly realistic characters (shockingly realistic especially in light of the generic romantic-comedic characters that developed from her template) to make the same dumb, insecure, egocentric judgments and decisions that normal people do. And that makes sense. I mean yeah, that works. But that's not the only solution. *Shakespeare in Love*, for its part, utilized Elizabethan gender norms and Queen Elizabeth herself to get in the way of Shakespeare (Ralph Fiennes) and Viola de Lesseps (Her GOOPness, Gwyneth Paltrow). And that also works. The script, written in part by Tom Stoppard, makes history fun as well as obstructionist, and the result is a Shakespearean romantic comedy that has the urgency of a contemporary crime thriller.

Best for when: You think the past can't be rewritten for the better.

3 *TAKEN*
DIRECTED BY PIERRE MOREL (2008)

So *Taken* is a movie that takes Liam Neeson—a man that everyone agrees should be punching, kicking, knife-fighting, and swearing at as many things as possible—and then gives him a character resembling a daughter, so that said daughter can then be kidnapped, enabling Liam Neeson to get down to the business of punching, kicking, knife-fighting, etc, as a form of retribution. It takes a long time to say all that, but it doesn't take very long for it to happen, especially with the aid of a few "Armenian" sex traffickers. Yeah, you know what I'm talkin' about: foreigners.

Note to Armenian sex traffickers/foreigners of all stripes: You steal Liam Neeson's daughter, Liam Neeson hunts you down. If you can add two and two, you should know that much. But no matter how transparent the set-up may be (very), or how exploitative (very), the fact is, it really is fun to watch Liam Neeson be pissed, have a mission, and go chasing after bad guys. In the end, L-Neezy is obviously going to get his daughter back, but still, just imagine how Liam Neeson you would have gone on Liam Neeson's ass if he hadn't actually succeeded in his mission. It would have been the righteous knife fight to end all righteous knife fights—and Liam Neeson would have won. And then stabbed himself in the chest ("oof!—just a flesh wound!") as a punishment for failing his earlier mission. That is how Liam he is.

Best for when: You need an excuse to just burn all your bridges and stomp on all your forts.

2 THE VENGEANCE TRILOGY (INCLUDING *SYMPATHY FOR MR. VENGEANCE, OLDBOY,* AND *SYMPATHY FOR LADY VENGEANCE)*
DIRECTED BY PARK CHAN-WOOK (2002-2005)

It really shouldn't be this fun to watch this much pain. In each of Park Chan-wook's three vengeance movies, the crimes are horrific, the vengeance missions are ambitious, the characters are compelling, and the twists are plentiful—but if you ever do press Play on any of these, be forewarned: it is not over 'til it's over, and when it's over, everyone will probably be dead or shaking with grief. Does that sound like fun? Well, it is. The movies look incredible and could not be more thrilling. They could be a little happier and less hammer-murder-ish (I'm looking at you, *Oldboy*), but hey, you can't have everything.

Best for when: You think that vengeance is yours.

1 DJANGO UNCHAINED
DIRECTED BY QUENTIN TARANTINO (2012)

Homer's *Iliad* is famous for many reasons, but one of the most impressive things about it is the way it displays beauty in everything—even in death. (Hold on, Tarantino's coming.) The deaths of the Trojan War are described in such elaborate yet beautiful detail that, as we read, we can't help but view mortality with a new respect. At one point a chariot race is held with a gravestone serving as the turning point: the closer you come, the more extreme the angle and the greater the risk, but the further afield you stray, the less chance you have of victory.

Death is something that touches on life yet also ends it; it is silent, terrible, profound, and poetic. Homer, for his part, is celebrated for his descriptions of death, but Quentin Tarantino is faulted for his proximity to the very same idea—perhaps because he comes too close to it; perhaps because he does not come close enough. (Perhaps also because he loves to use the N-word. And watch people die. And kill people in creative new ways. But hey, to each their own.)

In *Django Unchained*, Tarantino splatters retributive blood—elegantly and ostentatiously—over virginal white flowers and catapults villains backwards when they are shot with a righteous gun. The violence becomes more extreme the closer we come to justice (and the further away we move from it). It looks like comedy and schlock, but it plays like melodrama, and it feels like justice.

Violence and death are serious topics, and when Tarantino treats them offhandedly, it's hard for him to not seem crass; but when he treats them seriously, it's hard for him to not seem pandering. So what's the middle ground? Oh, that's Django. Django (played by Jamie Foxx) is first a slave, then an ex-slave; first a bounty hunter, then a bounty; first a failure, and then a hero. He is a testament to the vagaries of history, and when he gets his way, it is hugely entertaining, even if it isn't history, per se. And sometimes that is enough. Sometimes entertainment is its own form of justice. We want to hear the story we deserve. And sometimes that's the last laugh. Sometimes, that's justice.

Best for when: You don't mind playing Monday morning quarterback and you don't mind watching your quarterback win.

FIND YOUR HAPPY PLACE
MAGICAL, FICTIONAL WORLDS

Sometimes, during hard times, it's a good idea to be in the company of friends; but at other times it's a good idea to avoid friends entirely, and just do the thing we want to do in the cozy little place we want to do it. Yes, that sounds very dirty, but still, it's true. If you don't trust me, then trust pop culture: Where would the Pevensie children have been without Narnia? (I personally have no idea, because Narnia is a very easy place in which to get lost—especially after seven volumes—but I think the answer is "killed by bombs.") And how would Superman have maintained his steely demeanor if he hadn't had his crazy Arctic ice cave? (It seems likely that he would have gone mad, and fire-farted humanity into a pile of ashes. Or whatever Superman does when he wants to make a point.) The point is, everyone needs a break sometimes. So take a cue from Superman, and take a serious load off, in the place that works for you. (Again, sounds dirty, but is not.)

10 DINGY BASEMENTS IN *FIGHT CLUB*
DIRECTED BY DAVID FINCHER (1999)

Ideal for: The angry times, the grungy times, the no-good-dirty-feel-bad-times.
[PS: Punch you in the mouf.]

Is there anything better than a dirty, blood-spattered basement when you're feeling under the weather? As it happens, I think there are a lot of things that are better than that thing, and I do not think that many of those better things are improved by adding bloodthirsty week-night warriors into the mix. But I have already broken the first and second rules of fight club, so I am clearly not the market for this product. But if you are in the market for just slammin' dudes heads on things, punchin' yourself in the [wherever hurts most], kickin' loose-lying objects (like cans and such) all up and down the street, and otherwise just gettin' Saturday-night-crazy every single night of the week, and twice on Tuesdays (because why does Tuesday think it gets to change the way we spell the second best number ever invented?), then this is the movie for you. And all jokes and bloodshed aside, *Fight Club* does make a pretty strong case for the things we left behind when we joined up for civilization. Fight clubs may not be a good idea, exactly, but that doesn't mean we get to ignore their appeal.

9 THE DANCE ROOM IN *FISH TANK* DIRECTED BY ANDREA ARNOLD (2009)

Ideal for: When you're out of options.

Mia's bad days are not as bad as bad days get, but they are close. She has few prospects, few friends, and little talent. She lives in an estate, however, so that sounds promising, until you remember (or are reminded) that estates mean projects when you're in England. And, sad to say, Mia is very much in England. Her one escape lies in dance. She's not a great dancer, but when she dances, you can feel the hope quotient rising. That's about all you need to know about Mia. Oh, except she's just discovering her sexuality as a teenager in Britain, and Michael Fassbender just started dating her mom. So that seems dangerous.

Growing up means learning how to survive a broken heart, but Mia's heart seems broken in all the right ways at the end. That is to say, she's learning how to heal. (And by the way: Here's to all the not-promising dancers out there. Just because we can't dance doesn't mean we shouldn't!)

8 THE WELL IN *THE WIND-UP BIRD CHRONICLE* WRITTEN BY HARUKI MURAKAMI (1994-1995)

Ideal for: People who want a little peace and quiet. (But even better for those who want a lot.)

Before he wrote *The Wind-Up Bird Chronicle*, Haruki Murakami was a popular Japanese author who wasn't all that popular outside of Japan—despite the fact that his books were loaded down with references to American pop culture. But after this novel came out, he was an international superstar. This career detail is worth noting because *The Wind-Up Bird Chronicle* is, if anything, weirder than your average Murakami novel. It's got psychics, dream-sex, dream-mysteries, wig-factory employees, and cats—important cats. But it's also got a plot that won't stop, a main character that everyone can relate to, a series of ever-profounder mysteries, and a deep well of deep wells. Literally.

When the going gets rough, Toru Okada (the protagonist of the novel) heads down into the well in his backyard. And there he finds solace, flashbacks, and a second world—or perhaps just a new perspective on the first. This well is a place of deep metaphorical significance, yes, but it's also, at one and the same time, a place of progress and a place of peace. Toru goes there to find existential repose, but until he has calmed the spirits around him, there is no peace to be found. Rest assured, however, that if you go to the bottom of Toru's well, you'll wind up at the bottom of your own well as . . . well (sorry). That's a threat, but it's also a blessing. Enjoy.

7 NEVERLAND IN *PETER AND WENDY* (AKA *PETER PAN*) WRITTEN BY J.M. BARRIE 1911)

Ideal for: Anyone who's having trouble remembering what it's like to wonder. (And not ideal for: crocodiles.)

Childhood is not a place for wimps, but once all of us nonwimps have grown up and retired from the playground, then all of a sudden it's hard to look back upon our formative years without a sense of wonder, pleasure, and joy. Normally we classify (and dismiss) this schizophrenic experience as "nostalgia," but in *Peter Pan*, J.M. Barrie manages to distill all of these contrary impulses into their respective parts. The novel begins in an idealized bedroom, where the Darling children (pun intended—as for the Darling dog as well) are being put to bed. This scene is delightful and utterly prosaic. The Darling kids are kids, and kids are charming, but kids are real bastards, too. One minute they love you, the next minute they hate you, and in between they have drawn a picture of you on your favorite shirt and called that picture "Love." No enemy is more canny than these ingenious babies.

But back to the point. As a child, there is hardly anything more exciting than the departure of your parents. The moment when they leave the house brings on the sense of loss (which is bitter) and yet along with it the taste of freedom, too (which is sweet). And when a magical little pixie creature enables the Darling children to fly away to Neverland, that tension is, if anything, increased. The Darlings are both more isolated and more free. When in Neverland, they want to fight Captain Hook every day and sleep at home every night. But the best parables, like the best metaphors, are the ones that make the most sense on their own terms, before they are applied to normal human life as well. And in its own strange way—despite the ticking crocodiles, and the flying children, and the timeless time—almost nothing makes more sense than Neverland: the place where children never age.

6 FLOATING ON THE WIND IN *FLOWER*
DEVELOPED BY THATGAMECOMPANY (2009)

Ideal for: Times when you just need to let go.

So this won't take too long. Flower is a video game without plot and without character. You control the wind and the wind directs petals across a beautiful, changing landscape. It's not a game that you win. There's not really a point. You just play it, and then it's over. It is cheap and short and it changes your mind. Does that sound vague? Well, this game is an emotion, not a story.

It's like, you thought you were a human, and prone to irritation when you realized that the empty seat on the bus was empty for a reason, and oh sweet Caroline, that reason was not a sterile reason at all, and oh holy smokes, what should you do now? But then, after you got home and showered thrice, you turned on Flower . . . and then you were the wind, and then your soup-stocky rug didn't smell quite so bad anymore, because you were floating above it all, and your destination was the end of nowhere, and your speed was: slowly.

5 THE NA'VI FOREST IN *AVATAR*
DIRECTED BY JAMES CAMERON (2009)

Ideal for: When reality seems too limiting.

It's kind of weird how humans live every second of their lives in 3-D, but then when a movie comes out in 3-D, it makes us lose our three-dimensional minds. *Avatar* is a film of many virtues (mainly technological) and many flaws (mainly dialogical), but whatever its defects may be (the way its aliens are American Indians, for instance), it does at least remind us of how truly miraculous it is to see three-dimensional objects on a two-dimensional screen. Especially when James Cameron has specially designed the 3-D cameras so that they are even more 3-D than usual. Because he can do that. Because he is the king of the world.

The plot of *Avatar* doesn't matter so much, but as you may have guessed there's conflict and a native species and evil humans and you've heard it all before. But before the proverbial fecal matter hits the proverbial whirly-blades (I'm not so good at proverbs, I guess), the main character—who only regains the use of his legs through the use of his Na'vi avatar—also gets to spend some quality time with the forest where the Na'vi make their home. And man, if that is not dorky; and man, if that is not great. 3-D fairy dust! Monster creature battles! Tree limb acrobatics! Gimme *all* of us!

4 THE METROPOLITAN MUSEUM OF ART (AFTER HOURS) IN *FROM THE MIXED-UP FILES OF MRS. BASIL E. FRANKWEILER*
WRITTEN BY E.L. KONIGSBURG (1967)

Ideal for: Anyone who's forgotten what it's like to break the rules and for anyone who still wants to remember.

Claudia Kincaid is an eleven-year-old girl who wants to run away from home but doesn't want to be uncomfortable. Nowadays, a Greenwich, Connecticut, preteen would have little trouble pocketing a cell phone, a credit card, and a Metro North ticket, and finding at least a few hours of indulgence at an upper east side hotel before it all came crumbling down. But in the 1960s, things were not that simple, and things did not crumble as fast as they do now. Lacking convenient or easy answers, Claudia opts for a crazy answer and takes her brother with her to the Met. (. . . roplitan Museum of Art, that is). This is a crazy idea because museums are a terrible place to sleep, live, and bathe; but eleven-year-olds are idiots, so how was she to know any better? Her idiocy, however, enables her to have the time of her life hiding from staff, getting to know her kid brother, and solving art mysteries. And that is clearly the ultimate preteen, high-society tri-fecta. We could all use some more of that. And if you want to spend the night in a museum but don't want to be arrested for trespassing (or don't have the patience or the initiative to time-travel back to ancient Egypt, rise to power, and get yourself expertly mummified), then it's best to do your sneaking and your scamming while you're still a minor.

3 THE BATHROOM IN *GIRLS*
CREATED BY LENA DUNHAM (2012-)

Ideal for: A moment of solace in a turbulent world.

The girls in *Girls* are not struggling to survive, but that doesn't mean they're not struggling. After all, if young adult life can be described as a tightrope walk over a murky pool of failure, disappointment, and embarrassment (and since I just described it in those terms, it seems that it can, in fact, be so described), then having a crutch—whether financial, emotional, or cultural—only adds a new level of difficulty to your travels. The girls in *Girls* begin the series with crutches aplenty, but as the traumas pile up, the crutches are tossed aside, and even though they do each plummet to Earth on occasion, there's always a nice bathroom waiting for them when they do. The bathroom is a place for basic needs. It levels the playing field. And if you're trying to stabilize a relationship or find an even keel, it's a good place to start. So get in that tub, and start healing.

2 NEW YORK CITY IN "EMPIRE STATE OF MIND" PERFORMED BY JAY-Z AND ALICIA KEYS (2009) 🎵

Ideal for: Anyone who ever dreamed of a better future.

New York City is a city in America, but it's also an escape, a metaphor, and a dream. To some people New York means Broadway, to others it means Harlem, and to others Wall Street, but the beauty of the city lies in the fact that when you say "New York" everyone gets to imagine—as everyone gets to live—their own version of that place. "Empire State of Mind" takes the impossible contradictions of New York and makes them make sense. It combines the infectious optimism of Alicia Keys' chorus with the highs and lows of Jay-Z's own experience, and it's all 100 percent hip-hop and pure pop gold. If you want to be there, then this song's for you; if you haven't made it yet, then this song's for you; and if don't think you ever really want to visit, then this may change your mind. "The city of New York...!"

1 HOME IN *THE ODYSSEY* COMPOSED BY HOMER (CIRCA EIGHTH CENTURY BC) 📖

Ideal for: People who yearn to find their place. (AKA humanity at large.)

There's no place like home. It's where the proverbial heart is, and it's definitely the location where chickens come to roost (as you would know if you've ever roosted chickens). It's the base we want to land on and the slice we want to know. We can't wait to leave it when we're young and we cant wait to get back to it when we're old. It is, in other words, a pretty weird and very metaphorical place. When, as a young man, Odysseus left Ithaca, his home, he also left his wife (Penelope), his young son (Telemachus), and peace. Then the Trojan War happened, and Achilles hogged all the attention in *The Iliad*, but Odysseus must have known his time was coming soon. The story of his voyage back to Ithaca is also the story of his trip back to himself. It is not an easy trip. It takes ten years, involves much sacrifice, and only haltingly proceeds to its resolution in peace, harmony, and reconciliation.

The Odyssey has been adapted innumerable times since it was first pronounced in Greek, but any summary of its influence would be insufficient. Every road movie is *The Odyssey*; every coming-of-age tale is *The Odyssey*; and every adventure story is also *The Odyssey*. And if you want to make a movie in Hollywood, you have to either start where *The Odyssey* starts (with a poignant separation) or end where *The Odyssey* ends (with a profound reconciliation). This is the journey we all take, but sadly we each have to find our own way home. Whatever that means.

LAUGH SO HARD YOU SOIL YOURSELF
RELIABLE SOURCES OF UNDENIABLE JOY

Laughter is an extreme form of human expression. We laugh in joy (when, for instance, pumpkin-flavored ice cream returns to ice cream stores in the fall), we laugh in embarrassment (when, for instance, we plopdrop our newly acquired pumpkin-flavored ice cream cone on the [dirt-flavored] floor), and we laugh when we don't know what else to do (during the great pumpkin blight of '07, for instance). So clearly, laughter is as broad a form of expression as humans are a species. There are times, however, when we laugh purely, helplessly, and willingly. Times when we can't help from laughing, even if we tried—and we wouldn't want to try anyway. And the transparency that we feel at those moments is something liberating, almost sublime.

We all have our own sense of humor, but this list contains an honest effort to replicate, in ten items, that sense of utter cosmic joy. In other words, lettuce laugh, cabbage heads.

10 *"JACK SPARROW"*
PERFORMED BY THE LONELY ISLAND, FEATURING MICHAEL BOLTON (2011) 🎵

The Lonely Island bros—Akiva Schaffer, Andy Samberg, and Jorma Taccone—have a recipe that sounds good in theory and works even better in practice. They blend hot musical styles (including hard-core rap, electro pop, R&B, and auto-tuned R&B), random celebrities (sometimes hot, sometimes not), trademark *SNL* humor (boiled geese and a variety of other nonboiled animals make appearances), and enough LOLs to make you forget that what you're listening to is also kind of great, kind of smart, music. They've had a lot of hits and collaborated with a lot of talented people, so it's hard to pick out a single song or video, but when in doubt, go with Michael Bolton. That's as true in music as it is in a survival scenario, and that truth is borne out in "Jack Sparrow," where Bolton arrives in the Lonely Island studios with a "big, sexy hook" for their latest track. Michael Bolton never lies and the track is indeed big and sexy, but it's also not on topic. The song's about ballin' in the club, but Bolton, as it turns out, is a "major cinephile"—and he's currently obsessed with the *Pirates of the Caribbean* franchise. Johnny Depp (aka "the jester of Tortuga") has never been used to greater comic effect.

9 THE SIMPSONS
CREATED BY MATT GROENING (1989-) 🖥

The year 1989 was auspicious for television sitcoms. Both *Seinfeld* and *The Simpsons* had their premieres, and each took a pretty basic idea and used it to influence an entire generation of entertainers, comedians, and TV executives. *Seinfeld*, for its part, abandoned the normal sitcom formula; instead of providing moral lessons, it allowed the essentially depraved main characters to suffer the hilarious consequences of their very poor behavior. *The Simpsons* offered its own small tweak: It ended with standard-issue moral lessons, but its characters weren't people. They were yellow things with four fingers, and they were animated.

That key distinction, which in the early days seemed like little more than a marketing tool ("Don't have a cow, man!"), eventually turned into something truly revolutionary. Because the real world is great for a lot of things, but it is not so great for joke efficiency. You can't strangle child actors on prime time television, no matter how funny it may be; and you can only film so many nuclear meltdowns on an actual set before your budget explodes. *The Simpsons* has no such problems. The animated world can simply do more jokes, and do more kinds of jokes. And as a result *The Simpsons* has been able to cultivate an almost endless string of top-tier talent, from writers like Conan O'Brien to animators like Brad Bird. The show has been on the air for over 20 years now, but you can still pick an episode at random and find plenty of reasons to laugh out loud. *The Simpsons* is the place where laughter found a home.

8 CHAPPELLE'S SHOW
CREATED BY DAVE CHAPPELLE AND NEAL BRENNAN (2003-2006)

Chappelle's Show is almost as famous now for the way it ended (when creator and guiding comic light Dave Chappelle suddenly abandoned the project in the midst of its third season) as it is for what it actually accomplished. But for anyone who cares to play a clip from the show, there's no reason to get caught up in the drama of the conclusion, because the comedy itself has hardly aged a day. Race and other "issues" offer a steady stream of content for the program, and that kind of content generally doesn't age very well. Usually, as time passes, the commentary becomes less and less pointed, but Chappelle's underlying goofiness ensures that nothing is ever sacrificed for a laugh. Consequently, the show at large seems impervious to age.

Perhaps the best example of this is the "Charlie Murphy's True Hollywood Stories" sketch, in which Eddie Murphy's brother Charlie Murphy tells the (actually true) story of the occasions when Rick James, in various states of elation, was beaten by one or both of the Murphy brothers, whom he abuses in a variety of incredibly outrageous ways. The sketch gave birth to the phrase "I'm Rick James, Bitch!" which is both utterly insipid and utterly inspired. To watch Charlie Murphy tell his version of events, Rick James mumble his, and Dave Chappelle re-enact the sequence, is to gain insight into what it means to be punched in the face by Rick James at the height of his fame. It means little, but it results in a lot of deep, deep laughs.

7 DEEP THOUGHTS
WRITTEN BY JACK HANDEY (1984)

It's not easy to write a joke. Anyone who has ever tried, on any level, to make someone laugh out loud via pen on paper must be aware of this fact. (This is especially frustrating when you consider how easy it is to make a LOLcat.) But that doesn't mean it's not worth doing. Not every deep thought that Jack Handey (real name) wrote was deep, thoughtful, or funny, but over the course of 100 or so pages in his first book, he accomplished a minor miracle. With about as many words as it takes to write a haiku, he composed absolutely hilarious story-jokes. For an example of this ability, search "deep thoughts" on the Internet, because a lawsuit will follow if we include one here. And lawsuits are the opposite of deep thoughts, in almost every respect, but most of all in terms of overall hilarity. So search, read, laugh, and thank me later.

PS: Some say that our names are our destiny. Bearing this in mind, is it any surprise that a man named Jack Handey turned into an absurdist comic genius? Well, if you ask Seymour Butz (aka the wit of West Texas), he'll tell you the same thing I will: The answer is no.

6 BORAT: CULTURAL LEARNINGS OF AMERICA FOR MAKE BENEFIT GLORIOUS NATION OF KAZAKHSTAN
STARRING SACHA BARON COHEN (2006)

It's hard to be likeable when your job requires that you make fools out of people on a weekly basis, but Sacha Baron Cohen somehow managed that trick while filming two seasons of *Da Ali G Show* in 2003-2004. The characters that he created for the purpose of shaming the world's elite—these characters being Ali G (a wannabe rapper), Bruno (a flamboyantly gay party animal), and Borat (a simple and intolerant Kazakhstani with a heart of gold)—went on to have film careers of varying quality, but Borat was filmed in a style similar to that of da original *Ali G Show,* and the guerilla style really pays off. Borat may be simple, but Cohen is brilliant, running a mile with every inch that his interview subjects give him. And when he doesn't have a good comeback or quip, Borat/Baron Cohen is not at all opposed to either putting on a neon over-the-shoulder groin-cover-up, or wrestling in the nude with a fellow traveler in order to fill the void (no pun intended . . . at all). As a result, there is no dead air in *Borat.*

5 THE OFFICE
WRITTEN BY RICKY GERVAIS AND STEPHEN MERCHANT (2001-2003)

Before Ricky Gervais became the British Seth MacFarlane (tailored T-shirt, tailored laugh, very scary outlook), he also created the television series that reinvigorated sitcoms and updated the way the world looks at office life. The innovation of the faux-documentary style provided David Brent (played by Gervais)—the boss of a small paper company—with the necessary outlet to air his hilariously transparent insecurities even as he insists on playing the role of a contented and successful middle-aged businessman. Now that we have the American version of *The Office,* however, what seems even more impressive is the fact that the original series was able to cram so many jokes into such a short series without ever appearing to resort to exaggeration. This really is a boring office. It seems like a really horrible place to work. And it seems real. And for that very reason, the office has never been more gratifying. Will a boy ever outswim a shark? Is an elf a mythical creature? Can David Brent ever find happiness in this life? These are all real questions that we will all have to come to terms with at some point.

4 "THE SHREDS"
CREATED BY SANTERI OJALA, AKA STSANDERS (2008-) ♫

European comedy is usually funny to Americans in the same way that a chipmunk with a bottle cap hat is funny. We laugh at it because it is ridiculous, and we don't care to figure out how it happened or what it means. As proof of this fact, please ask yourself when you last laughed at a European comedy that wasn't taking place in the world of your imagination. Okay, that's settled then. "StSanders" is the internet alias of a young Finnish man who takes videos from famous bands and then composes music and lyrics to match what's happening on screen. The music and the lyrics are both complete and utter nonsense, but they will make you giggle like you have never giggled before. They will make you giggle like the giggly baby that conquered the YouTube with the power of its baby giggles. They will make you giggle like the carefree teenager you always wished you sometimes used to be. And if they don't, well, then you clearly don't know the meaning of "Frustration B.O. void." Press play on the updated video of the Rolling Stones' "Start Me Up" and prepare to move to the front of the avant-garde. Or go insane. (Whichever comes first.)

3 THE HITCHHIKER'S GUIDE TO THE GALAXY
WRITTEN BY DOUGLAS ADAMS (BEGUN IN 1978) 📖

Sci-fi is a genre that a lot of people have trouble getting into. (Which makes sense, since people are people and not aliens.) But laughter is a great equalizer, and after Douglas Adams, it almost seems surprising that more sci-fi authors haven't begun tilling the ripe comic soil of the genre. I mean, after all, anything is possible here, and it doesn't always have to end in darkness. And even if it does, it doesn't all have to end in tears. That was Douglas Adams's key insight, and it's that fundamental outlook (of irony, absurdity, and fatalistic optimism) that led to such iconic phrases as "So long, and thanks for all the fish" (the message that dolphins leave for humanity upon leaving Earth, just prior to its utter annihilation) and "42" (the answer to the ultimate question of "Life, the Universe, and Everything").

Our tour guides on this essential tour of the universe are Arthur Dent (an everyman if ever there was one), Ford Prefect (his friend, an alien), Marvin (a robot), Tricia McMillan (the only other ex-Earthling in the current universe), and, of course, the actual *Hitchhiker's Guide to the Galaxy*—which is exactly as sharp, pithy, and witty as Douglas Adams himself was. Which is to say, very. He's the human who wrote the book on aliens, and he couldn't have written a better book if he tried (unless he was a mouse).

2 "CELEBRITY JEOPARDY"
FROM SATURDAY NIGHT LIVE, HOSTED BY (WILL FERRELL AS) ALEX TREBEK, STARRING (FAKE) SEAN CONNERY (1996-)

"Celebrity Jeopardy!" isn't officially retired, so we can still reasonably state it has had a pretty long run on *SNL*, but even so, there have been a few staples. These staples include: Will Ferrell (as the host), potent potables (as a category), and a base level of stupidity that is close enough to what we read about in the (unbelievable) tabloids to be absolutely hilarious. The show generally begins with all of the celebrity guests in the red, and when things get predictable you can always count on the categories ("States that end in 'Hampshire,'" "Words that end in 'amburger'") or a cameo from a real celebrity to liven things up. And when even that fails, well then there's Sean Connery's final wager to make up the difference. Sean Connery will be the cock of the walk, and we will be the beneficiaries of his cock-walkery. Each and every time.

1 RICHARD PRYOR LIVE ON THE SUNSET STRIP (1982)
STARRING RICHARD PRYOR

Richard Pryor's performance in *Live on the Sunset Strip* was his first after free-basing cocaine, setting himself on fire, and spending a significant amount of time in recovery at the hospital and at his home. That is not an easy thing to recover from or address, and although it's outlandish enough to perhaps contain some element of humor, it's not usually the burn victim himself who provides the laughs. But in his words, "Fire is inspirational. They should use it in the Olympics, because I ran the 100 in 4.3."

There's often an edge to great comedy and often a darkness, too. That was always the case with Pryor, but here there's also the sense that he has almost stepped beyond that realm of danger and destruction and entered into some place new. The crazy thing is that even here, in the midst of self-reflection and self-discovery, he's still funnier than just about anybody else has ever been.

HAPPINESS, AS DEFINED BY

MARK TWAIN

"Sanity and happiness are an impossible combination."

BUT...

Not for the Insane Clown Posse.

OPRAH WINFREY

"I define joy as a sustained sense of well-being and internal peace—a connection to what matters."

BUT...

Oprah's audience defines joy as: "going to aw-STRAYLLLLLL-YUHHHHHH!!!!!!!"

STEPHEN KING

"No one ever *does* live happily ever after, but we leave the children to find that out for themselves."

BUT...

It's terrifying to think of Stephen King "leaving the children." Leaving them to what, Stephen!? Leaving them to what?!
[Enter the langoliers.]

NICOLE KIDMAN

"I kept looking for happiness, and then I realized: This is it . . . It comes, and it goes, and it'll come back again."

BUT...

This also sounds a lot like the bogeyman? *Is happiness the bogeyman!?*

THE BEATLES

"Happiness is a warm gun."

BUT...

Not a *hot* gun. (George Harrison once made the claim that a truly happy gun is located between 70 and 80 degrees Fahrenheit.)

TEN RANDOM CELEBRITIES

JOHNNY CARSON
"Happiness is a tiger in your tank and a pussycat in your back seat."
BUT...
Johnny Carson was eaten alive by a motley band of feral cats shortly after providing this quote.

INGRID BERGMAN
"Happiness is good health and a bad memory."
BUT...
Who's going to destroy the photographic evidence?

GARBAGE
"I'm only happy when it rains."
BUT...
This is also true of actual garbage. Should we be heeding life lessons that pertain to both humans and discarded cigarettes? Do dumps know best? TBD ...

DREW BARRYMORE
"I think happiness is what makes you pretty."
BUT...
That means the key to happiness is just surrounding yourself with less attractive people.

SHERYL CROW
"If it makes you happy / It can't be that bad."
BUT...
By that rationale Sheryl Crow winds up endorsing heroin, reality television, deep-fried Twinkies, and the exquisite pleasure of unloading multiple rounds of semiautomatic gunfire into a starlit country night.

NEW YEAR'S DAY
THE INSPIRATION YOU
NEED TO KEEP YOUR RESOLUTIONS

"**I**nspiration" has become a kind of dirty word. Not in the sense that you would tell someone at a stoplight to "go inspiration your-self, you inspiration-hole!" (No, because that would be very confusing for everyone.) But rather in the sense that, if you describe something as "inspirational," you might as well be saying it's "interesting" or "weird." We use this term because it's insufficient. We use it to damn with faint praise. It's hard to find inspiration in an unlikely success story if we hate the hero and don't care about who wins a given football game. The fact is, we're inspired by the things that we love. We're inspired by the things that stir us up—and formulaic entertainment is decidedly un-excellent at stirring human souls. So this list takes a different approach to inspiration: The items here exist as entertainment, first and foremost. They're lovable because they're great. And even though they weren't made to make us better people, that doesn't mean they can't serve that purpose as well.

10 "MAN ON FIRE"
PERFORMED BY EDWARD SHARPE AND THE MAGNETIC ZEROES,
MUSIC VIDEO DIRECTED BY BRADY CORBET (2012) 🎵

For those who want to keep their resolution to: Take more risks and have more fun.

The hippie movement has faded a bit since the Summer of Love, but Edward Sharpe and the Magnetic Zeroes have kept the fire burning. They make music that is joyous and all-embrac-ing; and despite the fact that the world has since moved on (to a more cynical, less optimistic way of being), there's no denying the sheer joy that's present in these songs. "Man on Fire" is about the instinctive urge to dance. The lead singer insists that he's a "man on fire" in the same tones that Johnny Cash used to sing about annihilation and salvation, and the song's rhythms are just as firm and straightforward as Johnny Cash appeared to be. BUT. In the video, those straightforward rhythms and lyrics are augmented (and disrupted) by the most thrilling assortment of dancers and dance instructors that you could ever hope to see.

The video begins at the Brownsville Rec Center (where Josh Cooper, a young tumbler, tumbles magnificently) and then, after a rapid-fire tour through cheer leagues, double-dutch competitions, and dance studios, ends with the New York City Ballet company engaging in an impromptu hoe-down in an anonymous New York City alley. You hear the music and you see the dancing and that's the entire video. But before you know it, your body will move you. And once you start, there's no reason to stop. This music video will make you want to dance forever no matter how bad a dancer you may be. So just do it. Just dance.

9 *Z* DIRECTED BY COSTA-GAVRAS (1969)

For those who want to keep their resolution to: Save the world (despite the world's essential un-save-ability).

The easiest way to deal with a hopeless situation is to not deal with it at all. But if we all ran away from everything then we would live in a world of blameless scapegoats—and that is just not tenable. At all! First of all, what is a scapegoat and what does it eat? Scape-oats? NO! Scape-oats are a myth! And second of all, a scapegoat isn't a scapegoat if it can't be blamed. So let's take a moment to put politics (and the hatred of politics) aside and just appreciate the fact that some people really do work hard to get beyond the confusing issue of scapegoats, and seek to right injustices, confront hypocrisy, and make the world a better place. To the point . . .

Greece in the late 1960s was ripe for apathy. The military ran the government, the government had its fingers in every piece of every pie, and everything was a mess. If you weren't in power, you were helpless, and most of the power was collected around a very few people. Grigoris Lambrakis was a Greek politician who advocated for pacifism and nuclear disarmament despite the fact that this was not a view shared by those in power at the time. He was assassinated in front of many witnesses, and the conspiracy behind his murder went all the way to the top. This hyper-realistic, semi-documentarian film begins with his death and ends with our disappointment (when we realize that almost all of the villains have found a way to escape any real form of punishment), but if you're looking for a reason to believe in change, then this is a good place to start. It's also one of the most thrilling stories you'll ever see on film.

8 CAVE OF FORGOTTEN DREAMS
DIRECTED BY WERNER HERZOG (2010)

For those who want to keep their resolution to: Keep things in perspective.

A lot of smart people have logged a lot of smart-people-thinking hours trying to figure out how time works. But basically we already all agree on the answer: time is as we perceive it. Sometimes time is fast, and sometimes time is slow, and sometimes (most of the time) time is utterly invisible. That's what's really so upsetting about the whole idea of time: the fact that, even though time is subjective, it also has a tendency to take great strides when we're not looking. We are born and all of a sudden we are grown. We have kids and all of a sudden our kids are adults. And that kind of sucks. (Give us a minute, Time!) When things are happening, they are both within our grasp and then, all of a sudden, beyond us. So it's good to have a reminder every once in a while that even though time goes on, there is something that is truly static and timeless.

The prehistoric art on the walls of the Chauvet Cave is tens of thousands of years old. LITERALLY OLDER THAN THE WHEEL (and far, far older than the reinvention of the same). But to call it human would be an understatement. It is profoundly human and profoundly alive. These humans were alive before history existed, and yet their art lets us know that they are us, and vice versa. It's incredible. How many contemporary art shows can make the claim to show humanity? This very uncontemporary art show can. Herzog makes many connections between the past and the present in the course of his documentary, but nothing is more poignant than the fact that Herzog has to struggle to use 3-D technology to capture the 3-D effects of flat lines painted on the surface of a moving, timeless wall. Holy smokes, humans. You guys never change.

7 CHARIOTS OF FIRE
DIRECTED BY HUGH HUDSON (1981)

For those who want to keep their resolution to: Exercise more.

It's not hard to be inspired by the idea of looking better and feeling healthier, but that idea is also kind of hard to bear in mind when your hard work doesn't pay off and when you end each workout looking no different than you did when the workout began (except for all the new sweat you've accrued). So it's not surprising that we often turn to more abstract forms of inspiration, like a mantra (*love* a mantra) or a playlist. *Chariots of Fire*, in a way, is both of those things. It provides a thrilling message—that will get you where you want to be—along with a thrilling Vangelis score. Watching people run on their feet should not be this fun watch, but it is.

6 LOUIE
CREATED BY LOUIS C.K. (2010–) 🖥

LOUIE

For those who want to keep their resolution to: Live life more consciously.

Good stand-up comedy is inspiring. Richard Pryor, George Carlin, Roseanne Barr, Chris Rock, Jerry Seinfeld, Sarah Silverman, Louis C.K.—they all seem to be, in their own way, fighting for clarity. Uncompromising honesty, however, isn't something that's in very high demand, and for good reason. Louis C.K. struggled for many years to find a way to deliver his own brand of comedy in a way that was true to his vision and still appealing to a wide audience. His stand-up always (or often) had a way of walking that line, but when he was given the opportunity to run a show, it took him a while to find his groove. *Lucky Louie* bombed, and *Louie* wasn't an immediate hit either, but it had something; and after a while that something became truly original and truly great. As in a Hitchcock movie, you can feel Louis C.K.'s presence in every shot, and that involvement and intimacy allows his fundamental punch line—that he himself is the thing he least understands and most resents—to really hit home, time and time again. The intense focus that he places on himself gives us the little bit of leeway we need in order to say, "Oh man, that is a funny joke and that is a funny guy, but that is not me" (even though, in the end, the reason why it's funny is because we also know it is, in fact, totally us).

5 REVANCHE
DIRECTED BY GÖTZ SPIELMANN (2008) 🎞

For those who want to keep their resolution to: Start fresh. (New Year, new you.)

So the thing about dramas is, why do we watch them? They are very sad, and if they're good, they make us feel sad, too. This is very weird! There are a lot of theories about why this thing ("dramas") is a thing, but basically in the end the answer is, we just don't know. It's a "philosophical question." Well, *Revanche* is a philosophical movie then, I guess, because it is very sad and very hard to watch; but it's also very enjoyable and very hard to turn off, because, for lack of a better explanation, it's beautiful.

Revanche tells the story of a bank robbery gone (as usual) very, very bad—but then it goes on to show how that bad ending plays out in the lives of both the bereaved criminal and the guilt-ridden cop who stopped him (and killed his girlfriend). Everyone is sympathetic, and that's what makes the movie so unbearable. We start in a hopeless situation, and yet when everything ends in utter despair, we find hope and a new beginning. If you think you've got it bad and don't know how to turn things around again, this movie will show you how much further there is to fall, and how close we all remain to a kind of simple salvation.

Note to bank robbers: Do not bring your spouses with you whey you go out robbing banks. Also, note to dramas: You're the worst.

4 THE QUEEN OF VERSAILLES
DIRECTED BY LAUREN GREENFIELD (2012)

For those who want to keep their resolution to: Save more money.

Great movies are, as a rule, made and not born—but *Queen of Versailles* is the exception to that rule. It's the *Citizen Kane* of accidents. Director Lauren Greenfield was originally drawn to the story for the simple reason that Jackie and David Siegel were building one of the biggest private residences in the United States, but the movie that she wound up making is an incredible study of the privileges, pitfalls, and pratfalls of wealth in America. David Siegel built his massive fortune during the housing bubble on a timeshare company and began construction on his enormous estate just before the housing bubble burst. To watch this couple as they come to terms with their new reality is to watch the American dream in meltdown mode. Nonetheless, it's charming. It's a testament to the seduction of the American dream even at the worst of times. With so many cute dogs. So very many. With so very much poop. So if you need some help keeping your spending in check, yeah, start here.

3 TROUBLE THE WATER
DIRECTED BY CARL DEAL AND TIA LESSIN (2008)

For those who want to keep their resolution to: Make a difference in the world.

It's easy to take things for granted. There are lots of good (and bad) reasons for this, but certainly one of the things that makes it so easy is the fact that we don't often find ourselves confined to an attic during a massive hurricane, surrounded by rising waters and a growing sense that really we are on our own—that no one is coming to help. That's the situation that Kimberly Roberts and her husband (and her dog) found themselves in during Hurricane Katrina. The fact that Kimberly filmed her experiences (on a recently obtained $20 camera) allows us to see that situation through her own eyes and ask ourselves what we would do if presented with a similar set of circumstances.

Would we survive? Would we help others survive? Where would we turn for help? And would those people give us the help we had sought? These are tough questions, but hardly as tough as Kimberly, given the world in which she suddenly finds herself. It's inspiring and enraging in equal parts, and it provides a helpful reminder that nothing is ever guaranteed; that even when we feel most comfortable, in our homes, and in our hometowns, we're always just one big disaster away from a whole new world entirely.

2 FRIDAY NIGHT LIGHTS
DIRECTED BY PETER BERG (2004)

For those who want to keep their resolution to: Connect with others.

Great speeches usually end with a bang—with a fiery Scot screaming to the heavens and leading a charge or with a Jack Nicholson talking about the capital T truth and what we can or cannot handle. But just because that's the way it's usually done doesn't mean it's always right. The original film version of *Friday Night Lights* (based on the incredible journalistic work of Buzz Bissinger) adopted the atmospheric music of Explosions in the Sky and the small-town rhythms of Permian, Texas, in order to tell an inspiring story that wasn't based on the idea that the good guy always wins or that there's even a good guy in the first place. Instead, this movie makes the point that in real life there are real people, and that real people have real struggles, and then we either meet them or don't and life gets better or worse accordingly. Plus, a lot of really great football footage. And then it's over and life goes on, and bring a handkerchief.

But Coach Gary Gaines (played by Billy Bob Thornton) delivers one quiet speech during halftime of the team's championship game that has to be up there with the best speeches ever captured on film. If you can watch this and not want to adopt the first wild animal you see, and then try and help that wild animal become a great human being and an even better outside linebacker, well, then you are truly heartless.

1 "HURT"
BASED ON THE SONG BY TRENT REZNOR, PERFORMED BY JOHNNY CASH (2002) ♫

For those who want to keep their resolution to: Drop a bad habit.

There are a lot of ways for covers to be great, but there's something especially great about a cover that just allows the cover artist to be himself. The closest analogy is in film or television, when actors are often given the opportunity to revisit aspects of their own personality (or persona) via a certain character. So the opportunity that Jimi Hendrix seized with his cover of "All Along the Watchtower" finds a kind of soul mate in the late action career of Liam Neeson (for better) or the late comedy career of Charlie Sheen (for worse). In all of these cases, what we appreciate is the apparent insight we get into a celebrity's "essential nature." And Johnny Cash's cover of Trent Reznor's "Hurt" is the perfect example of this phenomenon. The words were clearly written by a younger man, and the references are intended for a younger generation, but in Johnny Cash's iconic voice we get to listen as Reznor's seeds of regret blossom into something truly heartbreaking. This is not for show anymore. Instead, this is a reckoning. And if you want to find the courage to drop a bad habit, get healthier, or work to stay alive just a little bit longer, there's no better motivation than the sound of bitter death crooning at you, from just beside the grave. Youch.

VALENTINE'S DAY
HALLMARK-PROOF LOVE STORIES

Valentine's Day is indeed a day, but is it a good day? No! Of course not! Not at all! It's like a clown punching bag. It's tacky and crass and unceasingly optimistic, but every effort we make to get away from it (or "punch it in the face," in this analogy) only brings our nemesis hurtling back toward us with even greater force. As Valentine's Day approaches (stalks its human prey), we can't risk taking a leap with someone exciting (too much pressure too early), and we can't dump someone who's not exciting enough (too mean). It obstructs our moral progress, ruins what appears to be working in our lives, and never stops telling us how great it is.

But the fact remains: It is not great. Love is challenging. Sex is complicated. Dating is hard. And romance is fleeting. Valentine's Day is, in brief, a lie. But once a year, every year, it pops up and beams at us, and that's where this list comes in. The items here are intended as a tonic. They show the aspects of love that people try and discount on February 14—so things like regret, unrequited passion, passive-aggressive apathy, and outright emotional warfare—but if it weren't for these bitter and malevolent forces, we wouldn't know what love was if it clown-punched us in the face. (And that's a fate that's best avoided.)

10 LOLITA
WRITTEN BY VLADIMIR NABOKOV (1955) 📖

It seems cowardly to say "you can't say anything about *Lolita* that hasn't been said before" (even though that's true), because *Lolita* is, above all else, a love story, and there's nothing older or more hackneyed than a love story. But then again, love is an evergreen topic, and with Nabokov's language in the role of fertilizer, love blossoms into something strange, vibrant, disturbing, and beautiful. Into something that is, in a word, overwhelming.

Humbert Humbert's voice is overwhelming. We fall in love with his voice just as he falls in love with Lolita's essence—if that is indeed what he falls in love with; if indeed he falls in love at all. Is he in love? Is love a lie? Has language seduced us? Can forgiveness be possible where guilt hasn't been assumed? These are important questions—they are at the heart of Nabokov's much celebrated (and much castigated) novel—but the book is also a work of poetry, and poetry is notorious for its lack of easy answers. Read it, fall in love, feel elated, feel ashamed, lose the thread, find yourself, doubt your conclusions, and then start all over again. Some people say it's the best thing ever, and some people are sometimes very wise, despite their collective anonymity.

9 LAURA
DIRECTED BY OTTO PREMINGER (1944) 🎞️

Director Otto Preminger was a great filmmaker, but he stands out among his peers for the number of films he made in which the main character was dead. Dead as in not present. Not alive. And yet the center of all the action. And still, at least two of the films that Preminger produced in this micro-genre (namely, *Laura* and *Anatomy of a Murder*) can take their place in the pantheon of American cinema classics. In one of these two films, death isn't permanent, but you'll have to watch at least one of them to figure out which is which.

Laura begins the movie as a dead woman—a beautiful dead woman with a creepy apartment and too many people who like her a bit too much (including Mark McPherson, the new detective on the case who only knows Laura by her portrait and by the things he hears about her). But it doesn't take long for Laura's death to take on a life of its own; and anyway, you don't have to go much further than the film's opening scene to find the dark underbelly of the sacred truth that "love knows no bounds." Because when what you love is dead, then maybe love should stay in bounds. No offense to necrophiliacs (well, some offense), but seriously, good luck getting your dead partner to take on an equal share of the chores! (Also: "Hey!

Welcome to my dinner party! Oh, what's that smell? Well, that's my dead spouse; she is dead and therefore does not smell fresh. Oh. Goodbye, friends."

8 DEAR OLD LOVE: ANONYMOUS NOTES TO FORMER CRUSHES, SWEETHEARTS, HUSBANDS, WIVES & ONES THAT GOT AWAY
COMPILED BY ANDY SELSBERG (2009)

Speaking of death, you know what dies? Love. More specifically: old love. *Dear Old Love* began as a Tumblr feed, but after enough people had submitted hilarious, poignant, and heartfelt letters, a book was basically inevitable. The idea was too good, and the response was too strong. There are no pictures. There is no follow-up. There are only brief reminisces, brief recriminations, and titles pithy enough to make you wonder: "What is pith? Where can I get some? And what can I use it for, after I have purchased it?" Sometimes punchlines come at the end, and sometimes they come at the beginning, and sometimes punchlines punch us back. In *Dear Old Love*, the answer is all of the above.

It sort of makes you wonder, what would you say to your old love? I would probably say something like "Hey, what are you doing here and why does my room smell like maple syru—ohhhh. You poured maple syrup all over my stuff."

7 THE UMBRELLAS OF CHERBOURG
DIRECTED BY JACQUES DEMY (1964)

The unexpected pregnancy is now something of a trope in romantic comedies and romantic dramas. If there's a pause in the action, then believe this: Pretty soon that lady over there (that one looking mildly concerned right now, just as someone attractive is approaching to talk to her) is going to do something kind of not in keeping with her surroundings (like barf at a black-tie event or puke on a kindly, yet slack-jawed, stranger), and then make a trip to the drug store, and then [cut to next scene] O. M. G. baby is officially on board, and the movie is officially back on the rails. This shortcut happens for a reason though; it happens because BABIES HAPPEN. I mean, look around you right now. Do you see some humans? Well, guess what? Those humans you're looking at right now? They're all ex-babies. And inside some of those humans? Guess what else: more babies are happening. GESTATING. Babies are on the rise, adults. [Taps forehead, knowingly.] Always.

So, on to *The Umbrellas of Cherbourg*. The plot turns on an accidental pregnancy, but it does so in a way that feels kind of honest and real. That might seem like a minor accomplishment, but how many movies containing zero percent spoken dialogue/100 percent sung dialogue would you describe as honest or real? The answer is zero. Zero number of zero percent. The movie also looks beautiful, sounds beautiful, and feels tragic even though it tells the story of a doomed young couple (Catherine Deneuve and Nino Castelnuovo) that is just about entirely believable. It ends with desolation in the snow (at a gas station), but it ends on a high note (in a minor key). And if that's not the story of first love, writ large, then I don't know what is.

6 IN THE REALM OF THE SENSES
DIRECTED BY NAGISA ŌSHIMA (1976)

Love is a dangerous drug—and that is not a metaphor. In middle school, high school, and even college, most human beings experience romantic obsessions that are deserving of the term. They are all-consuming, and they get in the way of a lot of other things. But by the time we become real adults, most of us have enough friends and family members who are in functional, adult relationships that it's easy to forget how both inspiring and intrusive a love life can be. *In the Realm of the Senses* seeks to correct that lapse.

It tells the story of an innkeeper (Kichizo Ishida) and a maid (Sada Abe) who enter into an obsessive sexual relationship of ever-increasing intensity. They have sex many times together, and these sexual episodes are filmed with great earnestness. (It is intense for the viewer, too.) The film ends after Abe strangles Ishida to death in the throes of passion, cuts off his genitals, and writes a tribute to their love in blood on his chest. Based on a true story!

In normal human words that sounds almost mundane. Let me try again with some more expressive language: Sometimes, when two people really love each other, they make a special time to have sex festivals of world-historical proportions. And sometimes, when even the sex festivals aren't enough, and they still need bigger and better ways of loving one another, they look to the worlds of death and animals, and there they find things like near-death experiences and castration, and they think, let's give those ones a try, and then blood and penises are flying all over the place and it is like the apocalypse as imagined by a probing psychiatrist who is married to the reigning Empress of the Vaginal Realm. That's *In the Realm of the Senses*. But it will also really make you think.

5 SHORTCOMINGS
WRITTEN AND ILLUSTRATED BY ADRIAN TOMINE (2007) 💬

One of the weird things about dating other people is that even though we are who we are (because that's who we are) and they are who they are (for the same reason), both parties also take on something of their partner's identity and status as well. Ben Tanaka, to take an example from *Shortcomings*, is a young Japanese American man who, when the novel opens, is dating a young Japanese American woman who also happens to believe (somewhat justifiably) that Ben is obsessed with blonde American white girls. The question of what that obsession says or doesn't say about Ben's own identity is central to the book, but really so is everything else. Everything is about Ben's identity because Ben is obsessed with himself. Even so, he's an interesting guy, and to see him falter in an old relationship and stumble through several new ones is to watch the kind of romance (so-called) that we rarely see in pop culture: it's a romance that seems real and actually original. It also looks amazing. So even though it might hurt a little, it's medicine worth taking.

4 "NO CHILDREN"
WRITTEN AND PERFORMED BY THE MOUNTAIN GOATS (2002) 🎵

Speaking of love, let's talk about hate. Love and hate have a very close relationship. What makes me so sure? Two reasons: (1) because of reality television, and (2) because Fyodor Dostoevsky said so (and clearly if your name is that hard to spell and you are still famous, then you are a very wise type of Russian artist and very much worth listening to). Fyodor's exact words were: "To fall in love does not mean to love. One can fall in love and still hate." From nineteenth-century Russia to in your face! young lovers. Wadda guy.

Anyway, in the album *Tallahassee*, singer-songwriter John Darnielle (aka the Mountain Goats) explores this idea in depth and with a stunning array of carefully observed details. Every single word is simultaneously subtle and yet also clearly out to kill. Normally, we see the love before we see the hate, but in this case that process is reversed. These two people are lost from the first. They now spend their days loving and hating each other at their ramshackle house in Tallahassee, which seems to have been built as a shrine to their failed relationship. They are more full of bile than a 10-ton bile bomb. But the intensity of that emotion and the bond they share in their mutual hatred is something that we can't help but identify as genuine. They know each other too well to scale back the warfare. The only way forward is destruction: "And I hope you die. I hope we both die." Love, your husband.

3 GONE GIRL
WRITTEN BY GILLIAN FLYNN (2012)

This is the one that really stings. For all of the cynicism in the other entries on this list, *Gone Girl* is the book that takes ideas like "love is a disease," "love and hatred are the same emotion," and "all relationships are doomed," and shows that that's not even half the story. Does that sound dark? It is. But it is also insightful, endlessly surprising, and endlessly entertaining. The novel begins as a murder mystery, then expands into the autopsy of a dead marriage, then becomes a procedural, and then the twists start twisting, and you don't know who to trust or who to root for or why we don't just give up and play video games all day if this is what humans are like. Humans aren't all that bad, of course, but the two main characters in this novel really are. It's hard to imagine two more unbelievable characters in the end, but at no point is there ever any room for a reader to doubt their existence. They are just too well realized to be dismissed.

Welcome to relationship Hell—the best place on Earth.

2 ETERNAL SUNSHINE OF THE SPOTLESS MIND
WRITTEN BY CHARLIE KAUFMAN (2004)

I haven't personally conducted any studies on the topic, but it seems likely that, in terms of sheer numbers, more relationships end in sadness than they do in anger, so let's put away the righteous fury for a minute and take a deep dive into the swamp of sorrows. That's what *Eternal Sunshine* is for. It reminds us that knowledge is power and that power corrupts, that when things get serious they usually get complicated, and that everyone dies in the end. That sounds, at first glance, like a Nordic art film if ever there was one, but in the hands of Charlie Kaufman (and director Michel Gondry), those angsty ideas are filtered through a truly innovative plot, becoming fresh, funny, beautiful, and profound.

There are few scenes as romantic or prosaic as the scene that sets the movie on its course, in which the two main characters (played by Jim Carrey and Kate Winslet) meet on a train platform in Long Island. And to see the tragedy inherent in that same meeting, later on, is what people mean when they say "climax." *Eternal Sunshine* is philosophy, poetry, cinema, and prose. It's an elegy to the act of falling in love, and there's nothing more tragic than that.

1 BLUE VALENTINE
STARRING RYAN GOSLING AND MICHELLE WILLIAMS (2010)

Dean Pereira (Ryan Gosling) and Cindy Heller Pereira (Michelle Williams) are two young and attractive people who meet cutely and then fail familiarly. That's basically what happens in the course of *Blue Valentine*. But to watch two people be themselves, be likeable, and yet each, on their own, fail to be the person their partner expected them to be, is heartbreaking in the extreme. And relatable. And poignant. And beautiful. Raymond Carver wrote a lot of stories about this experience and a lot of writers have followed in his footsteps, but to see this story put on film is something almost entirely new. We expect short stories and novels to be subtle and deep; we don't expect that from our movies. Maybe we should, though, because this is, without a doubt, a serious form of entertainment. But entertainment nonetheless.

In conclusion, let us feed on the nutrients of human tears, shall we?

MARTIN LUTHER KING JR. DAY
SPEECHES WORTH HEEDING

From "Give me liberty or give me death" to "Four score and seven years ago" to "I Have a Dream," American history is ripe with big statements and iconic speeches. But in order for a speech to really have an impact, there also needs to be a cause. Martin Luther King was a profoundly eloquent man (as with Lincoln, we don't need to hear him speak to feel the impact of his words), but he also had a cause whose inherent justice was hard to ignore. And that tension—between justice and injustice, and between the dreams that we have and the reality that we face—is what makes his speech so enduringly poignant. When you watch him deliver his "I Have a Dream" speech, you can feel his truth and sense the way that his own experiences interact with his restrained yet still beautiful language.

The problem is, this is now a very hard speech to actually watch—unless you have the DVD. So if you're in the market for good causes and great oratory, you'll have to look elsewhere. The items included here can't match the importance or the impact of MLK's address, but they can provide that cathartic sense of shifting fortunes and righting wrongs. So, without further ado, LET'S DO IT! [Runs, screaming, out of nearest exit.]

10 MARLON BRANDO'S "I COULDA BEEN A CONTENDAH" SPEECH FROM ON THE WATERFRONT
DIRECTED BY ELIA KAZAN (1954)

Marlon Brando was already a huge celebrity by the time *On the Waterfront* released. He'd starred in the Broadway production and the film adaptation of *A Streetcar Named Desire*, and it was immediately clear that he was the next big actor and that he was bringing the next big thing (his hyper-intense, all-in acting style). His rise to fame was so quick and his persona was so unique that he's often used as a kind of a joke today, but there's an easy remedy for the temptation to laugh him off: All you have to do is watch him. In this scene from *On the Waterfront*, down-and-out boxer Terry Malloy explains to his brother, Charley, the difference between being somebody and being a bum. It was the thrown fight that cost him a shot at the title but also, "It was you, Charley." The lines are direct and heavy, but when Brando delivers them, they land with more than the force of a punch; they land with the weight of a lifetime.

Martin Scorsese revisited the moment in his 1980 film *Raging Bull* (about another ex-boxer, Jake LaMotta, played by Robert De Niro). Amazingly, Scorsese and De Niro manage to put the weight of yet another life behind these words. That's a testament not only to De Niro's ability, but also to the influence that Brando had on the larger world of acting and film. It's a scene that is deep and profound not because we don't know exactly what's going on within it, but because we feel like we're watching a soul in motion.

9 GREGORY PECK'S CLOSING SPEECH IN TO KILL A MOCKINGBIRD
BASED ON THE NOVEL BY HARPER LEE (1962)

There's nothing like the closing argument in a trial if you're looking for a well-written, well-delivered speech. But once you're in the courtroom, the pressure of that looming moment can often prove overwhelming and pull us, as viewers, out of the scene. Some of the greatest courtroom dramas ever produced (including *Anatomy of a Murder*) have opted to forsake such a scene entirely rather than risk it. But there's another option: You can always go quiet. Rather than amping up the volume, you can tone it down. That's the route that Gregory Peck takes as Atticus Finch in his defense of an innocent black man in *To Kill a Mockingbird*. The case is clear enough in its facts, but the town's white majority wants to see the defendant, Tom Robinson, hanged. No matter what. The speech is eloquent, reasonable, and just. But it's not enough. And sometimes it's gratifying to see the enduring injustice of our world actually reflected, at least in some small part, in a film.

8 BILL MURRAY'S CHAPEL SPEECH IN *RUSHMORE*
DIRECTED BY WES ANDERSON (1998)

Speaking of justice, Herman Blume (Bill Murray's character in Rushmore) sees only one truly valid form of justice, namely, personal justice. In his world, he is the winner and he deserves to be the winner. And if he is not winning, then someone else needs to pay. This outlook in perfectly summed up in Herman's brief speech to the students at Rushmore Academy High School, whom he tells to "take dead aim . . . on the rich boys. Get them in the cross hairs . . . and take them down." ("Best chapel speaker I have ever seen," notes his soon-to-be-protégé/antagonist Max Fischer.) This sounds like a recipe for tragedy or parody, but in fact *Rushmore* evolves into a tender, childish (in the best sense) romantic comedy. This speech is an essential reminder that, once someone gets up on a podium, we generally expect to know, pretty much, what they're about to tell us. But surprises are still possible up there. And when surprises happen, history is made. So rich boys, watch out.

7 BILL MURRAY'S SPEECH IN *MEATBALLS*
DIRECTED BY IVAN REITMAN (1979)

Bill Murray again?! No, not true. Not "again," because this is not the same Bill Murray. The Bill Murray that we know today lives his life at the bottom of a metaphorical pool of depression, littered with cigarettes, black-eyed squirrels ("hey squirelly") and empty beer cans. The original Bill Murray, however, was like dynamite in a paint can: he was threatening, lively, and likely to end in a mess—but a mess that would leave you laughing and shaking your head for days afterward. Is that a confusing metaphor? Well, so is Bill Murray. *Meatballs* is your standard '80s summer camp comedy. There's a good camp and a bad camp, and in the year-end tournament, the bad team is winning. That's where counselor Murray comes in. His speech is brief (again), but pointed. They have more money, resources, and talent, he says, but in the end "it just doesn't matter." This outlook quickly transforms from a fact into a mantra into a wail and then into a chant and finally into a rallying cry. "IT JUST DOESN'T MATTER!!" the campers cry. And they believe it. Whatever that means, they believe it. Sometimes, that's rhetoric. Always, that's funny.

6 KURT RUSSELL'S PREGAME SPEECH IN *MIRACLE*
DIRECTED BY GAVIN O'CONNOR (2004)

You can't have a list of speeches and not include at least one locker room speech. And although *Miracle* may not have the emo-cred of a *Hoosiers* or a *Rudy*, it does have a sports moment that's hard to beat (the 1980 US Men's Olympic hockey team's victory over the USSR in the midst of the Cold War), and it's got a speech to match. There's nothing unexpected here. The USSR is bigger, faster, stronger, and icier, but the USA is the USA—and it has Kurt Russell. And even when Kurt Russell is wearing suit pants that would make a beige disco ball blush, you still cannot say no to him. "One game. If we played 'em ten times they might win nine. But not this game. Not. Tonight." So many clipped sentences in this man. And so much intensity. There are no surprises in this movie, but when something truly unbelievable has occurred, then that lack of surprises only adds to the suspense. And to the pleasure.

5 THE "ST. CRISPIN'S DAY" SPEECH FROM *HENRY V* WRITTEN BY WILLIAM SHAKESPEARE (CIRCA 1599)

Motivational speeches exist for a reason. They exist because there are a lot of things that people would otherwise much prefer not to do. Few people, if given a choice between hand-to-hand combat and a nice nap at home, would prefer the battle scenario (especially given the state of surgeons/barbers in 1415); and even less would choose the battle option if outnumbered to the extent that the English were during the Battle of Agincourt. That's where King Henry (aka Prince Harry; aka his royal drunkenness) comes in.

Death, under these circumstances, seems not unlikely, but instead of bluffing past this prospect he doubles down on it. He says yes, we may die, but if we do, there could hardly be a better death. (And a lot of other things, too, and with a much better sense of rhythm and timing and all that other Bardy stuff). *Henry V* is more or less explicit propaganda, but its entertainment quotient remains high because Shakespeare populates his stage version of England with people we really do like and care about and want to root for. Plus, the play is packed full of memorable lines. If you're feeling bold, throw on Kenneth Branagh's version, but if you're in the mood for something a little less Little Lord Fauntleroy-y, just go back to the original script. Even today, the words ring out like destiny.

4 GENERAL GEORGE S. PATTON'S SPEECH IN *PATTON* DIRECTED BY FRANKLIN J. SCHAFFNER (1970)

. . . And then there's the other kind of motivation. The kind where instead of generating goodwill, troops either grow extra testicles or retire to Smurf village. That's the kind of speech that General George S. Patton specialized in, and that's the speech he delivered, in secret, to thousands of American soldiers before the Normandy landings in World War II. That speech is replicated almost line for line in the film version (with an enormous American flag included as a backdrop), and it was an instantaneous hit. The speech changed slightly as the real Patton delivered it in different places, but the essential points remain the same: you don't win a war by dying for your country, you win it by making other people die for theirs; Americans want winners and Americans want to fight; and cowards and the German enemy both need to be killed—along with a few *Saturday Evening Post* contributors for good measure.

General Patton was not an inoffensive man. Nor was he un-violent. But his speech has certainly got panache and personality. And if you've got troops that are anxious and tired, it can't hurt to loosen them up a bit. And calling everyone bastards and spitting at your enemies seems like it was probably pretty effective in that respect. The speech has stuck around. And even though America has lost a few wars in the meantime, Patton was right about one thing: America loves obscenity and "real talk" almost as much as Patton loved revolvers and riding crops. It's a winning recipe. Just ask HBO.

3 NIKE'S *"LEAVE NOTHING"* TELEVISION SPOT DIRECTED BY MICHAEL MANN (2007) 🖥

Now before going any further, it is worth noting that this advertisement contains zero spoken words. So it's not technically a speech. BUT. If actions speak louder than words, then who needs words anyway? The 60-second ad shows two NFL stars at the time—linebacker Shawne Merriman and running back Stephen Jackson—as they, respectively, tackle all the way up the field and then run the ball all the way back. The ad ends with Jackson struggling to break the plane of the goal line despite the bets efforts of six or seven defenders. Does that sound intense? It is. And then director Michael Mann went back into his toolbox and pulled the score from *The Last of the Mohicans* and slapped that on top of everything. Then he (presumably) proclaimed "Fin," dropped the mic, and walked out of the production studio, never to return again. Not sure if that is factual, but it seems right.

2 OPRAH'S LIFETIME ACHIEVEMENT AWARD ACCEPTANCE SPEECH DELIVERED BY OPRAH WINFREY (1998) 🖥

Speaking of an eloquence that transcends words: Oprah. If you are not careful, then Oprah will make you feel and then Oprah will make you cry. And if she is careful, then it doesn't matter what you do, because you are now subject to Oprah's whims. That sounds diabolical in those terms, but the deeply un-diabolical secret of her power lies in her reliance on empathy. She can only make us feel what she herself is experiencing. So if she's losing, we're losing, and if she's winning, we're winning (often literally). That's why, despite their reputation, the Emmys really aren't that bad. They give us moments like this, when Barbara Walters presents Oprah with her Lifetime Achievement Award, and Oprah manages to be both self-possessed and enraptured. Looking back on her life, we can all feel the staggering surprise of her success. She can feel it, too. And yet here she is, the undeniable fact of the matter. This speech shows that she doesn't take her success for granted and (more shockingly, from a now-superstar) that she doesn't think it means the problems of the world have thus been solved. "We are all beacons of light for each other," she says. And she appears to really mean it. Huh.

1 MEL GIBSON'S "FREEDOM" [AKA "FREEDOMMMM"] SPEECH IN *BRAVEHEART* DIRECTED BY MEL GIBSON (1995)

Well, here we are. There's no getting away from it. "It" in this case is *Braveheart*, and if the topic is speeches and the question is what's number one, then "it"—*Braveheart*—is the answer. *Braveheart* is the great film of American independence that America never got. Plus, face paint, accents, Mel "Jesus" Gibson, and fart jokes. It's easy to laugh at it from a distance, but from up close it's hard not to cry. If you gave a Muppet long odds, periwinkle face paint, a galloping horse, and the rallying cry of "Freeeee. Dommmmmm!!!" even that silly little Muppet couldn't have failed to have had an effect, and with a wild-eyed Mel Gibson, man do those lines land. This wasn't the first motivational speech captured on film, not by a long shot, but it has become the speech that parodists mock, that imitators imitate, and that competitors have to cope with. Like the shower scene in *Psycho* or the closing scene in *Casablanca*, it's a game-changer.

[Cut to Mel Gibson on a craggy rock, surveying landscape. Scene.]

BONUS! 40 INSPIRATIONAL SPEECHES IN 2 MINUTES CREATED BY MATTHEW BELINKIE (2008)

If you can't get enough of motivational speeches, then you should definitely check out this supercut, which uses all the stock moments and much parodied tropes of "inspirational" films to tell a story entirely its own. It's revealing and hilarious and, surprisingly/unsurprisingly, pretty, um, captivating. Okay, just pass the handkerchiefs and SHUT UP. Just watch.

INDEPENDENCE DAY
THE BEST SOURCES OF AMERICATTITUDE

The Fourth of July is a holiday that begs the question: fourth what of July? Day? Well, sure, maybe. But who knows? Maybe some segment of America the beautiful celebrates the "Fourth Mesh-Shirt Sighting of July" instead. In this nation of free speech, free Yellow Pages, and *Free Willy* sequels (we made four movies about a whale escaping from humans!), anything is possible. Just when you think that you have us pinned down, we slip out of your grasp and show you something new. Oh, you thought Americans were citizens of England and loyal subjects to King George III? WRONG! Don't tread on us! Or maybe you thought that Americans were a sexually repressed people who flinched at the very notion of human bodies in motion? Sorry, you lose. We put nudity in everything now. Or maybe you thought that we loved money, just money, and that that was the point of everything we did? Ha-ha, nice try, Euro-skeptics! Look at our national bank account! We disdain money.

We are slippery like a snake, but hardy like a bear, and bold like a sassy peacock. We are the bear-snake-sassy-peacock-thing that you fear in your nightmares but admire in your dreams. And this list shows us as we truly are—sometimes, but not always. This list is, so to speak, the Fourth America of July.

10 THE CALL OF THE WILD
WRITTEN BY JACK LONDON (1903)

When we think "great American novels with animals in them," we think *Moby-Dick*—and that response is as natural as it is right. *Moby-Dick* is a work of genius. But it's also long. So sure, if you've got some time to spare, or if it's not Independence Day and you're not going to be distracted by fireworks and sirens, then go ahead and read about the whale. But if you're with Poor Richard in thinking that a stitch in time saves nine (and if you do think that, please first tell everyone else what that phrase can possibly mean), then go with the much shorter, much breezier, much doggier *Call of the Wild*. Author Jack London knew whereof he wrote. He lived a wild life, but he wrote with a fairly stunning degree of control.

Even though his books were written for a paycheck and even though he wrote to entertain, there's hardly a word out of place in *The Call of the Wild* (or in his other works, such as *White Fang* or "To Build a Fire"). It's impossible to tear yourself away, so you're forced to just stick with Buck (a domesticated St. Bernard-Scotch Collie) as he is kidnapped, shipped to the Arctic, and forced to either fight for life or die. The longer he lives the more bestial he becomes, but there's a kind of genius in that, too. And there's certainly genius in this story. It takes us to the extremes of civilization and asks if that brings us closer to who we are, or if it bears us farther away. It's a good question.

9 ROBOCOP
DIRECTED BY PAUL VERHOEVEN (1987)

What's a Robocop? Well, it's just like a robo-duck or a robo-dog, but its duty is to serve and protect. Oh, and also, a Robocop is made of a mostly dead, very betrayed, very shot-up cop (played by Peter Weller), plus lots of extra robo-parts. The film takes place in "the future," but as soon as the first robot turns on its human programmers and shoots the proverbial shit out of everyone in sight, then you know that we have now entered the political commentary zone. There's ultraviolence, melodrama, comedy, and also a real point. And its main character is a sympathetic cop who is also pretty excellent at stopping gun violence. And is a robot! Or at least robot-ish. What's more (or less) American than that!? Plus, it's directed by the same non-American filmmaker who brought us *Starship Troopers* and *Showgirls*!

8 THE AMAZING ADVENTURES OF KAVALIER & CLAY
WRITTEN BY MICHAEL CHABON (2000)

Superman is the American superhero. But if you examine him as a character, he's not that interesting. He's uncompromising, he's moral, and his romantic life is straight out of (and straight into) a thousand Hollywood scripts. As a phenomenon, however, he is absolutely out of this world. That's the key insight of Michael Chabon's hilarious, thrilling, and prize-winning novel. Superman was a character of maximum strength created by people of minimal power. The entire comics industry, in fact, arose at the hands of some poor, dorky Jewish kids just when Hitler was marching German troops all over Europe. It was the baldest projection ever, but it was pure genius. Chabon follows the career of his two proxy Superman creators (Kavalier and Clay) as they develop their own superhero (the Escapist), profit from their creation, and then deal with the fallout. The American dream is a great idea, but most great dreams lack a plot; this book doesn't.

7 ILLMATIC
WRITTEN AND PERFORMED BY NAS (1994)

Have you heard of beats? It's okay if you haven't. Nas has.

Do you like it when early-'90s hip-hoppers drop knowledge into little windows between beats? Do you like it when that happens on one of the greatest rap albums of all time? Do you like it when the rap genre as a whole is reinvented and rediscovered? Well, whether you do or don't, you should. Nas's *Illmatic* is a reminder of what something new sounds like. It's always great. Always fresh. And always all-American in a way that may be surprising. But it's like Walt Whitman's poetry or Ernest Hemingway's prose or Janis Joplin's voice: Before it came around there was nothing like it, but after it arrived, it was part of the America we had always known. Our country has always been associated more with optimism than fatalism, but Nas's central chorus of "life's a bitch, and then you die," isn't just the end of the story, it's also the beginning. Most of the '90s sounds dated and even laughable now, but this album still sounds immortal.

6 AMERICAN GODS
WRITTEN BY NEIL GAIMAN (2001)

America is a young nation. In terms of our politics, this was a boon, because we were able to look back on the mistakes of other nations and try to create a perfecter (or "more perfect," if you prefer) union. But in terms of our cultural identity, this presented a lot of problems. For many years, we were not bound under a single name and we did not have a single past to reflect upon. So here we are now, hyphenated Americans marked in colors red and blue, sharing a culture but wondering what our culture is and looking to ourselves for answers. Individually we might find them, from time to time, but collectively? Good luck.

American Gods is about the tension of identity. It follows a character named Shadow after he is released from jail, begins a new life, and rapidly finds himself embroiled in a battle between old and new. Before long we realize that his mentor, Mr. Wednesday, is one of the old Gods who followed early immigrants to America and thrived (or died) in the same measure that those immigrants believed in them, and he is now engaged in a massive struggle against the new *American Gods* (like credit cards and the internet) who have modernity on their side. This great American novel (written by an Englishman) is surprisingly mundane for an epic, but sometimes that's the way it should be: Sometimes we show our fidelity to a national spirit by ordering eggs for breakfast, and sometimes we betray ourselves by simply saying "nay."

America is deep terrain, and Neil Gaiman picks up the plow like few Americans ever have.

5 ROSEANNE
STARRING ROSEANNE BARR AND JOHN GOODMAN (1988-1997)

Roseanne Barr is the kind of woman who's capable of both spitting on America and running for president of the United States. She's bold and smart and thoroughly unpredictable. So in retrospect, it's not surprising that she was the lynchpin of *Roseanne*—a show that celebrated normal, blue-collar Americans while also calling attention to everything that was eternally doomed about normal, blue-collar life in the actual United States. What's more surprising, in retrospect, is the hit sitcom's subtlety. The Conners—the family at the center of the show— had real problems. Problems paying the bills (the lights went out in one famous episode), problems raising teenagers, and problems even just treating each other like family. It might be an exaggeration to call the show "profound," but looking back it doesn't seem unfair to say that it was "revolutionary." (Also, so very many excellent guest stars.)

4 JESUS' SON
WRITTEN BY DENIS JOHNSON (1992) 📖

The French have their poetry, the Italians have their sculptures, and we Americans—sticking with these stereotypes—we Americans have our action movies. But the thing is, the French also have the guillotine (a not very subtle instrument), the Italians have Silvio Berlusconi (again, not indelicate), and we Americans have the short story. We have Ernest Hemingway, Flannery O'Connor, Raymond Carver, Tim O'Brien, and Denis Johnson. These writers have all helped to establish a genre that is now equal parts poetry and prose. They all write with the poetry of the human voice—as it actually exists in the real world, with real problems. *Jesus' Son* contains 11 stories, one voice, and, with apologies, pretty much infinite beauty. Every sentence feels like it has been dragged through the dirt and raised up to heaven and blessed on both occasions. We tend to pass by people who seem "down and out" or "crazy as all hell"—but this book provides us with the occasion to stop and wonder. That's it. It's miraculous.

3 AT FOLSOM PRISON
PERFORMED BY JOHNNY CASH (1968) 🎵

Is there anything more American than a middle finger to The Man? With the possible exception of a bald eagle cooking the perfect steak, the answer is no. And is there anything more The Mannish than a warden at a state prison? Probably not. (And if there is, then that other thing is probably best left alone.) In *At Folsom Prison*, Johnny Cash performed before a literally captive audience, but that captive audience got just about the best show that anyone is ever likely to see. They saw Johnny Cash at a turning point, fighting for fame, success, and for his life as a musician. He was fighting against himself, against his past, and against the present, and he was going to win. Part of the reason why he has the reputation he does today is because of this performance, which contains a thrilling blend of measured music and riotous energy; but it's also got the weariness and rawness that comes of performing a private struggle on a public stage. It's honest, it's brave, and it's up yours, Warden. In conclusion: America, fuck yeah.

2 HE GOT GAME
WRITTEN AND DIRECTED BY SPIKE LEE (1998)

Before the opening credits have finished rolling in *He Got Game*, it has already become apparent that Spike Lee is not interested in making a small movie. He is going big or going home. How do we know this? "Music by Aaron Copland. Songs by Public Enemy." It sounds bold and it is, but it also sounds like a recipe for a hilarious disaster. It is not.

Aaron Copland was the classical composer who adapted traditional American folk songs like "Simple Gifts" into majestic orchestral events; Public Enemy is the hugely influential '90s rap group behind "Fight the Power." *He Got Game* blends their polarized aesthetics into something that's shockingly intuitive, organic, and subtle. How does he manage this? The answer is by adding basketball, and because he's Spike Lee. The movie examines the prospects and perils of a highly recruited basketball prospect living in Staten Island (played by actual basketball star Ray Allen). It's a drama that centers around a sport, but it's not a sports movie. This is a human drama, first and foremost, and the drama here is something that is distinctly American. It's big, brash, loud, and honest. And just when you think you know what it's up to, Denzel Washington falls in love with a prostitute. From start to finish, it's a beautiful surprise.

1 "THE STAR SPANGLED BANNER"
AS PERFORMED BY WHITNEY HOUSTON AT SUPER BOWL XXV (1991)

When a song has been performed as many times as "The Star Spangled Banner" has, you had better put on your best pair of spangling pants if you want to stand out. Or, if you are not a practiced spangler, you had better be Whitney Houston. She wore a plain white tracksuit to her performance at Super Bowl XXV in Tampa, but then she sang like a Whitney Houston and smiled like a star. Confidence? Check. Charisma? Check. Bravado? Discount double check to the power of ten. She sounds great (as it should—it was recorded in a studio), she looks like she's not even trying, and she makes us remember that our national anthem really is a kind of alright song. (Even if "America the Beautiful" is better.) This performance is what the phrase "holy smokes" was invented for. Because holy smokes, what a pair of lungs on that gal! (Said the oldest man in attendance in attendance at Super Bowl XXV.)

Trivia question: Who won Super Bowl XXV?
(Hint: The Buffalo Bills were in it, and the Buffalo Bills have never won a Super Bowl. And the New York Giants were the other team).

Trivia answer: Whitney Houston.

MOTHER'S DAY
CELEBRATING SOME UNDERAPPRECIATED ACTS OF POP-CULTURAL PROCREATION

Just because Mother's Day and Father's Day were created as part of a massive conspiracy to sell Hallmark cards and commit us all to brunches we don't want to attend, that doesn't mean that these holidays are not also deeply valuable. No one wants to get ontological, but the fact remains that, had someone not made us with someone else, we would not exist. So yeah, hey, waddup parents. And thanks.

But one quick question for "parents:" Are you our parents, really? I mean, moms are pretty hard to dispute, but dads? Less so, at best. In honor of that enduring uncertainty we offer this list. Here, we go beyond the apparent parents and try to root out the real and metaphorical ma- and pa-ternity behind the shows, genres, and people we love.

10 EDGAR ALLAN POE BEGETS . . . THE DETECTIVE STORY

Most of the world's genres have been around pretty much forever. *The Iliad* and *The Odyssey* are older than the written word is in Greece, and they set the templates that we still use for action movies, revenge tales, and the road-trip genre. St. Augustine wrote his *Confessions* (the first autobiography) nearly a thousand years before Gutenberg's printing press arrived on the scene in Europe. And it's hard to think of any story that doesn't have a precedent in the Bible (more on that in a moment). But the detective story is a true outlier here and a true newcomer. Edgar Allen Poe wrote *The Murders in the Rue Morgue* in 1841, and with that, the detective story was born—and with it the character of the detective as well. C. Auguste Dupin is smart, methodical, and determined, and even in his first appearance you can see where Sherlock Holmes and Hercule Poirot (among others) learned their trade and gained their sense of style. The only thing missing here is the butler. And thank goodness for that, because otherwise we'd be deprived of what is, still, a shocking conclusion.

9 MEDIEVAL HISTORY BEGETS . . . GAME OF THRONES

There's a moment in the second season of *Game of Thrones* when Tyrion Lannister (played by Peter Dinklage) opts not for a standard trial (which he knows would not be just), but instead for a trial by combat. It's a pretty awesome idea and a pretty awesome scene, but it's also a choice that real human beings were actually able to make in the actual real world. That is nuts! But it is far from the only nuts thing that *Game of Thrones* borrows from the Middle Ages. In fact, much of the power dynamics and even the personality types are lifted from the England's War of the Roses. The names are changed, of course, and the dragons are added, but it really is astounding to think that there is a real precedent for the deeply cynical and astoundingly cruel actions of the characters in the series. It's also astounding to think that people fought to the death with so many weapons that are, essentially, variations of "metal on a stick." Trial by combat is bad enough in the case of a duel, but if you're shot in the head at least you die quickly. Death by war hammer is, I think, not a fast or pleasant way to go. (Unless you are fighting Thor.)

8 GEORGE R. STEWART BEGETS . . . THE NATURAL DISASTER FILM GENRE

George R. Stewart's novel *Earth Abides* (1949) is a landmark work of post-apocalyptic (post-plague, more specifically) fiction and was the inspiration for Stephen King's own classic, *The Stand*. His academic work of non-fiction, *Names on the Land*, provides an incredible history of America through the names of its cities, towns, counties, lakes, and mountains. But his most lasting contributing to American pop culture is

GEORGE R. STEWART

perhaps found in *Storm* (1941) and *Fire* (1948)—two books in which a natural disaster plays the roles of villain and main character. These books set the stage for films like *Backdraft, Twister, The Perfect Storm, Contagion*, and even *Jaws*. *Storm* is also the reason that we now give female names to hurricanes. Stewart doesn't get a lot of credit these days (perhaps because of the existence of more disastrous disaster films like *Dante's Peak, 2012, Deep Impact*, and many, many more), but for an academic, he certainly had an eye for profitable genres. Give that man a movie studio! (And then, please, take that studio back away from him; storms don't really need a hype man.)

7 DISNEY'S MOUSEKETEERING PROGRAM BEGETS · · · ENTERTAINMENT SUPERSTARS 🖥

The peripatetic school of Athens. The mail room at William Morris Endeavor. FC Barcelona's training program. Disney's Mouseketeers.

The alumni for these programs are, as a rule, extraordinary. They turn into great philosophers, revolutionary entertainers, sublime soccer players, and 'N Sync. And look, this level of success is not surprising if the founder of your program is a world-historical genius—but it is surprising when your students are collectively known as "Mouseketeers." The list is truly shocking: Keri Russell, Christina Aguilera, Britney Spears, Justin Timberlake, and Ryan "Hey Girl" Gosling. They may not all be sane, they may not all be happy, they may not all be non-Canadian, but they are all absolutely entertaining. I don't know who finds these Mouseketeers, and I don't know who makes sure to keep them far away from the Elephantsketeers, but I do know this: That old mouse has to be the smartest and most well-compensated rodent on the face of planet Disney.

6 BRIDESMAIDS BEGETS · · · MONEY FOR COMEDIES WITH ACTUAL WOMEN 🎞

Funny women have been around for exactly as long as unfunny men have said that funny women aren't really that funny. What has not been around forever, however, is funding for movies written by female comedians. The ascendancy of Tina Fey in recent years has definitely changed the look and feel of comedy on film and television, but the rapid release of ensemble comedies like *For a Good Time Call* (starring Ari Graynor and Lauren Anne Miller) and *Bachelorette* (written and directed by Leslye Headland)—along with dramas like *Take This Waltz* (starring Michelle Williams and Sarah Silverman) and *Save the Date* (starring Lizzy Kaplan and Alison Brie)—shows that movie producers are not blind (to money when it piles up in front of them).

Bridesmaids isn't a revolutionary movie. The romance in it is pretty standard (if charming); the laughs are solid but also often reliant on bowel movements (a joke as old as time); and the absurdity is straight out of *SNL*. The one thing it has (missing from other movies of the time) is a believable and hilarious scene in which two comedians (and friends) just talk and laugh together. Not every movie can count on the hyper-dirty, ultrahilarious comic alliance of Kristen Wiig and Maya Rudolph, but female friendship is definitely not a unicorn. Nor are female comedians. So here again, this is a replicable formula. Prior to *Bridesmaids*, this fact was not in evidence. (If you need some convincing on this point, do a search for "Bechdel test.") After *Bridesmaids*, it kind of is. And when this formula gets old, that will be a good thing. It means we will be on to something new.

5 THE LAST TEMPTATION OF CHRIST BEGETS . . . DONNIE DARKO 🎞️

Some adaptations (like almost every period drama based on a book) are literal. Others (like the films of Stanley Kubrick) are spiritual. Still others (like the films of Quentin Tarantino) are pointillstic mash-ups. But the best adaptations, in my (unadapted) book, are all of the above. *Donnie Darko* is in that last camp: It combines a fairly literal adaptation of Graham Greene's incredible short story "The Destructors" with a spiritual adaptation of *The Last Temptation of Christ* (directed by Martin Scorsese). It also injects both of these works into the larger movie organically (by having the students in Donnie Darko's class read Greene's story and then setting the film in the 1980s, when *Last Temptation* first made waves).

There's no doubt that these references are part of the reason why *Donnie Darko* has developed a huge cult following, but due to all of the additional references that the film makes (to *Lolita*, *The Smurfs*, the 1988 US presidential election, and so on), it's easy to lose sight of the fact that, on a macro scale, this really is *The Last Temptation of Christ* set in the 1980s, with Donnie as Christ, science-fiction taking the place of spirituality, and love, once again, as the answer. It's a testament to the value of reinventing the wheel every once in a while.

4 RICHARD WAGNER BEGETS . . . POLITER THEATERS, THE LORD OF THE RINGS, TERRENCE MALICK'S THE NEW WORLD, AND ALMOST EVERY EPIC MOVIE SCORE EVER WRITTEN 🎵 🎞️ 📖

The headline says it all, right? And it sounds crazy, but it's true. Richard Wagner was an immensely talented, hugely revered composer (and a less talented, less revered, more despised philosopher and anti-Semite) who has had a strangely enormous impact on the world of pop culture. Before his arrival, operas were performed with the lights on, with audience members chattering away, and with a lot of people paying no attention whatsoever to what was going on. He said the German word for "oh, hell no," and turned the lights off, made the performers on stage more visible, and told the audience to zip the proverbial lip . . . or else. Then, with his Ring Cycle, he sought to make opera into something that was bigger than it had been.

He borrowed heavily from Northern European folklore to create an epic, four-part series that fused music, dance, stage-design, and philosophy into an overarching Gesamtkunstwerk—a "total work of art." This cycle, in turn, provided the philosophical underpinnings for Terrence Malick's poetic ode to early America, *The New World*, but also the thrilling, warmongering chorus behind the cynical masterpiece *Apocalypse Now*. It also provided the narrative framework and many of the themes for Tolkien's *Lord of the Ring* series.

Perhaps his most ubiquitous innovation, however, was his use of leitmotifs—recurring musical themes that were used to identify each character and whose alterations and combinations over time were also intended to offer some insight into a given character's evolution and/or degeneration. The idea of the leitmotif is now pervasive in almost all dramatic art, but it remains most present in musical scores, where it's now often used to simply set a scene or announce an arrival. Like the ring, it's not the tool that matters, it's how you use it.

So in summary: Wagner—bad man, great artist.

3 THE BIBLE BEGETS . . . A LOT OF THINGS, QUIETLY

It's hard to say that the Bible is "underappreciated" since it's been translated into nearly every language, imported into nearly every country, and put to bed in every open hotel drawer, but the Good Book's very omnipresence can also make it invisible. This lack of visibility is exacerbated by the fact that the Bible has A TON of different stories in it. So even if you were looking for biblical elements in a space opera, say, or in a song, you'd need either a heads-up that a certain story was coming your way or else a very explicit reference. And since explicit references don't usually make for great art, well, there we are: a lot of Bible shout-outs go slipping through the cracks.

Star Wars is a relatively recent example of a case where biblical elements were kind of smuggled in, but an even more telling case is contained in Thomas Mann's multivolume classic *Joseph and His Brothers*. This was a work that Mann undertook after immigrating to America prior to World War II, and he was inspired by the similarities between Joseph's ancient story and the classic tale of the American dream. So to put it another way, Mann was hoping to tell a new story by telling an old story and letting us see how American it had become. Or, to invert the formula again, how biblical we now are. It is, in the end, a great story and a great novel because of how little has changed. We're still human and so is the story and, even when it's stretched over 2,000 pages, this is still a story that we all want to hear.

2 THE HEADLINES BEGET · · · EVERYTHING, ALL THE TIME

Here is just a small sampling of the things that the news provoked, inspired, and/or promoted: the collected works of Fyodor Dostoevsky, *In Cold Blood*, *The Onion*, *Law & Order*, *The Wire*, crossword puzzles, *The Daily Show*, *South Park*, *Zero Dark Thirty*, *Thirty Rock*, the collected quips of Jay Leno, a rash of gorilla attacks in New York City (because of copycat gorillas), an equal and opposite rash reaction of tabby cat ingenuity in Long Island (because of copy-gorilla cats), future presidents, ex-presidents, presidential cats—if it's happening in real life then it happened in the headlines first and it's coming to a theater near you. Don't fight it. Just consume it, fear the world, expect the worst, and enjoy your nightmares.

1 THE BROTHERS KARAMAZOV BEGETS · · · ARRESTED DEVELOPMENT 🖥 📖

This is a crazy thing to say. *The Brothers Karamazov* is frequently included in discussions about the greatest book of all time. *Arrested Development* is frequently included in discussions about the greatest and most-elaborate auto-fellatio puns of all time. If that last sentence makes no sense, be alerted that Tobias Fünke (played by David Cross) hopes, someday, to become a member of the Blue Man Group, and thus has occasion to report, in his words, "I blue myself."

That joke provides a very small sampling of the tone and reach, as it were, of this much beloved comedy. It also gives a sense of its utter frivolousness. That's why it came as such a surprise when, in January of 2012, Helen Rittelmeyer wrote an article for *First Things* (a magazine published by the Institute on Religion in Public Life), in which she outlined the very close similarities between both the families and the plots at the center of these two works. It's a convincing case. And the realization that a profound work of theology, philosophy, and fiction could be at the heart of something so utterly silly and fun is, I think, a testament to how hard it is to be entertaining, no matter what genre you may be working in. You work with what works. Sometimes the thing that works is drawn from world literature and other times it's drawn from the intense weirdness of Liza Minnelli—either way, it's genius.

THANKSGIVING
AD HOC FAMILIES THAT WILL DO IN A PINCH

Theory: Thanksgiving is a trap. When you look at it from afar, it looks peaceful, calming, and pleasant. All you can see is a four-day weekend, lots of food, some movies, and a nice little spot on the couch. It's only when you've committed yourself that the day reveals its true intentions. Your four-day weekend is three days with family and one day spent in recovery—if you're lucky. There's lots of food but you'll have to pass a pop quiz ("What are you thankful for") before you can enjoy it. And that fantasy about movies and a couch? Well, good luck. So in conclusion, Thanksgiving is a holiday like that sun-dappled patch of leaves and grass over there is a nice place to si—OH MY GOD I'M FALLING ONTO SHARPENED BAMBOO POLES!! For those that have not already fallen into a metaphorical tiger pit, there's only one real means of defense: Find a new family made of make believe people and go treat yourself to dinner (alone) at Boston Market.

This list is your guide to the very best fictional, nonfamilial families. Find the one that works for you, queue it up on Netflix, smash your computer to bits (or turn it off), and flush your phone, and I guarantee you'll have a relaxing and heartwarming holiday. (Do anything else and you have only yourself to blame.)

10 L'AUBERGE ESPAGNOLE
DIRECTED BY CÉDRIC KLAPISCH (2002)

The excitement over the European Union may have waned somewhat, but the interest in what attractive and intelligent young people will do when they share the same space and pursue the same goals remains just about exactly as interesting and engaging as it ever was. French superstar Romain Duris plays Xavier, a French college student who leaves his girlfriend (Audrey Tautou) and postpones his future in order to spend a year studying in Barcelona. The stakes are high in the sense that he needs to figure out what kind of a life he wants to lead, but they're also low in the sense that he doesn't really need to make his mind up quite yet. Everyone else that he winds up living with (in the titular auberge) is in the same situation. The movie never oversells its importance, and that's they key to its charm: It matters because we care about the characters—not because their year in Barcelona is going to change very much.

9 PITCH PERFECT
DIRECTED BY JASON MOORE (2012)

Most teams in the movies—whether they play basketball or lead cheers or sing songs—adhere to the same basic formula. There's the talented group leader who's hard to get along with, the gifted but injured one, the charming but mediocre one, the emotional wildcard, and so on. The college a cappella team in *Pitch Perfect* doesn't stray too far from these basic types, but they make these types come alive again. Rebel Wilson, for instance, plays the character "Fat Amy." That is not her real name, though; she just uses it so "twig bitches like [group leader Aubrey] don't do it behind my back." In a moment of honesty later on, she reveals her name is really "Fat Patricia." That's *Pitch Perfect*. The old formula with great music and better jokes.

8 STAND BY ME
DIRECTED BY ROB REINER (1986)

In the last scene of *Stand by Me*, the narrator (played as an adult by Richard Dreyfuss) types, "I never had any friends later on like the ones I had when I was 12. Jesus, does anyone?" The movie is based on the semiautobiographical story *"The Body,"* by Stephen King, but this concluding thought is more than just semitrue. Childhood friendships are a serious business, but in looking back on them, it's hard to say quite why they meant so much. That Stephen King and Rob Reiner were able to capture this poignancy without insisting on it is what makes the movie so special. The four young actors in the film (Wil Wheaton, Jerry O'Connell, Corey

Feldman, and River Phoenix) were hired to play kids out on a childish adventure, but they were also given a script that didn't demand that they remain children. Their characters have moments of innocence, flashes of insight, and reversions to utter immaturity. They act like humans on their way to something, which is what they are. And, of course, what we are as well. The moral? "That's life."

7 THE AVENGERS
DIRECTED BY JOSS WHEDON (2012)

Captain America goes for glory while Hulk goes for smash. Hawkeye and Black Widow both have some growing up to do. And Iron Man wants to be number one (and Thor does, too). This is the stuff that great dysfunctional families are made of, and great superhero superteams, too. This is *The Avengers*. What are they avenging? Profits unearned? Perhaps. But I prefer to think that what the Avengers are avenging is stupidity in summer blockbuster films. And they achieve their vengeance by simply speaking well, fighting hard, and enjoying themselves, no matter what. Under Joss Whedon's steady hand, no fight can keep them from joking, no joke can keep them from fighting, and despite the now traditional two-hour plus running time, nothing really ever gets in the way of anything—except, of course, for the main characters, who trip each other up with an equal degree of stubbornness and relish. In the end they save the world, but in this unique blockbuster, it's the journey that matters, not the destination.

6 SHAUN OF THE DEAD
DIRECTED BY EDGAR WRIGHT (2004)

Shaun of the Dead is what happens when really smart nerds are entrusted with time, resources, and a really good metaphor. The nerds in question are writer/director Edgar Wright, writer/actor Simon Pegg, and actor/actor Nick Frost. The time and resources in question were provided by the studio. And the metaphor in question is zombies. Admittedly, zombies have been done before, and they have been done "like this" before as well, but they have never been done like this before for comedy; this is something new. (And if that sounds like faint praise, go eat a brain and see how far that gets you. Not so nutritious, dum-dum!)

Here, the fundamental metaphor of "we are all zombies" is put into the foreground, which has the double benefit of turning a hungover commute into something truly poetic and also putting the developing relationships among the main characters into the background. And as anyone who has ever wondered why so many terrible horror movies have such great opening scenes can attest, the answer is because when the threat is palpable, there's hardly any pressure to entertain. Which makes the humans on the screen seem all the more real. So in summary, trust in this: If you've ever been intrigued by the idea of "running for your life," this is the best place for a trial run.

5 THE GOONIES
STORY BY STEVEN SPIELBERG, DIRECTED BY RICHARD DONNER (1985)

Goonies is like *Stand by Me* in that it puts children onscreen and lets them behave like actual adolescents rather than Hollywood kids, but instead of using that realistic sensibility for poignancy, here it's used to maximize the overall effects of its comedy and action. To say that another way, it's a Spielberg picture. It's Baby *Raider of the Lost Ark*, plus pirates, a hunchback, and music by Cyndi Lauper. It was made by hit-makers (including *Home Alone* director Chris Columbus, who wrote the script, and *Superman* director Richard Donner), so it was born to be a hit, but its endurance as a family favorite is a testament to both their abilities and to the appeal of the kids who were cast as the *Goonies*—including Sean Astin (who would later play Samwise Gamgee), Josh Brolin (who would later play Llewelyn Moss in *No Country for Old Men*), and Corey Feldman (who would only ever play Corey Feldman).

4 THE PERKS OF BEING A WALLFLOWER
WRITTEN BY STEPHEN CHBOSKY (1999)

A lot of books would wilt (wallflower pun alert!) under the pressure of all the sex abuse, verbal abuse, drug abuse, and insecurities that occur in Stephen Chbosky's classic high school novel. But *Perks of Being a Wallflower* has Charlie, and Charlie has friends, and together this ad hoc circle of rebels and misfits offer an open, honest, and unpretentious look at both the thrills that make teenage life so exciting (and the threats and embarrassments that make it so unbearable). MTV published this book two years before the first season of *The Real World* premiered and, although this is fiction, it still offers a blend of entertainment and interest that reality shows struggle to achieve. (Plus, no reality show has ever been better cast.) The movie version, also directed by Chbosky, isn't too shabby either.

3 NEW GIRL
CREATED BY ELIZABETH MERIWETHER (2011-)

It's hard to find a sitcom that isn't also a domestic drama. Whether we're talking about *All in the Family* or *The Cosby Show* or *Friends*, there's always a coherent kind of family structure at work. There's the character who sets things on fire, the character who puts out those fires, and then the character who pops up after the fact with a grocery bag full of left shoes and wonders why everyone's standing outside. Or you know, whatever. Anyway, the point is that in order to make this formula work, the characters need to maintain a natural balance while also continually pushing each other's buttons and providing the fodder for future jokes and fires.

It took *New Girl* a while to come to that point of entropic equilibrium, but it is definitely there now. The absurdity of Zooey Deschanel's childish outlook provides the necessary counterweight (and spur) to Schmidt's consumerist koans ("Damn it! I can't find my driving moccasins anywhere!"); Nick's howls of frustration give Winston the space he needs to mock his roommates while also opening himself up to their return-thrusts. It's fun, hilarious, absurd, and even though they're all just friends (except when they're more than that), it's also very family.

2 THE BREAKFAST CLUB
WRITTEN AND DIRECTED BY JOHN HUGHES (1985)

Back in the nineteenth century, all the best quasi-family stories were set in orphanages. But that became depressing after people realized that gruel was not just a word that people sometimes said—it was also a thing that neglected children sometimes ate. So that fad eventually passed and now all of our best fake families either come from, or take their inspiration from, John Hughes's classic film, set in detention (aka, the secular, high school version of purgatory). To put that another way: We are all born of detention. That's where we rebel, that's where we reflect, that's where we give up, and that's the place where we all find each other. We're all a hopeless mess, and the sooner we admit it the better off we'll be. Fist pump.

1 SATURDAY NIGHT LIVE
CREATED BY LORNE MICHAELS (1975-) 📺

The family that gaffes together, laughs together. Right? I think that's the line. Well, no one gaffes harder than the cast of *SNL*—because no one else really has the same opportunity. Live television with live microphones is just a tough proposition. Thirty-seven years on, they're still doing it, and they still appear to be mostly having a good time. And despite the intense pressure of working on the show and competing for airtime and preeminence, the people on the show seem to really like each other. You can sort of see it in the Stefon skits, for example, where there's a standing challenge to Bill Hader not to laugh when he reads out his advice for NYC tourists ("If you're ordinary and love salt, New York's hottest holiday club is [bellows like a goat]"), and you can definitely see it when someone like Kristen Wiig leaves the show. Her final slow dance with Mick Jagger, fellow cast members, and Lorne Michaels is a beautiful, beautiful thing. [Chills.]

CHRISTMAS
TEN WILDLY DIFFERENT INTERPRETATIONS OF THE MEANING OF CHRISTMAS

Christmas is a riddle wrapped inside an enigmatic lockbox (which is then gathered up by elves, swaddled in rags, roasted next to chestnuts, and placed underneath an enormous fir tree—as per tradition). Its mascots include a red-nosed elk, a drummer boy, a snowman, and a flaming log called "Yule." It's a Christian holiday, but pagans were the ones who gave it to us, and today it's presided over by a jolly old fat cat who breaks into people's homes and steals cookies on a global scale. So what does it all mean? Here are some of the most popular theories from pop culture, in chronological order.

10 A CHRISTMAS CAROL
WRITTEN BY CHARLES DICKENS (1843)

Dickens gave us almost every hallmark of the Christmas we now celebrate. He gave us Christmas charity and holiday feasts and, of course, "bah, humbug!" But more than that, he gave the holiday an irresistible storyline. When we celebrate Christmas today, we celebrate the sentimentality of Charles Dickens as much as anything else. At every other time of year we live our lives as Scrooges, but in December, we get to think like Tiny Tim. We get to emote. And for once, we're happy to be suckers. (It's also worth noting that almost all of the best Christmas movies—from *It's a Wonderful Life* to *Scrooged*—borrow heavily from this iconic tale.)

Verdict: During Christmas we can sob over coffee commercials without having to explain ourselves.

9 THE NUTCRACKER
COMPOSED BY PYOTR ILYICH TCHAIKOVSKY (1892)

Christmas and music have a very strong alliance. Christmas carols tend to use simple melodies—often borrowed from old religious hymns—to tell a simple story, and, if nothing else, they do an excellent job of getting inside your head and never leaving again. In other words: do-you-hear-what-I-hear-jingle-bells-jingle-bells-jingle-all-the-way-in-a-manger-no-crib-for-a-bed-the-holly-and-the-ivy-pa-rum-pa-pum-p-LEASE MAKE IT STOP! So as a result, when you get to hear music that sounds like Christmas but at the same time doesn't make you want to kill yourself, that's a great feeling. And that's a feeling that *The Nutcracker* provides in spades. Watching the ballet or even just listening to the score is like going back to childhood and experiencing these beautiful songs again. It really is magical. (Especially during "Dance of the Sugar Plum Fairies.") Also, new rule: every ballet has to have a rat king in it.

Verdict: Christmas is all about restoring a sense of childlike wonder.

8 IT'S A WONDERFUL LIFE
DIRECTED BY FRANK CAPRA (1946)

Since we were kids, everyone's been telling us that this movie is the great Christmas movie. It's on all the time, it's old, and it has Jimmy Stewart wobbling with his wobbly mouth all over the place. This is all true, but *It's a Wonderful Life* shouldn't be dismissed as naïve or simple. The climax comes after the main character—George Bailey, by name—has given up on his dreams and decided to commit suicide. And although the movie ends with tears of joy,

George Bailey is still a man who has sacrificed his own dreams to support the people that he loves. Most movies would sink under the weight of that kind of sadness, but *It's a Wonderful Life* works because it has so much life in it—it has the hard glare of reality, the disappointments of adulthood, and dozens of little moments that make George Bailey's small little life seem wonderfully real. It's basically Charles Dickens's book all over again, but with an even better (read: less saccharine) climax. If you're not sobbing at the end, or beaming at the end, or both, you must be a piece of coal.

Verdict: Christmas is a time for taking stock, but remember: "No man is a failure who has friends."

7 MIRACLE ON 34TH STREET
DIRECTED BY GEORGE SEATON (1947)

Despite the fact that both Jesus and Santa Claus thrive on belief, Christmas stories didn't find a really solid place for the theme of belief until after World War II, when *Miracle on 34th Street* was released. By placing a sweet, gentle, and childish Kris Kringle, opposite a jaded single mother (played by Maureen O'Sullivan) and her deeply cynical daughter, the movie turns Santa Claus—who up to that point had been a fairly flat symbol of joy and goodwill—into a character with the power to really change lives. And in the end, that transformation seems like much more than a simple contrivance, because in order to empower Kris Kringle, they had to first strip him of his magic. They asked what such a character would look like in everyday life, and the answer was: He'd look absolutely, totally insane. We love him immediately and we also learn, in the end, to respect him (after his optimistic brand of honesty wins out over dishonesty and disbelief), but we also have to suffer some serious doubts over Kris and his status in the real world before we get to reap the satisfaction of triumph and happy tears. Santa Claus may be the incumbent now, but this movie proves that his natural role is that of the underdog.

Verdict: Sanity and logic be damned! Christmas is a time to believe!

6 A CHARLIE BROWN CHRISTMAS
WRITTEN BY CHARLES M. SCHULZ (1965)

It turns out that Christmas and Charlie Brown were, in a way, really made for each other. For a brief period of time, Santa Claus was a real possibility in the minds of most kids, and it's hard not to look back on that time with a sense of loss and sadness. Charles Schulz always did have a way with sadness, and in the Peanuts Christmas special, he's able to indulge his affection for melancholy while at the same time providing its cure—that is, even more sadness. When Charlie Brown has to select a Christmas tree, he moves past the artificial ones and picks instead a real—and really sad—tree (in fact, it's really more of a twig). When Linus goes up onstage to explain the meaning of Christmas, he tells the story of the first Christmas, but he tells it sadly; and when the climax arrives, it's centered around the fact that Charlie Brown is even more sad than usual.

Verdict: The best Christmas is the saddest Christmas.

5 HOW THE GRINCH STOLE CHRISTMAS!
WRITTEN BY DR. SEUSS (1957)

Never one to shy away from controversy, Charlie Brown was again on the front lines of the culture wars when he asked the sprawling universe, "Isn't there anyone who knows what Christmas is all about?" Linus, as it happened, had an answer for Chucky B. (and provided it in style, with an exquisite reading of Luke 8:14), but still the debate raged on. Luckily for them, Dr. Seuss was in the hoose! (Please don't shout out rude reprisals; there's only one true Theo Geisel!) HTGSC offers a greener, rhymier version of the original Scrooge story, but the lesson has been updated. Now, in order to learn what Christmas is about, the Grinch has to first learn what it's not about. And—spoiler alert!—Dr. Charles Brown was right: It's not about the gifts. In the end, that's a lesson worth learning, because it gives you access to Who Village, and you haven't really partied until you've partied with the Whos.

Verdict: Christmas is a spirit, not a thing.

4 THREE DAYS OF THE CONDOR
DIRECTED BY SYDNEY POLLACK (1975)

Although an entire office is murdered in the opening scene, and although it's a spy thriller first and foremost, *Three Days of the Condor* thoroughly deserves a spot in the Christmas movie rotation. Instead of using the holiday season to celebrate family, friends, and goodwill for men, this film uses Christmas to show what loneliness really looks like. At the end of the movie (spoiler alert!) Robert Redford's character—code name: Condor—has no job, no contact with any friends or family, and no one he can trust; and that's the point when "God Rest Ye Merry, Gentlemen" pipes up, just to pour a little extra salt on his copious existential wounds. It's an amazingly poignant moment, and, if you've ever had a sad and lonely Christmas (and who hasn't!), it's surprisingly easy to relate to—even if you're not on the run from a ruthless assassin.

Verdict: At Christmas we have a special opportunity to be alone, together.

3 A CHRISTMAS STORY
DIRECTED BY BOB CLARK (1983)

Families are pretty weird, and Bob Clark (who also directed the Christmas horror classic *Black Christmas*) decided to make a Christmas movie exploring that topic. "Spare the pink bunny suit and spoil the movie," Bob Clark's grandmother had told him, and boy, was she ever right. Ralphie is the uncomfortable child in all of us, and I think it's safe to say that the more we can identify with Ralphie, the less likely we are to be boring as adults.

Verdict: At Christmas it's okay to be dysfunctional.

2 ELF
DIRECTED BY JON FAVREAU (2003)

Elf is the ultimate in Christmas movie mash-ups. You've got stop-motion animation references, Christmas carols, a Scrooge, an elf, Santa Claus, a redemptive plot, the theme of belief, and also reindeers, department stores, and New York City. It lacks for nothing, but like all great mash-ups, it also creates something entirely new as well: namely, a justification for eating spaghetti with syrup.

Buddy the Elf, as played by Will Ferrell, is obsessed with candy. And this makes perfect sense. Elves are sweet (except in *Scrooged!*), and therefore, elves must eat sweet things! In this way Christmas begins to take on its closest holiday competitors. You thought candy was for Halloween? No way, man—that's a Christmas thing. If you want to eat a chocolate bar on Christmas morning, now you can; and if you prefer to go whole hog and hit that spaghetti con syrup, then go for it. After all, sometimes there's no sauce left, and what are you supposed to do then. The store's closed on December 25.

Verdict: At Christmas we should binge on sugar.

1 *LOVE ACTUALLY*
DIRECTED BY RICHARD CURTIS (2003)

Lots of people talk about "the end of print" or "the end of marriage" or "the end of helium balloons." But authors still write bestsellers, people still go to Vegas, and I don't really see how helium balloons will ever truly disappear so long as their fuel can be used for making chipmunk voices. (Also, helium balloons float like four days longer than you think they will, right? They sink down to an altitude of 3.5", and then they just sit there. Do they think that's what we humans mean when we talk about "victory"?) Generally, these "end of" comments are an overstatement, but in regard to *Love Actually,* they're apt, because *Love Actually,* for all its merits, has definitely annihilated any meaning that Christmas may have had before.

The screenwriters of this blasphemous delight decided that they could just MAKE UP the meaning of Christmas. As though there were no such thing as its "real meaning!" Despite all evidence to the contrary (see previous entrees), they insist that "Christmas is the time to tell the truth." (Incidentally, I can promise you that if you try and organize a drinking game around truth-telling in this film, you will have a very hard time.) Christmas is a time for Santa Claus, even though Santa Claus doesn't exist. Christmas is a time for Rudolph, even though same. But Christmas can't be a time for telling the truth if that statement itself is already a lie. It's a contradiction, dummies! And anyway, lord knows there is a long tradition of lying in Christmas. ("No. I did not ransack the closet for future gifts." "No. You ate the fruitcake.")

But that's not to say that this movie is without value. It makes you emote like a bastard, if you can avoid the *Titanic* parts. And it also allows us all to pause and think about what Christmas really is time for, since clearly there are no rules at this point. In that vein, here are some ideas that I had, just off the top of my head: (1) Christmas is a time to bathe in eggnog; (2) Christmas is a time to play the sousaphone, regardless of musical ability, or sousaphone availability; (3) Christmas is a time to engage in battles of wit with lobsters (at gunpoint, should Christmas fall on a Thursday); and (4) Christmas is a time to eat Bart Simpson's shorts, should any such shorts remain.

Christmas is dead. Christmas is risen. Christmas is now more powerful than ever.

Verdict: Christmas is the one chance you get to construct traditions out of whole cloth.

NEW YEAR'S EVE
PARTIES THAT WILL GET YOU PUMPED FOR PARTIES

New Year's Eve is a great holiday that, by all accounts, no one actually enjoys. It's a huge party night, but since the stakes are high, no one wants to commit too early, so no party really looks that good until too late, so then oh god it's 11:30 and here we are with Dick Clark again and honestly it is impossible what year is happening now and what year is happening next. Every year looks exactly the same, and every year ends in exactly the same way—with a ball dropping, a panic mounting, and then chaos. Or depression. And either way almost everyone generally loses, except for those on TV.

So yeah, it's hard to get up for New Year's Eve. BUT! The greater the challenge, the greater the reward. So let's pre-game with great games. Let's watch the parties that did turn out well to pump ourselves up for the parties that won't turn out well. (Eeeeeee-yore.) Let's start the new year off right.

10 THE HANGOVER
DIRECTED BY TODD PHILLIPS (2009)

Party style: All-in.

Party motto: "Four of us wolves, riding around the desert together . . . in Las Vegas, looking for strippers and cocaine."

So far, the twenty-first century has been very kind to dudes in comedy. Judd Apatow's mini-empire has given rise to a steady stream of smart and original movies that feature as many or more laughs than before and as many penises (or more), but which also have real, recognizable characters as well. Not always, but a lot of the time. That has represented a real step forward for comedy as a whole. Now the onus is on the filmmakers to not just make us laugh but to also make a movie. Even when bachelor parties are involved.

The Hangover is a clear indication of that general progress. It's not hard to imagine this movie—which, when it comes down to it, is really just about getting into a mess and then getting out of it again (plus roofies, and Mike Tyson, and Mike Tyson's tiger)—as a pretty crass grab for summer movie dollars, but the pressure of the comedy competition at the time mandated that they at least try something new. So what they did was just keep everything they already had and then lay over it an entirely new genre: a mystery. So now, instead of just laughing as they get hit with things, we also wince as time begins to run out on their desperate effort to reconstruct the events of the night before, find the bridegroom-to-be, and get him back home in time for the wedding. It's a simple innovation but it makes all the difference. And when it begins to fall flat, well, there's always Zach Galifianakis (aka the cause of and solution to all of *The Hangover's* problems).

9 "GANGNAM STYLE"
PERFORMED BY PSY (2012)

Party style: Absurdist.

Party motto: If life isn't a party then why is everyone spending so much money on party pants?

PSY's elevator pitch of the concept behind "Gangnam Style" (as described on *Ellen*) is "dress classy and dance cheesy." Metaphorically speaking, this is almost definitely the secret to a happy life. Literally speaking, it's doubtlessly—without a doubt—the secret to effective party-going. By dressing classy, we show our willingness to commit fully to a social event and treat it with respect; by dancing cheesy, we show that fun comes first and that we shall judge not, lest we be judged. (And by screaming at butts, emerging spontaneously from hot tubs, and lounging at playgrounds we insist that, although the world may be absurd, we will always be absurder.) This video is the twenty-first century equivalent of an etiquette guide for the culture-critiquing, horse-imitating, trash-ignoring socialites of the future. Over a billion YouTube views after the video released, the entire world is Gangnam now.

8 BACHELOR PARTY
STARRING TOM HANKS (1984)

Party style: Messy.
Party motto: "Uh . . . no, that's incorrect."

Tom Hanks is now most famous for *Forrest Gump, Saving Private Ryan*, and for turning a bloody volleyball into his friend. But once upon a time, Tom Hanks was just a goofball. He was funny. *Bachelor Party* happened at just about the perfect moment: just before everyone stopped being surprised to see such a normal-looking dude starring in major motion pictures. At this point, he is clearly not looking for Oscars—he's just happy to be working. And you can't really do this movie unless you're willing to give in to it entirely. *Bachelor Party* sets the template for offensive, immature, prewedding party movies. It's got animals, Tawny Kitaen, sex, drugs, and a bus driver. Bus drivers in movies: as rare as party donkeys in real life.

7 BLACK ORPHEUS
DIRECTED BY MARCEL CAMUS (1959)

Party style: Samba.
Party motto: Party in the front, business in the back.

There are three basic contenders for best party in the world: Carnival in Brazil, Oktoberfest in Germany, and New Year's Eve on planet Earth. New Year's Eve has a giant ball, Oktoberfest has giant beer mugs, and Carnival has heat, the streets, and a serious beat. It's a party as pervasive as sunlight; it touches every inch of the country, and you can feel it in every scene of *Black Orpheus*. The film retells the mythical story of Orpheus (a man who has the power to charm beasts with his music) and Eurydice (his beloved wife). After Eurydice dies, Orpheus ventures down to the underworld to retrieve her with depressing results. The movie transports the story to Rio during Carnival, and the sheer vitality of the surroundings— not to mention the light and the music—makes the ultimate annihilation at the end seem that much more poignant and profound. It's a great party movie because it all takes place at the best party on Earth, but it's a great movie because nothing is exclusively joyous. Everything here implies its opposite. And so when the sun rises in the film's final scene, it makes the deaths seem all the more final and complete.

6 VANITY FAIR
WRITTEN BY WILLIAM MAKEPEACE THACKERAY (1847-1848)

Party style: Desperate.
Party motto: We're all gonna die.

There's no kind of party like an end-of-the-world party cuz an end-of-the-world party don'—oh, whoops. An end-of-the-world party definitely stops, but that's also the whole point. When the world ends tomorrow, there's just no point in holding back today. Becky Sharp, the heroine of the novel (which contains, it should be noted, the subtitle "A Novel Without a Hero") doesn't want to hold back anyway, but her own passionate outlook is generally shunned by the more staid society around her. Until, of course, Napoleon comes to town. Then it's time for everyone to party. The ball scene in the novel is based on a real event, on the Duchess of Richmond's ball on the night before the Battle of Waterloo. Things are going to end badly. That's the case for the soldiers—and also for the characters in the novel as a whole. The world is a rough place. So pass the champagne and let's party like it's 1899.

5 CAN'T HARDLY WAIT
DIRECTED BY HARRY ELFONT AND DEBORAH KAPLAN (1998)

Party style: Cathartic.
Party motto: "There is such a thing as fate, but it only takes you so far."

During high school the tension between the things that we want to do and the things that we fear to do is at an all-time high. Some kids throw the shackles of embarrassment off earlier than others, but whenever that moment of release happens, it feels good. The four seniors at the center of *Can't Hardly Wait* each have one great hope (and one great fear) on graduation night, and in the end, they all get what they're after—even if what they're after isn't exactly what they had in mind at the outset. The "party of the year" that everyone is heading to is the place where it's all going to come to a head, and the only thing that's surprising, in retrospect, is that more teen movies don't take place at their own version of the party of the year. It's a revealing night and a pretty solid stand-in for the blowout graduation party that everyone wants but few people actually have. Also, lots of future stars! Also, so much 1990s!

4 REPRISE
DIRECTED BY JOACHIM TRIER (2006)

Party style: Open to interpretation.
Party motto: "More crackers, please . . . more crackers, please . . ."

When we're teenagers, we don't always get to make our own decisions (curfew), and when we do, we often make the wrong ones (hence the near universal desire to keep old yearbook photos from ever seeing the light of day again). When we're in our thirties, many of our decisions have already been made, and when we are given the opportunity to make a choice, we are often hampered by the past. But in our twenties, we do get to make our own decisions, and those decisions seem to have real promise. (We haven't learned our lessons yet!) To put that another way: The twenties are a good time for parties—rock stars know it, party girls know it, and pretentious Norwegian literary types know it, too.

Reprise takes us deep inside the lives of a few close but competitive friends as they struggle to make their names in the world. That sounds stressful, but these close but competitive friends are also young and eager and that paves over a lot of what could be grating and obnoxious. In one pivotal scene, a stale party, attended by a number of apparently supercilious types, is disrupted by the song "Deceptacon" by Le Tigre. The party comes to life because people want to party. And then the music is turned off, because the host is worried about the noise. There's a pause as the future hangs in the balance and then, behind the host, the sneaky DJ cranks the music on again and that's the end of that. This is the time for deferred payments, and sometimes you just have to seize the moment. Even if you're writing a novel. Even if you're European.

3 DAVE CHAPPELLE'S BLOCK PARTY
DIRECTED BY MICHEL GONDRY (2005)

Party style: Inclusive.
Party motto: Gotta spend all this money on something, right!?

For parties, as for life, the lower your expectations are, the happier you'll tend to be with the outcome. Dave Chappelle went even further than low expectations for his enormous Brooklyn block party: He created a party with almost no expectations. Until the day of the concert the location was a secret, the nature of the entertainment was a mystery, and to some of Chappelle's neighbors that he bussed in from Dayton, Ohio, even once the performers were revealed, they remained a mystery. Despite (and because of) these unknowns, the day was a huge success. It rained, Kanye West showed up, the Fugees reunited, Chappelle hosted, Gondry filmed, and everyone clearly had a really great time.

2 "PARTY ROCK ANTHEM"
PERFORMED BY LMFAO (2011) ♫

Party style: Infectious.
Party motto: "Everybody just have a good time."

This is the song and the video that everyone on the planet knows they should hate but can't quite manage to reject. It is cartoonish in the best possible sense. The outfits are crazy and the lyrics are unimportant, but the joy is infectious and the dance moves are head-explodingly amazing. If you invite someone to your party and that person can hurl himself up in the air and then land on his back in such a way that it looks like his back has "caught" his body (Is his back made of feet!? What is going on there!?), then you are the winner of party rocking. LMFAO already knew that, but that guy in the purple jacket puts their aristocratic standing beyond dispute. These guys are profoundly party.

1 GIRLS, "WELCOME TO BUSHWICK, AKA THE CRACKCIDENT" 🖥
DIRECTED BY JODY LEE LIPES (2012)

Party style: Haphazardness.
Party motto: Better sorry than safe.

Parties aren't usually transformative. They're meant as a diversion—as a way to forget or escape, or, most commonly, just relax. It seems possible that someone, sometime, might have discovered who they really were or become the person they really wanted to be while shouting conversation fragments over "We Didn't Start the Fire," but if you go through life betting on that chance, then you have a ton of money and a double ton (four thousand pounds' worth) of really weird bookies. But on television, reality doesn't matter; all that matters is that we believe. And this is the episode of *Girls* where realism finally gave way to sense. Almost every major character in the show does something that not many people in real life are ever likely to do, but whatever happens, we believe that that's exactly what they would have done, under the circumstances. Every mistake takes us forward and every sudden decision shows us something new. And every accidental crack-smoking episode acts as the connective tissue, and it all ends in smiles. All is well that ends well, and all is party that is Bushwick.

TEN PROPOSED HOLIDAY AMENDMENTS

10.

January 1:
Open-Couch Day

New Year's Day is famous for two things: bowl games and hangovers. Open-Couch Day celebrates both of these traditions, but does away with the trouble of having to actually commute home from wherever you wound up spending the night. It also adds an interesting element of tension, because why is that hound dog cuddling that man on your couch!? The answer is Open-Couch Day! Ring in the new couch! Celebrate it!

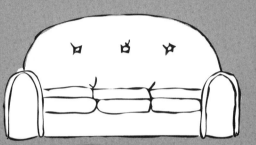

9.

February 29:
The Day We Leap Back

Once every four years we encounter a stunning anomaly. We call it "Leap Day." It is a makeweight, a sacrifice, in our ongoing battle against erroneous clocks. Enough with this callous pandering, I say; enough bowing down before Father Time; let's take the fight to him for a change. On every future Leap Day, humanity should take the chance to sock it to the clocks. If you see a watch, you smash it; if you hear some upstart bells trying to tell you what the hour is, you run screaming right back at them, and give 'em the old Liberty Bell treatment. In your face, Time!

8.
February 15:
Secret Valentine's Day

Frankly, it's shocking that Secret Valentine's Day is not already a thing. Valentine's Day itself is humiliating, expensive, and unpleasant. If you disagree, then it is probable that you are, or were, featured in the movie *Valentine's Day* and are contractually obligated to disagree on this point. For the remaining 15 percent of the population, it's time we made a move. Let's avoid the lines, the mark-ups, and the humiliation, and just go out for a nice date tomorrow night, on this, our secret Valentine's Day.

(PS: Don't tell Hallmark.)

7.
April 1:
April Spools Day

Dear fools: Why is there a day when we try harder than usual to "fool" one another? And why is that day April 1? This is arbitrary and stupid. Meanwhile, everyone needs thread at one time or another! So let's kill two birds with one stone! (Birds are easily fooled by our stones.) On April 1, from now on, let's give one another beautiful spools of luxuriant thread. What joy it will bring us all! How unfoolish we all will look when we collect our spools and go home rich in friendship, rich in joy, and rich in threads.
Huzzah!

6.
The Third Sunday in May:
Mayday

Did you know that the military phrase "Mayday!" comes from the French phrase "m'aidez"—as in, "help me"? Yeah, it's true, probably. So that's a fun little story about words. Also, that was always cool as kids when we would do that thing with the ribbons and the maypole, right? Did you guys do that? I think that was called "celebrating May Day" too, but I'm not sure if Mayday in that context was two words or one. This confusion is annoying, so let's get down to brass tacks. The new rule is: On the third Sunday of May, everyone has to run wildly through the streets screaming "Maydaymaydaymaydymayday!" until they are "aided" by a person who hits them with a Mayday egg. Why? Because it's Mayday, stupid, and America doesn't suffer fools on Mayday.

5.

July 4:
Independence Day . . .
with Bonus Slip 'n' Slides

This is a hard holiday to amend. People like beer and explosives and sports and barbecues, so there's not much demand for change here, but maybe we should add some more Slip 'n' Slides? Yeah, extra Slip 'n' Slides. Let's do that.

4.

Summer-ish:
Hallmark Day

Mother's Day, Father's Day, Valentine's Day, come on. Let's just cut out the middleman and have a day where we all send notes of appreciation directly to Hallmark. Maybe then they'll cut us some slack with these extra appreciation days. Here's the thing though: On Hallmark Day you don't have to write anything in the card. You just send the Hallmark card to Hallmark, and then they have to read them all. Because those are the rules. (See you in Hellmark, Hallmark.)

3.

October 31:
Nothing Scary Day

Dressing up is fun. That makes sense. Eating candy is enjoyable (except when the candy is chocolate stuffed with coconut). That also makes sense. And I admit, begging at strangers' homes is strangely thrilling. So we're good up to that point. But why this strange obsession with death, murder, ghosts, and goblins on the last night of October? Let's keep it clean, guys! Think about the children. (And if you must watch horror movies, at least have the decency to save it until Christmas [more on that in a moment])!

2.
That Thursday in November:
Turkey Day

For so long now, we, the American people, have just had our way with the turkeys of the world. In the autumn, when that fateful Thursday rolls around, we look at a turkey and just see meat. Because we are thankful, we get to murder and dine on turkeys. They could have been our national bird!! (And just imagine that scene, if we were to dine on bald eagles every November!) So I say again: Enough. This next Thanksgiving, it's time we gave something back. It's time we gave the turkeys back their freedom. We can still have the mashed potatoes and the brussels sprouts, but from now on, we buy our turkeys live from the farms, we take them home, and then we free them.
Turkeys on the loose!

1.
December 25:
Not *This* Christmas Day!

Fear not, fans of *Halloween V* and *Psycho*! For as long as there are men like Santa Claus, there shall be room for horror and for violence. This deathless symbol of corpulence and manic joy rampages around the globe and invades our homes, taking and leaving as he sees fit, and yet we celebrate him? No. No more. This year, we pack the chimneys with explosives, turn off all the lights, lock the doors, and turn up the volume on *Hostel 2*. If he's still brave enough to try and breach our walls behind the freakish lead of his freakish polar horses, then he will have us to deal with. Not this year, Santa.
No. Not this year . . .

APPENDIX

As you might imagine, I had to rely on a large number of print and online resources in order to come up with the hundreds of items included in this book. I needed to find pop-cultural material that I could both personally vouch for and that I felt other people would be able to enjoy, and as a result, I needed resources that could both serve as inspiration (in finding new authors, reconsidering movies that I'd otherwise dismissed, delving into new musical subgenres, etc.) and aid in more traditional research as well. There are hundreds of such resources out there for people looking for even more recommendations, but the list here focuses on what I have relied on the most—both for personal use and in the creation of this book.

TOP TEN RESOURCES FOR PEOPLE WHO STILL WANT MORE

10 "THE BEST 1,000 MOVIES EVER MADE," COMPILED AND WRITTEN BY FILM CRITICS OF THE NEW YORK TIMES

In addition to linking to reviews from many of America's greatest film critics, this constantly updated online resource (which is available in a less constantly updated book form as well) provides a great overview of "the classics"—and, unlike many other lists, really does balance foreign and American masterpieces.

9 "500 GREATEST ALBUMS OF ALL TIME" AND "500 GREATEST SONGS OF ALL TIME" COMPILED BY THE EDITORS AT ROLLING STONE

This is another great online resource if you're looking to cover your bases and conquer the canon. Clicking through each of the 500 selections can take a little/lot of time (or you can buy the *Rolling Stone* special issues), but at least the album covers are there to keep us company and remind us how variable the quality of cover art really is.

8 THE PITCHFORK 500: OUR GUIDE TO THE GREATEST SONGS FROM PUNK TO THE PRESENT, WRITTEN AND COMPILED BY SCOTT PLAGENHOEF AND RYAN SCHREIBER

For the commentary, you need the book, but if you just want to listen to the musical cutting edge as it swerves through the decades, it's worth listening to this chronological playlist all the way through.

7 "IN WHICH WE COUNT DOWN THE 100 GREATEST SCIENCE FICTION OR FANTASY NOVELS OF ALL TIME," WRITTEN AND COMPILED BY ALEX CARNEVALE

Of all the more specialized lists I relied on, this (available at ThisRecording.com) was the most personally inspirational. I am not *not* a fan of SFF, but, well, there it is. No list left me with a longer reading list than this one.

6 "ALL-TIME 100 VIDEO GAMES"
COMPILED BY **TIME** STAFF

There are a lot of great video game lists and discussions out there and the Time list (available on Time's website) is perhaps not the most respected among these, but it has the benefit of being the only one that is easy to scroll through and more or less pleasant to consume. So there's that.

5 "THE TOP MUSIC VIDEOS OF 2012"
COMPILED BY THE STAFF AT **PITCHFORK**

There's nothing like a music video to get you pumped for music, and this annual list—available online from *Pitchfork* with embedded videos and without commentary—is always a good resource for new music and for a "Gangnam" break (or a "Gangnam" indulgence).

4 "YOUR FAVORITES: 100 BEST-EVER TEEN NOVELS"
VOTED ON BY NPR LISTENERS AND READERS

There are so many great books "for kids," but whether you're a kid or a "kid," this list, published on the NPR website, contains all the classics and contains a lot of reminders about forgotten favorites as well.

3 THE NRYB CLASSICS IMPRINT
CURATED AND PUBLISHED BY THE **NEW YORK REVIEW OF BOOKS**

For movies there's the Criterion Collection (more on that in a moment), but for books there's NYRB Classics. If you're looking for something really new to read or if you just want more books with bold and beautiful spines, this is the place.

2 THE "INVENTORY" SERIES
COMPILED AND WRITTEN BY STAFF AT THE **A·V· CLUB**

This ongoing online series (also available in book form) is essentially a factory for pop-cultural rabbit holes. I love it.

1 THE CRITERION COLLECTION
CURATED BY STAFF AT THE CRITERION COLLECTION

My all-time favorite attempt to create a new film canon, complete with free access to extraordinary essays on many titles in their ever-expanding list of diamonds in the rough and diamonds in the treasure box full of other diamonds.

INDEX

ABOUT THE AUTHOR

Daniel Harmon is the editorial director at Zest Books and a longtime editor of pop culture projects for a variety of publishers. He is a former staff writer at Brokelyn.com, a current provider of unsolicited feedback on a wide variety of topics, and the author of "Oh, Hi Humanity"—an essay about Tommy Wiseau's film *The Room,* published in the anthology *Cult Pop Culture* (2011). Daniel loves free podcasts, midnight movies, and other things that are both cheap and fine.